Tacitus and the Principate
From Augustus to Domitian

Chris Burnand

CAMBRIDGE
UNIVERSITY PRESS

University Printing House, Cambridge CB2 8BS, United Kingdom

One Liberty Plaza, 20th Floor, New York, NY 10006, USA

477 Williamstown Road, Port Melbourne, VIC 3207, Australia

314–321, 3rd Floor, Plot 3, Splendor Forum, Jasola District Centre, New Delhi – 110025, India

79 Anson Road, #06–04/06, Singapore 079906

Cambridge University Press is part of the University of Cambridge.

It furthers the University's mission by disseminating knowledge in the pursuit of education, learning and research at the highest international levels of excellence.

www.cambridge.org
Information on this title: www.cambridge.org/9780521747615

First published 2011

20 19 18 17 16 15 14 13 12 11 10 9 8 7 6 5 4 3 2

Printed in Great Britain by CPI Group (UK) Ltd, Croydon CR0 4YY

A catalog record for this publication is available from the British Library.

ISBN 978-0-521-74761-5 Paperback

Contents

Maps and figures

Preface

Tacitus is almost universally acknowledged as the greatest and most influential historian of ancient Rome. In his writings he offers a uniquely personal perspective on imperial Rome and the political system under which he had himself served. As a result, he is a vital figure in the development of the western historical tradition, not least because he was one of the first historians to explore and trace the history of a particular institution, namely the principate.[1] Augustus had established this system of government out of the ashes of the Roman Republic, which had been torn apart in the civil wars by rival warlords such as Pompey and Caesar. Following his victory over Antony at the battle of Actium in 31 BC, he developed the new system slowly, by a process of trial and error: he had to negotiate his relationships, as emperor or *princeps*, with the people, the Senate and the army, and importantly, he had to provide for the succession after his own death. Subsequent emperors chose to follow or diverge from Augustus' example with varying degrees of success: on particular occasions, such as following the deaths of Caligula and Nero, the whole edifice seemed to be on the verge of collapse, but each time it survived and evolved, proving the durability and resilience of the institution which Augustus had created.

Tacitus himself, in a way paralleling the development of the institution itself, did not trace the history of the principate in a linear fashion. In his first major work, the *Histories*, he gave an account of the period during which he had risen to political prominence, from AD 69 to 96. Then he looked further into the past in his greatest work, the *Annals*, which took the story back to the death of Augustus and the accession of Tiberius. It is not simply a story about emperors, though they do play the central part. Tacitus explores how the institution of the principate affected the lives of other Romans, such as senators, soldiers, and even historians like himself.[2] He is interested in not only what happened, but what people said and thought had happened, and the fact that the truth of events might be beyond anyone's knowledge.

The passages in this book are arranged chronologically, and in selecting them for inclusion, I have chosen those which I feel are particularly significant for Tacitus' portrayal of the workings of the principate. Half of the ten chapters (2–6) are concerned with the first six books of the *Annals* and the reign of Tiberius. However, this imbalance is justified not only by the fact that the vagaries of survival have been kindest to Tacitus' account of this period, but also because

---

1 On this term, see Introduction, pp. 1–2.

2 However, it is true to say that his senatorial bias perhaps leads him to neglect the ordinary people, the Roman *plebs*.

the historian seems to have viewed Tiberius and his contemporaries as crucial to the further evolution of the principate. I have tried to preserve the continuity of Tacitus' narrative as far as possible, not least because the way in which he juxtaposes different items is often so crucial to a full understanding. However, there are some chapters (notably 4–6), where I have traced a theme by selecting shorter passages from a more extensive narrative. Since the main focus of this book is the *Annals*, unspecified headings and references within the text and notes are always to this work.

It is a happy time to be writing a book on Tacitus, because scholars have recently been producing some very illuminating studies and articles about his historical works. However, I have been even more fortunate to have had the opportunity of learning with many excellent classical teachers. Of these none opened my eyes more to the complexities and intricacies of Tacitus than my undergraduate tutor, Michael Comber, a great teacher and friend, who is sorely missed.

In the production of this book, I have been hugely indebted to the suggestions and improvements of the series editors, but especially to James Morwood, who provided the initial encouragement and has chaperoned the work firmly towards its completion. In addition, I would like to thank Lucy Mitchell and her colleagues at Cambridge University Press for the care and professionalism they have shown in bringing the book to publication. I am also grateful to individuals who have read and commented on various sections of the manuscript, in particular Stephen Ridd, Mike Truran and Oscar Hird. Those whom I have been lucky to have as students and colleagues in my teaching career have enormously improved my understanding of Tacitus through sharing their perspicacity with me. I am particularly fortunate to have such excellent colleagues in the classics department at Abingdon School who are tolerant of my foibles and provide such a happy and thought-provoking environment in which to work. However, my greatest thanks are owed to my family, and especially my wife Katie: her efforts have allowed this book to reach completion during our son Charlie's first year; our conversations have always improved my understanding of all things classical; and her comments on my text have greatly improved it. Needless to say, those errors which remain are to be attributed to my own stubbornness.

I hope that this book will introduce new readers to the pleasures of Tacitus, and that they will use it as a stepping-stone to reading his complete works. However, if it were to encourage even one person to embark on the long and demanding process of learning Latin so that they could appreciate his writing in the full glory of his actual words, then I would be truly delighted.

Introduction

Tacitus

For the twenty-first century reader Tacitus can seem at the same time both a very familiar and a shadowy figure: familiar because his personality seems to come across so strongly in his writings, shadowy since there are such large gaps in our knowledge of his life and career.

We do not know for certain Tacitus' first name, the date or place of his birth, nor the year of his death. All we can say is that his full name was probably Publius Cornelius Tacitus, and that it is likely that he was born in southern Gaul (modern France) in about AD 56. By the year 75 at the latest he had arrived in Rome, where he embarked on a very successful career as a senator: this involved him in service in the provinces and holding office in Rome. In 97 he held the highest of these offices, serving as consul during the brief reign of the elderly emperor Nerva, before becoming governor of Asia in 112–13, the most senior provincial post in the gift of the Senate. He probably lived to see the first few years of Hadrian as emperor, and perhaps died in about 120.

Although Tacitus is best known to us as a historian of ancient Rome, he seems to have turned seriously to writing only after holding the consulship. Indeed it is essential to a full understanding of Tacitus' historical works[1] to bear in mind that he was writing as a successful senator at the very heart of the Roman political system. Tacitus himself is explicit about this in the preface to his first major historical work, the *Histories*, which covered the period in which he had risen to prominence in Rome (see *Histories* **1.1**, p. 17). One emperor had a particular impact on Tacitus' life and helped to shape the perspective with which he viewed earlier Roman history; this was Domitian. He succeeded his elder brother Titus in AD 81 and ruled until 96, when he was assassinated. Tacitus wrote in the *Agricola*, his first work, of how he witnessed at first hand in the Senate the descent of Domitian's reign into tyranny and bloody oppression (*Agricola* **45**, pp. 13–14). However, Tacitus is open about the fact that he did well under this emperor, and his consulship in 97 had almost certainly been approved by Domitian before his death.

The principate

Tacitus' personal experience seems to have made him reflect upon the Roman system of government and the opportunities and limitations it offered for individual senators. The Romans referred to this system as the principate, and

---

1 For an account of the works written by Tacitus, and the order in which he wrote them, see Chapter 1, pp. 9–22.

to individual emperors as *principes* (in the singular, *princeps*), the terminology which I use in this book rather than the traditional English usage of 'empire' and 'emperors'.² The term *princeps* literally means 'leading man', and had traditionally been used in Rome in the phrase *princeps senatus* to refer to the most senior member of the Senate. Augustus adopted it to refer to his own position following his establishment of what was essentially one-man rule after his defeat of Mark Antony at Actium in 31 BC. He was keen to disguise the realities of this power and wanted to create the impression that he had overseen the restoration of traditional republican institutions represented by the Senate and the individual magistrates. The term *princeps* was suitable as it was a traditional one (although now given a rather different use), and did not really stand in the way of the existing offices. It offered an inoffensive cover for the realities of Augustus' power, which actually relied on his permanent tenure of *imperium* (the Latin word for constitutional power bestowed on individuals by the people), and tribunician power, which gave him a particular responsibility for looking after the interests of the ordinary people.

Tacitus himself discusses the origins of this new system of government at the start of his *Annals* (see **1.2–3**, **9–10**, pp. 23–7, 35–40), but all his historical writing reflects his interest in exploring the institution of the principate and its evolution under the various *principes*. One term which he often uses in opposition to the principate is *libertas*; that is, freedom, but a freedom which has significantly different implications from the modern use of the word. Tacitus usually links *libertas* with the institutions of the republican constitution, before Augustus imposed his new system. This was embodied by the two chief annual magistrates, the consuls, who represented the executive (and military leadership) of the republican system. Their powers were carefully circumscribed: they were democratically elected (although in a way that gave far greater weight to the votes of the rich), they were only allowed to serve for a period of a year, and there were two of them, a fact which limited the scope for individual ambition. As a result the theory was that no one man held too much individual power.

In this system *libertas* meant the freedom of the politician to pursue his career free from the interference of others, but as this was eroded by the realities of the political situation under Augustus and later, the term became a slogan around which opponents of the regime could gather. As a result it took on more of the modern implications of the word 'freedom', and in particular the idea of freedom from tyranny by the powerful. As a result, the opposite of *libertas* became seen as servitude, an idea that was readily available in Rome thanks to the wide prevalence of slavery. Therefore, the system of the principate could naturally be understood

---

2 Not only is the traditional terminology less faithful to the Roman terms, but the word 'empire' is confusing, since it refers more obviously to the lands controlled by Rome rather than the system of government instituted by Augustus.

in republican terms as un-Roman, since it equated the Roman senators of the noblest families with a status traditionally held by foreigners who enjoyed little or no personal freedom.

This is not to say that Tacitus saw the republican system of government as an ideal to which it was desirable to return. He realized that the demands of the Roman empire had subjected that system to irreparable stresses and that the principate was a necessary evil (see *Histories* **1.1**, pp. 16–17 and *Annals* **4.33**, p. 107). Indeed he was more interested in the ways in which individuals could still operate within the new system, without demeaning themselves in debased sycophancy or pointlessly martyring themselves to no one's benefit. In men such as Lepidus (see **4.20**, p. 103) and Agricola (see *Agricola* **42**, p. 15), he recorded examples which he thought that others should aspire to follow in their lives. In doing so he was remaining faithful to the traditions of Roman republican historiography (the writing of history), which had always had a strongly exemplary nature, offering practical examples to avoid or adopt.

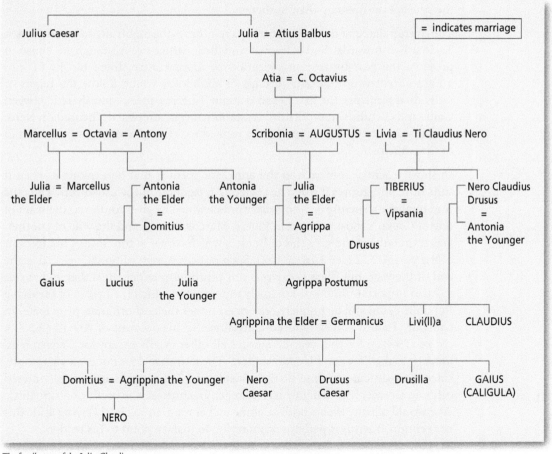

The family tree of the Julio-Claudians.

Tacitean historiography

It is striking just how faithful Tacitus is to the style of history which had been prevalent during the Roman Republic. This is perhaps surprising, since one of the major themes of his writing is his unmasking of any pretence that the political system has remained the same under the principate. He writes annalistic history (i.e. following a year-by-year account), which was a natural form under the republic with its annual change of consuls. In her ground-breaking book *Tradition and Theme in the Annals of Tacitus*, Judith Ginsburg was the first to explore the way in which Tacitus reshaped and exploited that traditional form to add to, rather than restrict, the meaning of his narrative. As a simple example, the naming of the consuls at the start of the year had in republican histories marked the entrance into office of a new 'administration', and they would dominate the following narrative; in Tacitus they remain, but almost as a mere dating device and usually in a subordinate clause or phrase, whilst the emperor continues to be the centre of events. So Tacitus suggests that the republican magistrates are in reality only the preserved fossils of an earlier political system, and exploited by the *principes* to dress up their autocracy.

The overall shape of the *Annals* perhaps reinforces the ambivalent attitude which Tacitus had towards the traditional annalistic structure. Although he chose to preserve the year-by-year organization of his narrative, these blocks fit into a bigger structure of hexads (groups of six books) which follow the reigns of individual *principes*: the first hexad is about Tiberius, the second shared between Gaius and Claudius, and the third (assuming it was completed) focused on Nero. In this way, the traditional pattern is refined to reflect the new political realities of the principate.

In short, Tacitus' approach to the annalistic form is that he exploits it when it suits him, but ignores it when he prefers. An example of the use to which he puts the annalistic structure is the obituary notice which he gives for Iunia (the sister of one of Caesar's most prominent killers, Marcus Brutus, and the wife of another, Gaius Crassus) at the very end of Book 3, which comes at the close of his account of the year AD 22 (see **3.76**, p. 102). Such notices were traditionally placed at the end of the year, but Tacitus exploits this position to anticipate a theme that was to be so important in Book 4, namely the extent to which the heroes of the dying Republic could still be publicly celebrated under the authoritarian principate. In contrast, Tacitus totally ignored convention in his account of AD 18 (**2.53–8**, see pp. 79–82): for that year he ignores all other events except for Germanicus' journey to the East and his actions there. The narrative does not even visit Rome, since Germanicus was one of the consuls and Tacitus tells us that he entered office in Greece, itself a highly irregular act. In contrast, the traditional annalistic year would narrate events both at home and abroad: in so clearly laying aside this convention, Tacitus is perhaps again trying to make a point to his readers.

Tacitean style

If the structure of Tacitus' writing is essential to a full appreciation of it, the same can be said of the style of his Latin. It is utterly idiosyncratic and often intentionally difficult, combining as it does extreme brevity with an often convoluted and complex sentence structure. In producing a translation it has been the greatest challenge to preserve some feel for this Latin, whilst making the English sufficiently accessible to readers. It is an especial difficulty to capture his brevity, not least because Latin, with its rich variety of word endings and inflections, lends itself to such brevity in a way that English does not. Tacitus' brevity takes two forms: sometimes it is simply the omission of unnecessary words, but more strikingly he employs it to produce an epigrammatic turn of phrase. One example may illustrate the point. He concludes his obituary of Galba (*Histories* **1.49**, p. 186), by saying of him 'omnium consensu capax imperii nisi imperasset', which in English means literally: 'by the agreement of all capable of power unless he had held power'. Even a literal translation cannot capture the brevity of the original, which is achieved in part by the fact that Latin has a verb which can convey in one word 'he had held power' (*imperasset*); but English cannot afford to omit all the other verbs in the clause in the way that Tacitus has done, and so I have rendered it as 'judged by the consensus of all to be capable of supreme command, had he only not held it', which rather lacks the concise and even lapidary quality of the original, even if it does now convey the sense clearly.

However, there are other occasions when the style of the original seems to be even more important to its sense. A clear example is Tacitus' description of the effects of the Great Fire of Rome on the inhabitants of the city: the confused structure of the sentences in **15.38** (pp. 164–5) seems to mimic the confusion of the victims as they struggled to escape. Another example is the description of the mutinous legions facing Germanicus in their camp in AD 14, where the confusion of the different cries, complaining and imploring him to help (**1.35**, p. 61) is mirrored by Tacitus' style, as the focus of each clause jumps from person to person and from group to group. The culmination of the passage is Germanicus' dramatic threat to kill himself: he 'snatched his sword from his side, lifted it up and was bringing it down into his chest, had not those closest to him seized his right arm and restrained it by force'. Tacitus has omitted the clause 'and would have done so' before 'had not' in order to heighten the drama of the moment. I have kept this one omission, but on countless other occasions he uses the same technique, and it just sounds too odd in the English.

The other important feature of this passage is that in it Tacitus studiously avoids any balanced clauses. Traditionally, rhetorical Latin – of which Cicero offers the prime example – revolved around directly parallel or directly opposed clauses for many of its effects. Tacitus studiedly avoids this, and on the contrary strives after variation (*variatio* in Latin). Nowhere is this more obvious than when he suggests alternative motivations for an action. A striking example comes again from **15.38** (p. 165), when he describes how some people were helping the spread of the flames during the Great Fire. According to Tacitus, they did so, whilst claiming that they had the authority to do so 'whether this was so that they could loot more freely, or because they really did have orders'. Tacitus expresses the first possibility as a purpose clause ('so that'), and the second using a noun: the latter does not really work in English, but I have tried to preserve the variation by using a different type of clause, a causal one ('because'). It is important to ask why Tacitus avoids balance in this way – in part, it may be a stylistic choice and a way of differentiating himself from writers such as Cicero, but it also has the important effect of making the reader think about every single word. Tacitus does not want the reader to be able to gloss over the balancing clause as a natural adjunct to the previous one, and by always avoiding the obvious parallel, he is perhaps trying to focus minds on exactly what he is saying all the time.

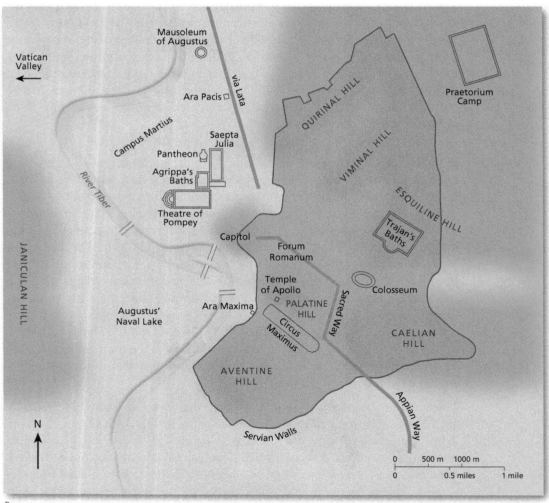

Rome.

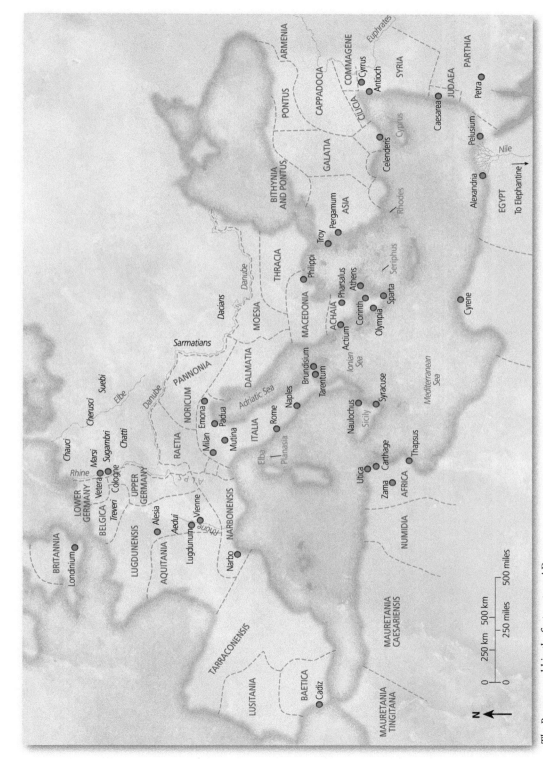

The Roman world in the first century AD.

1 The motivations for writing history

Tacitus reached the pinnacle of his career as a senator when he was appointed consul in AD 97, and his election must almost certainly have been ratified by Domitian before the *princeps'* murder in 96. Tacitus had already prospered under Domitian's rule, since he had been made praetor in 88, by which time he had already been appointed to a priesthood. It is likely that Tacitus began writing his first work during the year in which he had served as consul, and it seems to have been published in the early part of the following year. This work, the *Agricola*, was not a history, but a biography of his father-in-law, Gnaeus Iulius Agricola, who had won especial renown while governing Britain in the seven years from 77 (or 78). The *Agricola* is part of a long tradition of Roman biographical writing, but in it Tacitus makes clear his feelings about recent history, coloured most clearly by his opinions of the late emperor.

Writing biography: *Agricola* 1–2

1   The recording of the deeds and characters **of famous men** for future generations is a time-honoured custom, which even in the modern age our generation has not abandoned, indifferent though it is to its own achievements. This tradition has survived as often as **an individual of** great and noble **merit** has overcome and surmounted that fault which is common to both small and great states, namely 5 the jealous ignorance of what is right. But just as for previous generations there was an easier and more open field for achievements worthy of record, so too every man of the most notable intellect was encouraged to produce a record of distinction without partiality or self-seeking, but for the reward only of knowing

---

of famous men   these words (the first in the Latin sentence) are the same as those which opened a historical work by the elder Cato, called the *Origines*. This was the earliest Roman history written in Latin, and Cato himself had been a dominant political figure in the first half of the second century BC. Why might Tacitus be choosing to echo this early republican work in the opening words of his biography?

an individual of ... merit   this is a translation of the Latin word *virtus*, which Tacitus uses repeatedly in the opening of the *Agricola*. It is related to the Latin word for 'man', *vir*, and its range of meanings is based around excellence in those qualities which were seen as typical of a true man, although Tacitus also uses it (as here) to stand for human examples of excellence. It is not easy to use one English word or phrase in translation, and in these opening sections I have used 'merit', 'distinction', 'man of merit'.

he had done a good service. Indeed, very many considered the act of relating their own lives to be a sign of confidence in their own character rather than arrogance, and it was not incredible or a matter of censure for **Rutilius and Scaurus** to do so: to such an extent are men of merit best appreciated at the very times when they are most readily produced. But nowadays I have required indulgence as I am about to recount the life of a dead man, an indulgence which I would not have sought had I been about to write an invective: **so barbarous and hostile to merit is the age.**

> 1 Why do you think that Tacitus puts so much emphasis on the idea of excellence (*virtus*) in this opening section of the work? Does it suggest that Tacitus has greater ambitions than a simple biographical narrative for his work?
>
> 2 What impression does Tacitus give of contemporary Rome?
>
> 3 How does Tacitus portray the relationship between making history and writing history?

2 We have read that when **Thrasea Paetus had been eulogized by Arulenus Rusticus, and Helvidius Priscus by Herennius Senecio**, it was a capital offence: the rage was vented not only against the authors themselves, but also against their

---

Rutilius and Scaurus Publius Rutilius Rufus was a notable Stoic philosopher born soon after 160 BC, who reached the consulship in 105, but was in 92 prosecuted for extortion as governor in Asia. In exile, following his conviction, he wrote a personal memoir of his time, which became influential for later historians such as Sallust. Marcus Aemilius Scaurus, unlike Rutilius, came from a traditional noble family, defeated Rutilius for the consulship of 115 BC, and became the leading figure of the Senate for the following decades. Cicero refers to his autobiography as valuable but no longer read (*Brutus* 112). The works of both men are now lost.

so barbarous and hostile to merit is the age this is a typically pithy Tacitean comment, used to sum up the contents of a section in an epigrammatic manner.

We have read it is unclear from the Latin whether this verb is present or past. Tacitus perhaps chooses to use the verb 'to read' here because he was absent himself from Rome in AD 93, when these prosecutions occurred. However, the verb also emphasizes that the true account of events can be preserved in writing even in the face of the burning of books which Tacitus goes on to describe.

Thrasea Paetus … Herennius Senecio Publius Clodius Thrasea Paetus was a Stoic senator who had been influential under Claudius and Nero, but he became disenchanted with the latter and withdrew from public life in AD 63–4. He was subsequently prosecuted for treason and committed suicide in 66 (on Roman attitudes to suicide, see note on p. 19). Gaius Helvidius Priscus, another Stoic, was Thrasea's son-in-law and had been banished after his father-in-law's condemnation. Upon his return a feud had continued with Thrasea's prosecutor, Eprius Marcellus, and Helvidius flaunted his independence books, with the task entrusted to **the triumvirs** of burning the memorials of the most distinguished minds in **the comitium and Forum**. Certainly **they believed** 5 that the voice of the Roman people, the freedom of the Senate, and the awareness of the human race were being obliterated with that fire. In addition there followed the expulsion of the professors of philosophy, and all good practice was driven into exile, so that nothing honourable should confront them anywhere. We have certainly given a striking lesson in submissiveness; and just as antiquity witnessed 10 the extremes of freedom, so we have the extremes of slavery, once the interaction of speech and listening had been taken away through a system of spies. We would also have lost memory itself together with our voice, had it been in our power to forget as much as to stay silent.

1 How does Tacitus emphasize the tyranny of Domitian's reign in this passage?

2 When, and under what circumstances, have books been burnt in modern times? What does the act symbolize for us today?

3 What effect does Tacitus' use of the first person plural have in the last two sentences?

of opinion. He was banished and exiled in 74 under the emperor Vespasian. Quintus Arulenus Rusticus was also a Stoic sympathizer and served as consul under Domitian in 92; at some point he published an account of Thrasea's death, and was executed under Domitian in 93. Herennius Senecio was a friend of Pliny and refused to hold office under Domitian. He published an account of Helvidius' death and like Arulenus was prosecuted for treason and executed in 93. These men were seen as part of the 'Stoic opposition' to the imperial regime under Nero and the Flavian emperors.

the triumvirs   these three minor magistrates were known as *tresviri capitales* and had a police function in Rome under the command of more senior magistrates.

the comitium and Forum   the *comitium* was an open area at the north-western end of the Forum next to the Senate House. Although it fell into disuse after changes to the Forum made by Caesar, it had served as the main meeting place for the Roman people during the republican period. It remained a traditional location for carrying out punishments.

they believed   Tacitus presumably means Domitian and his close associates by 'they', but why does he choose to leave the subject unclear?

Tacitus describes Agricola's career and achievements in the main body of the work, culminating in what his son-in-law saw as his completion of the conquest of Britain. Tacitus believed Agricola's recall to Rome to be motivated by Domitian's envy of his achievements – which is hardly fair, given that he had been allowed to serve as governor for the extraordinarily long period of seven years. Tacitus then describes how Agricola prudently retired from public life before his death on 23 August AD 93, a death which he alleges was eagerly awaited by the emperor: however, he at least offers the consolation that in many ways it was a timely end.

The fortunate timing of Agricola's death: *Agricola* 44–5

44   With his daughter and wife surviving him, he can even seem to have been blessed to have escaped what lay ahead, while his status still remained intact, his reputation flourished, and his relatives and friends were unharmed. For although he was not permitted to live on until this dawning of a most blessed age and to see Trajan as emperor – an event which he used to predict in our hearing with prophecy and 5 prayers – he did enjoy the significant consolation of such a hastened death to

The Senate House in the Forum Romanum.

prayers   it is typical of Tacitus' style to make this addition even though it does not make sense with the verb he uses – it really means 'and wish for in his prayers'.

a hastened death   the Latin word for 'hastened' not only suggests that the death was premature but also hints that it might have been precipitated by foul play.

have avoided that final period, in which Domitian drained the state no longer with periods of respite and breathing-spaces, but incessantly and as if in one hail of blows.

45 Agricola did not see the Senate House besieged, the Senate beset with weapons, 10 the murder of so many ex-consuls in one and the same slaughter, and the exiles and banishments of so many of the noblest women. **Mettius Carus** still had only one victory to his count, **the noisy opinion of Messalinus was still confined to the Alban citadel**, and **Baebius Massa** at that time was still a defendant. Next

The cryptoporticus (semi-subterranean gallery) of Domitian's villa in the Alban hills.

Mettius Carus Mettius was a notorious *delator*, or prosecutor, under Domitian. Since there was no public prosecution service, such men were relied upon to bring accusations of treason against others. They received at least a quarter of the accused man's property if they brought successful cases, and were often seen as stooges of the imperial regime.

the noisy opinion of Messalinus was still confined to the Alban citadel Lucius Valerius Catullus Messalinus was another *delator*, who was known as 'the bringer of death'. Domitian had built a huge villa in the Alban hills on the site of the ancient city of Alba Longa, rather in the fashion of Hadrian's even more lavish subsequent villa at Tivoli. It is a 'citadel' in that it incorporated the ancient town, but the word also hints that it could be seen as the fortified base of the despotic emperor. Its ruins now lie in the grounds of the pope's summer residence at Castel Gandolfo.

Baebius Massa in AD 93 at the time of Agricola's death, Massa was being prosecuted by Senecio and Pliny for misconduct during his time as a governor in Spain. He was found guilty, but turned the tables and became an accuser, first of Senecio on the charge of impiety, and subsequently of his friends.

our hands delivered Helvidius into prison; the sight of Mauricus and Rusticus 15
shattered us, and Senecio drenched us with his innocent blood. Nero, however,
averted his gaze and simply gave orders for his crimes – he did not watch. An
especial aspect of the miseries under Domitian was to watch and be seen: our
sighs were recorded, and that cruel and ruddy complexion of his – a redness with
which he used to protect himself against a sense of shame – was able to take note 20
of the pallid faces of so many men.

You indeed were lucky, Agricola, not only for the distinction of your life, but also
for the timeliness of your death. As is related by those who were present for your
last words, you met your fate bravely and willingly, as if you could confer the gift
of innocence on the emperor as far as any man could. 25

---

1 What consolations does Tacitus offer for Agricola's death?
2 To judge from these extracts, what other interests besides the life and virtues
   of Agricola does Tacitus have in writing this work?
3 How does Tacitus portray Domitian's regime in this section?
4 How significant here is Tacitus' repeated use of the first person? What effect
   does it contribute to his account?
5 How would you describe the writing style of Tacitus in these sections?

Helvidius the son of the Helvidius mentioned in *Agricola* **2** (p. 10). According to
Suetonius (*Domitian* 10), he was put to death for writing a play in which he seemed to
allude unfavourably to Domitian's divorce.

Mauricus and Rusticus Rusticus, according to *Agricola* **2** (p. 10), was put to death for
his eulogy of Thrasea. Junius Mauricus was his brother and was banished at the same
time, but he did outlive the emperor to return to Rome and prominence under Nerva
and Trajan.

a redness with which he used to protect himself against a sense of shame the point is
that Domitian's naturally red face was able to disguise any blush that might otherwise
have revealed his embarrassment. There is also a striking contrast of colours between the
ruddy emperor and the faces of the senators, bloodless with terror. Physical description is
a frequent feature of ancient biography since in ancient thought a person's appearance
was believed to reflect inner character traits.

As is related by those who were present for your last words Tacitus was absent from
Rome at the time of his father-in-law's death and had been for four years, almost certainly
on official business in a provincial post, although it is not known where.

Other minor works

In the same year as the *Agricola* Tacitus also published a second short book, the *Germania*, the main focus of which is an ethnographic description of various German tribes. There is some comparison with Roman society and culture, both implicit and explicit, but Tacitus only returned to this subject more directly a few years later with the publication of a dialogue about the recent history of oratory in Rome, his *Dialogus de Oratoribus* ('Dialogue on Orators'). As Tacitus was himself a notable public speaker, this subject was close to his heart. However, he distances himself from the subject by inventing a fictional setting for the work in which he pretends to recall a discussion that took place in AD 75 between three men, Marcus Aper, Vipstanus Messalla and Curiatius Maternus. The narrative prompt to this memory is the repeated questioning of Fabius Iustus, a friend of the younger Pliny, over the causes for the decline of oratory in Rome. Of the three interlocutors, Aper denies that such a decline has taken place, Messalla ascribes it to a neglect of the training of the young, whilst, most interestingly from a historical point of view, Maternus argues that the present, stable political system of the principate has rendered oratory relatively obsolete: the golden age of Cicero had flourished in a time of virtual anarchy in the late Republic.

It is clear that none of the speakers in the dialogue acts as Tacitus' own mouthpiece, but Maternus' speech raises questions which were to be pertinent to Tacitus' major historical writings, and which he had already touched upon in the *Agricola*, namely the role left for men other than the *princeps* to play within the principate. In this particular case, could orators thrive in a situation where there was little value in persuading a mass audience of an argument, since in reality all power lay in the hands of one man? Or was there simply now a need for a new style of oratory to suit the changed political circumstances in which Rome now found itself?

Introduction to the *Histories*: 1.1–3

It may have been soon after the publication of the *Dialogus* that Tacitus turned to the first of his major historical works, the *Histories*, because we know that he was collecting material for them in AD 105–6, when he consulted the younger Pliny for details concerning the eruption of Vesuvius in 79. The *Histories* were published in about 109. They covered the years from 69 to 96 inclusively, and so offered what was very much a contemporary history.

1.1   **Servius Galba, as consul for the second time,** and Titus Vinius, as a first-time consul, will be the start of my work. For many authors have narrated the preceding period of eight hundred and twenty years following **the foundation of the city**, as long as **the achievements of the Roman people** were related with equal eloquence and freedom: after **the battle took place at Actium** and it served the interests   5

Servius Galba   he was the emperor in January 69, having seized power following the suicide of Nero in 68 by marching on Rome from Spain.

as consul for the second time   Tacitus begins his account with the opening of the year and the assumption of office by the two consuls. It might seem a rather arbitrary point at which to begin his narrative, but it sets Tacitus firmly within the annalistic tradition of Roman historiography. This organized its narrative in a strictly year-by-year fashion (the word 'annalistic' derives from *annus*, the Latin word for 'year'), which was appropriate to the Republic with its system of government where new consuls entered office each year; however, under the principate it might seem less appropriate (see Introduction, p. 4).

the foundation of the city   this was traditionally dated to 753 BC. The best known of such writers was Livy.

the achievements of the Roman people   i.e. the history of the republican period, when the Roman people were not under the rule of one man.

the battle took place at Actium   this happened in 31 BC, and Octavian (as Augustus then was known) defeated the combined forces of Antony and Cleopatra, leaving him the sole ruler of the Roman world. For all practical purposes it marked the start of permanent one-man rule in Rome.

of peace that all power should be entrusted to one man, that sequence of great intellects ended; at the same time truth was weakened in several ways, first by ignorance of affairs of state as if they were somebody else's concern, then from a passion for flattery, or in turn out of hatred towards the masters. In this way neither group – neither the hostile nor the servile – had a concern for posterity. But while you may easily reject **the obsequiousness of a writer**, malicious disparagement is received with ready ears; the reason is that flattery entails the shameful accusation of slavishness, while spite has the false appearance of freedom. Galba, Otho and Vitellius were known to me neither to my detriment nor to my advantage. I would not deny that my status was **first advanced by Vespasian, enhanced by Titus, and carried much further by Domitian**. But those who lay claim to unadulterated truthfulness must narrate each reign without **affection** and untouched by hate. However, if a long life permits, I have set aside the principate of Nerva and the rule of Trajan – more fertile and safer material – for my old age, since **rare is the blessedness of the times when you can think what you like and say what you think**.

---

the obsequiousness of a writer of such authors Velleius Paterculus is unfortunate enough for his work to have survived: under Tiberius he wrote a history stretching from Greek mythology to AD 29 in only two books, which included passages of the following sort, in this case praising the emperor's successful campaigning in Germany:

> By the great gods, what a huge tome is needed for what we achieved the following summer under the leadership of Tiberius Caesar! The whole of Germany was traversed by our arms, races were defeated whose names were almost unknown, the tribes of the Cauchi were conquered again. All of their youth, although countless in number, physically huge, and protected very securely by the terrain, handed over their weapons. Together with their leaders they were surrounded by the gleamingly armed column of our soldiers and prostrated themselves in front of the commander's platform (2.106).

first advanced by Vespasian ... carried much further by Domitian Tacitus came to Rome at some point in the reign of Vespasian (AD 69–79), who appointed him to some junior offices; he was appointed quaestor, and hence to membership of the Senate, under Titus in about 81, but rose to the highest ranks of the senatorial career during Domitian's reign (81–96): he served as praetor, the second highest rank, in 88 (when he was also appointed to an important priesthood), and finally as consul in 97, although his election must have been ratified by Domitian before he was deposed and killed.

affection the actual Latin word is *amor*, meaning love, an exact antonym of the hatred which is also to be avoided. Compare also Tacitus' claim in the preface of the *Annals* to write 'without anger and partisanship' (**1.1**, p. 22).

rare is the blessedness of the times ... say what you think this conclusion to Tacitus' introduction is very famous, and is traditionally read as a celebration of the liberality of the current regime under which he was writing. However, it is possible to understand the words differently: can you think of other reasons why Tacitus might put off writing about Nerva and Trajan?

1. What are the major handicaps which Tacitus identifies for the writing of history under the principate?
2. Is Tacitus right when he says that flattery in a historical account is easier to detect than unfair criticism?
3. Why do you think that Tacitus is keen to give an outline of how his own career progressed during this period? Are modern historians ever similarly explicit about their own careers?
4. Why do you think that Tacitus so formally adheres to the traditions of annalistic history, even to the extent of beginning his account on 1 January, when such a model perhaps seems less suited to writing a history where the emperors rather than the consuls are now the dominant figures in Rome?

1.2   I approach a work rich in misfortunes, terrible for its battles, riven with civil strife, violent even during periods of peace. **Four emperors died by the sword**; there were **three civil wars**, even more foreign ones, and very often a combination of the two; there was success in the East, failure in the West; **Illyricum** was disturbed, the provinces of Gaul faltering in their loyalty, **the whole of Britain** 5 **was conquered and immediately surrendered**; **the Sarmatians and the Suebi** rose against us, **the Dacians** were made famous by a series of battles in which success was enjoyed by both sides in turn, even the Parthians almost took up arms because of the laughable behaviour of **a false Nero**. Now indeed Italy was

Four emperors died by the sword   Galba, Otho and Vitellius (all in AD 69), and Domitian (in 96).

three civil wars   these were between Otho and Vitellius, Vitellius and Vespasian (both in AD 69), and Saturninus' failed uprising in Germany against Domitian (in 89).

Illyricum   this is the name often given to the three provinces of Dalmatia, Pannonia and Moesia, an area which rose up against Vitellius. They stretched from the eastern Balkans up to the Danube.

the whole of Britain was conquered and immediately surrendered   a reference to the successes of Tacitus' father-in-law, Agricola, against the Scots, which he felt were subsequently wasted by Domitian.

the Sarmatians and the Suebi   these tribes lay along the Danube frontier (see map on p. 7).

the Dacians   they occupied modern Romania, and fought a series of campaigns against Domitian; they were finally conquered by Trajan and their territory was turned into a Roman province, a campaign immortalized by the sculptural frieze on Trajan's Column.

a false Nero   Suetonius (*Nero* 57) records the appearance of this impostor at the Parthian court in AD 88 and his favourable reception there. Parthia had been Rome's great enemy in the East, defeating both Crassus and Mark Antony before a diplomatic settlement was achieved under Augustus. However, the Parthians remained a potential danger to Rome's control of her eastern provinces.

afflicted by fresh disasters, or at least those which it had not faced over a long 10
span of centuries. **Cities were consumed or buried** on the most fertile shores
of Campania; and Rome itself was devastated by fires, which devoured the most
ancient shrines – **the Capitol itself was burned by citizen hands**. Religious
rites were defiled, adulteries were committed by the most eminent people: the
sea was filled with exiles, **its rocky islands** were stained with murdered blood. 15
The violence was more shocking in Rome: good birth, wealth, rank – whether
surrendered or retained – served as grounds for accusation, and for merit death
was absolutely assured. And the rewards of prosecutors were no less detested than
their crimes, since some by taking priesthoods and consulships as spoils, and
others by winning **official posts** and power behind the scenes, held absolute sway 20
in all spheres through hatred and terror. Slaves were bribed to turn against their
masters, freedmen against their patrons; and those who lacked personal enemies
were overthrown by the agency of their friends.

1.3   However, the age was not so barren of merit that it did not also produce some
good examples. Mothers accompanied their children into banishment, and 25
wives followed their husbands into exile; relatives showed daring, sons-in-law
were steadfast, the loyalty of slaves was obstinate even against torture; the final
hours of famous men driven to their deaths were met with bravery, and their ends
matched **the much-trumpeted deaths of ancient men**. Beyond the numerous
misfortunes of humankind, in heaven and on earth there were omens, warnings 30
of lightning and forebodings of the future, both happy and gloomy, ambiguous

---

Cities were consumed or buried   a reference to the eruption of Vesuvius in AD 79.

the Capitol itself was burned by citizen hands   this happened in the fighting in the city
during AD 69; however, there were other major fires, most notably in 80.

its rocky islands   these were often the destination for those banished from Rome.

official posts   a reference to positions with the title *procurator*, held by men who were
essentially employed by the emperor in his civil administration, whether as governors
of smaller provinces, financial administrators in the imperial provinces, or in specialized
public roles, such as managing aqueducts, the mint or the grain supply. Some of these
posts could be held by imperial freedmen, but most were held by *equites*.

good examples   on the exemplary nature of Roman historiography, see Introduction,
p. 3.

wives followed their husbands into exile   Fannia, the daughter of Thrasea Paetus,
accompanied her husband, Helvidius Priscus, into exile on the two separate occasions he
suffered this fate, under both Nero and Vespasian (Pliny, *Letters* 7.19).

the much-trumpeted deaths of ancient men   Socrates had set the original example,
immortalized by Plato, but it had already long been emulated by Romans, perhaps most
famously by Marcus Porcius Cato, who had committed suicide in 46 BC rather than accept
Caesar's pardon. In this period steadfast death in the face of imperial repression (and
even compulsion) became a significant motif of the 'philosophical opposition' to the
various emperors.

and clear; for it was never proven by more terrible disasters to the Roman people or more legitimate evidence that the gods have care not for our wellbeing, but for our punishment.

> 1 How does Tacitus attempt to sell his history to the readers?
>
> 2 What does his reference to divine omens add to his account? Is it consistent with his usual tendency to avoid explaining events through reference to the gods?
>
> 3 Is there any emphasis on the usefulness of the history, or is it purely aimed at the enjoyment – albeit gruesome – of his readers?
>
> 4 Is the sort of history which Tacitus outlines here compatible with one which is written 'without affection and untouched by hate'?

After this preface, Tacitus includes a brief summary of the state of the Roman world in AD 69, the necessity for which is perhaps an indication that the annalistic style of beginning one's narrative with the start of any particular year is not the most helpful for the reader. In this survey he includes the state of Rome, the thoughts of the armies and the provinces and the general state of the empire, so that 'the reason and causes of events may also be known'. After this groundwork he then launches into his narrative of the 'year of four emperors' with all the complexities involved in trying to relate contemporary events which were occurring in so many different theatres. The surviving four and a quarter books take the narrative only as far as AD 70, and we have lost the bulk of his account of Vespasian, together with those of Titus and Domitian.

Introduction to the *Annals*: 1.1

I shall return to the narrative of AD 69 in the last chapter, but the bulk of this book is devoted to Tacitus' final historical work. This is conventionally known as the *Annals* (and will be so called here), but the actual Latin title was *ab excessu divi Augusti*, 'From the death of the divine Augustus'. Contrary to the suggestion that he had made in the preface to the *Histories*, Tacitus in fact turned not to more contemporary, but to more remote history and the dynasty of the Julio-Claudians. Beginning then from Augustus' death in AD 14, the *Annals* took the story up to the beginning of his earlier work with the death of Nero in 68. However, considerable chunks of the narrative – including its end – are again lost. Indeed, it is not even known whether Tacitus completed the work in full before his death, the date of which is uncertain. We do know that he served as proconsul of Asia in 112–13, something of a pinnacle for a senatorial career, and a reference within it seems to date Book 4 to 115: it therefore at least seems likely that he was still alive and writing when Hadrian replaced Trajan as emperor in 117, but we cannot be certain. He begins the work with only a brief preface.

1.1   **Kings held the city of Rome from the beginning; Lucius Brutus established freedom and the consulship. Dictatorships** were taken up according to the needs of the time; neither did the sovereignty of **the decemvirs** last beyond two years, nor did the consular rights of **the military tribunes** last for long. **The tyranny of Cinna and that of Sulla were short-lived**; the sway of Pompey and   5 Crassus quickly gave way before **Caesar, the arms of Lepidus and Antony before Augustus**: everything was exhausted by civil wars, and the last named took it all

---

Kings held the city of Rome from the beginning   after Rome's legendary foundation by its first king Romulus, it was said to have been ruled by six further kings until the overthrow of the last, Tarquinius Superbus ('Tarquin the Proud'). This sentence takes the form of a dactylic hexameter, the verse form in which epic was composed.

Lucius Brutus established freedom and the consulship   Brutus, the legendary founder of the republican system of government, was supposed to have been responsible for the expulsion of Tarquinius and subsequently to have served as one of the first two consuls in 509 BC. It is notable that Tacitus associates the idea of liberty with the institution of the consulship. However, what he understood by liberty was very different from what we would think now (see Introduction, p. 2).

Dictatorships   a dictator was a supreme but temporary magistrate appointed during a military or domestic crisis. Sulla and Caesar were perhaps the two most famous holders of the office; the latter was the last.

the decemvirs   this board of ten magistrates had reportedly been appointed instead of the consuls to draw up a new set of laws in 451 BC.

the military tribunes   these were appointed instead of consuls, according to Livy, for most of the years between 444 and 367 BC.

The tyranny of Cinna and that of Sulla were short-lived   Cinna was a supporter of Marius and opponent of Sulla. He had marched on Rome and captured it in 87 BC, and then illegally held the consulship for three successive years, before being killed in a mutiny. After Cinna's death, Sulla had in turn marched on Rome and become dictator in 81, before going into retirement in 79.

Caesar   Julius Caesar had formed an unofficial alliance with Pompey and Crassus in 60 BC (which is often known by the modern and anachronistic term 'the first triumvirate'); the latter had died fighting in Parthia in 53, and Caesar defeated the former at Pharsalus in 48. Caesar repeatedly held consulships and dictatorships until his death in 44.

the arms of Lepidus and Antony before Augustus   these three men had formed an official triumvirate in 43 BC (now often known as 'the second triumvirate'), but Lepidus was forced into retirement in 36, and Antony was defeated by Augustus at the battle of Actium in 31. Augustus was left as the last man standing.

into his power under the title of *princeps*. But the successes and failures of the Roman people of old were narrated by famous writers; **the age of Augustus did not lack fine intellects to relate it**, until they were discouraged by the rising tide 10 of flattery. The history of Tiberius, Gaius, Claudius and Nero was written falsely during their own lifetimes because of fear, and after they had died as a result of fresh hatreds. Therefore my plan is to narrate briefly the final days of Augustus, and then move on to the principate of Tiberius and the rest, **without anger and partisanship**, since I am far removed from the reasons for these. 15

---

1 Why do you think that Tacitus includes a brief summary of Roman constitutional history at the start of this preface?

2 What does Tacitus admire about the republican period of Roman history?

3 As mentioned above, the first sentence is written in such a way that it matches the verse form of epic poetry. Do you think that this has any significance?

4 Is the tone of this preface different at all from that of the *Histories*? Does it offer any other motivations for writing history?

5 Is it significant that Tacitus no longer begins his annalistic history with the start of a calendar year, but with the death of the first emperor?

---

into his power here Tacitus finally uses the official word for power in Rome, *imperium*. The previous lines have contained four Latin near-synonyms, but it is perhaps significant that Tacitus keeps this term for the power of Augustus and the subsequent lasting system which he instituted.

under the title of *princeps* there is a key Tacitean juxtaposition here, as he underlines the difference between the reality, the actual *imperium* held by Augustus, and the public image, that he was simply *princeps*, namely first among equals. This is underlined by his use of the word for 'name' or 'title' with *princeps*.

the age of Augustus did not lack fine intellects to relate it it is not entirely clear to whom Tacitus is referring here. Livy and Asinius Pollio have been suggested, but the latter stopped his *Histories* at 42 BC and the former at 9 BC. Tacitus may also have in mind men such as Cremutius Cordus (on whom see **4.34–5**, pp. 107–11).

without anger and partisanship in Latin this is *sine ira et studio* (compare Tacitus' use of the phrase 'without affection and untouched by hate' in the preface to the *Histories*). It is a much-quoted phrase when historians are comparing Tacitus' stated aims with his practice, and discussing whether he did succeed in writing without bias towards or against particular individuals.

2 Augustus and the first accession

After his brief preface tracing the history of Rome from the kings through to the emergence of Octavian, Tacitus gives a more detailed summary of the **Augustan principate** before moving on to Augustus' death and the accession of Tiberius. His account incorporates retrospective views on Augustus' achievements and focuses on the interaction between the new emperor and the Senate. However, the immediate question which springs to mind is just why Tacitus has chosen to begin at this point. He had explained in the preface that good accounts already existed of the Augustan period, but his starting-point also draws particular attention to the occasion of the first accession to the position of *princeps*, by Augustus' heir, Tiberius.

A statue of Augustus, veiled in a toga to depict his participation in a sacrifice.

The principate of Augustus and his plans for succession: 1.2–5

1.2   Following **the slaughter of Brutus and Cassius** there no longer remained any state forces, and **Pompeius was crushed off Sicily**, with **Lepidus cast aside** and

---

Augustan principate   Octavian received the name Augustus from the Senate in 27 BC, a title connected with the religious practice of taking the auspices. This most commonly meant consulting the flight of birds to predict the future or to check that the gods approved of a particular action. Therefore the title had the meaning 'someone divinely approved'. It was used by Augustus and all subsequent emperors.

the slaughter of Brutus and Cassius   both Brutus and Cassius committed suicide in 42 BC after being defeated at the battle of Philippi by Antony and Octavian, so the word 'slaughter' is, as Furneaux notes (p. 180), 'used with some rhetorical licence'.

Pompeius was crushed off Sicily   Sextus Pompeius was the son of Pompey the Great and in 43 BC had been made naval commander by the Senate. Outlawed under the triumvirs, he seized Sicily and used it as a base to blockade Rome from its overseas grain. He was finally defeated at the battle of Naulochus in 36 and fled to Asia, but was captured and put to death.

Lepidus cast aside   although Lepidus was forced to retire from the triumvirate in 36 BC, Augustus allowed him to retain the title of chief priest (*pontifex maximus*) until his death in 13 or 12.

Antony killed, and even the Julian faction had no remaining commander save Caesar, who abandoning the title of triumvir styled himself as consul and content with tribunician rights to protect the ordinary people; once he had won over the soldiers with gifts, the people with the grain supply, and all with

An aureus (gold coin) of 43 BC depicting Octavian (left) and on the reverse Julius Caesar (right). However, both are referred to by the name C CAESAR.

Antony killed   again there is some licence here, as Antony, like Brutus and Cassius, committed suicide.

Caesar   it is noteworthy that Tacitus uses the name Caesar of Augustus in this context, but this is in line with Octavian's own practice. After his posthumous adoption by Julius Caesar, he would have taken the name Gaius Iulius Caesar, but could also have used the further name Octavianus, to show that by birth he was an Octavius. However, Augustus never used this, as his adoptive name was far more important (unlike modern historians who use the name 'Octavian' to distinguish him from his adoptive father). A gold coin issued in 43 BC had the head of Octavian on one side and the head of Julius Caesar on the other, and both were labelled as C CAESAR. Octavian was at pains to emphasize his close ties to the dead dictator, and this is appropriate to the Tacitean context. However, in this section Tacitus is concerned with nomenclature (i.e. the use of names and titles).

consul and content with tribunician rights to protect the ordinary people   Tacitus telescopes a gradual constitutional evolution here. Initially Augustus seems to have determined to maintain his hold on power by serving as consul every year: he held the office without break between 31 and 23 BC. However, in 23 he abandoned this plan, perhaps because it was seen as an ostentatiously untraditional use of the annual magistracy, and it blocked the opportunities of others to hold the position. He may have held tribunician power already, but it was now the cornerstone of his position, and became 'annual and perpetual'. The office of *tribunus plebis* had been set up to create magistrates to champion the ordinary people (the *plebs*), and gave its holders among other things personal inviolability, the right of veto, and the ability to propose legislation. Although Augustus did not hold the office proper, he held its powers, and even dated his reign from 23 BC onwards by using the number of years that he had held this office. He also used it subsequently to mark out his successors by bestowing this power on members of the imperial family, as is noted in the case of Tiberius in the next section.

gifts   Augustus records these enormous gifts of money (as well as those which he made to the ordinary people) in his own account of his achievements, which he wrote to be inscribed after his death outside his mausoleum in Rome (*Res Gestae* 15–16).

the grain supply   free grain for adult male citizens had been established by Publius Clodius Pulcher as tribune in 58 BC. Its supply had been seriously interrupted during the civil wars, but Augustus restored it and fixed the number receiving it at 200,000. Suetonius records in his life of Augustus (*Augustus* 42) that he had considered abolishing the provision of all free grain, but realized that a subsequent politician would be bound to restore it at some point to win the favour of the people.

the pleasures of peace, he gradually rose up, and drew the responsibilities of the   10
Senate, magistrates and laws to himself with no opposition, since the fiercest had
fallen in battle or through proscription, and as for the rest of the nobility, the
readier each of them was for slavery, the more they were elevated by wealth and
honours, and after rising through revolution they preferred their present safety
to the dangers of the past. Nor did the provinces reject this state of affairs, as the   15
rule of the Senate and people was mistrusted because of the competition between
powerful individuals and the greed of magistrates, since the assistance of the laws
was feeble, shaken as they were by violence, corruption and finally bribery.

1.3   Moreover, as supports to his tyranny Augustus advanced Claudius Marcellus,
his sister's son, while only a young man, giving him a priesthood and a curule   20
aedileship, and Marcus Agrippa, who was not well-born, but a fine soldier and
an ally in his victory, whom he appointed to a repeated consulship; then, after

---

peace   the word that Tacitus uses here is not the usual *pax*, but *otium*, which has
the force of 'leisure' or 'relaxation'. In Roman historiography it often carries negative
overtones as the cause of moral decline.

through proscription   this was a murderous procedure by which a list of Roman citizens
was published declaring them outlaws and able to be killed. It had been used by Sulla, but
was also adopted in 43 BC by the triumvirate of Antony, Octavian and Lepidus, as a way
of removing political opponents and generating funds from their confiscated property.

they preferred their present safety to the dangers of the past   this is the end of an
exceptionally long sentence, which had begun with the start of the section. Just as
striking is the absence of a clear structure to the sentence, as Tacitus piles up details of
how Augustus gradually won total power for himself in Rome.

shaken as they were by violence, corruption and finally bribery   the government of
the various provinces of the Roman empire under the republican system was particularly
open to corruption, as officials often sought to recoup the cost of winning office through
bribery from those they had been appointed to govern. If prosecution did ensue it was
particularly hard for provincials to secure conviction in courts which were convened in
Rome, where many of the jurors knew the accused and had even perhaps been guilty of
similar crimes.

Claudius Marcellus   Marcellus, the son of Octavia, was born in 42 BC; he served under
Augustus in Spain and was married to Augustus' daughter, Julia, his own cousin, in 25. In
23 as curule aedile (a magistracy which was usually one of the next options for senators
following the quaestorship, the first step in the senatorial career) he had responsibility
for putting on lavish shows, which would have endeared him to the urban populace.
However, he died late in the same year.

Marcus Agrippa   Agrippa had been instrumental in Augustus' key victories over Sextus
Pompeius and Antony; he had also sought considerable popularity by his aedileship in
33 BC, during which he had taken particular interest in the infrastructure of Rome, most
notably in maintaining the sewers and repairing and building new aqueducts. He was
actually consul on three occasions (37, 28 and 27), and married Julia after the death
of Marcellus.

Marcellus died, he made Agrippa his son-in-law; he elevated Tiberius Nero and Claudius Drusus, **his stepsons**, with the title of *imperator*, even during the time when his own line was intact. For he had adopted Agrippa's sons, **Gaius** 25 **and Lucius**, into the family of the Caesars, and before they had given up **their children's clothes**, despite the pretence of reluctance, he had most passionately desired them to be called '**leaders of the youth**' and be marked out as future consuls. After Agrippa had passed away, death carried off Lucius Caesar as he travelled to the Spanish provinces and Gaius as he returned from Armenia, 30 weakened by a wound – **deaths hastened by fate** or **the plotting of their stepmother Livia** – and since Drusus had previously died, **Nero survived alone of his stepchildren**, and everything went in his direction: **he was adopted as son, colleague in command, and partner in the tribunician power**, and was

---

his stepsons   they were the sons of Tiberius Claudius Nero and Livia. They had divorced in 39 BC so that Livia could marry Augustus despite being pregnant at the time with Drusus.

imperator   the title was an honorific one traditionally bestowed on a victorious general by his soldiers, and was so won by Octavian. However, he subsequently adopted it as one of his permanent titles. As emperor he could also grant this honour to others: the date of Tiberius and Drusus winning the title is not certain, but its achievement is a sign of their military importance to the Augustan principate from 20 BC onwards.

Gaius and Lucius   Julia bore Gaius to Agrippa in 20 BC and Lucius in 17, when both were adopted by Augustus.

their children's clothes   the *toga praetexta* had a purple border and was worn by boys of high birth until they came of age (which tended to occur by the time of their seventeenth birthday).

'leaders of the youth'   this was an honorific title, but the Latin word *principes* used of them was the same as that used by the emperor himself. Its grant marked them out as potential successors.

deaths hastened by fate   Agrippa had died in 12 BC, Lucius in AD 2 and Gaius in AD 4.

the plotting of their stepmother Livia   stepmothers in Rome were caricatured as notoriously hostile to their stepchildren, but Livia is also the first in a line of powerful women in the *Annals*. This far-fetched allegation is repeated by Dio (*Roman History* 55.10.10), but note the way in which Tacitus adds this possibility as a barbed alternative to a simple blow of fate.

Nero survived alone of his stepchildren   Drusus had died in 9 BC. Here the use of the name Nero for the future emperor Tiberius is worth noting (in spite of his being called Tiberius Nero earlier in the section): again Tacitus implicitly draws the reader's attention towards the question of nomenclature, but there is probably also a suggestion for the structure of the work as a whole, since the final emperor whose reign Tacitus was to relate in the *Annals* was the even more famous Nero.

he was adopted as son ... in the tribunician power   this all happened in AD 4 after the death of Gaius Caesar; previously he had spent a period of voluntary exile in Rhodes (from 6 BC to AD 2), perhaps out of pique at the fact that he felt marginalized by the new-found prominence of Gaius and Lucius.

paraded before all the armies, not through the dark arts of his mother, as before, 35
but at her open instigation. For she had got such a tight grip on the elderly Augustus
that he had banished to the island of Planasia his sole grandson, **Agrippa Postumus**,
who was indeed devoid of decent qualities and foolishly headstrong in his physical
strength, but found guilty of no scandal. In contrast, he put **Germanicus**, the son
of Drusus, in charge of the eight legions on the Rhine and gave orders for him to be 40
adopted by Tiberius, although **there was already a son in Tiberius' household** who
was approaching adulthood, in order that he could rely upon further protection.
There was no ongoing war at this time except against the Germans, which was being
continued more to remove the stain caused by **the loss of the army with Quinctilius
Varus** than from a desire to extend the empire or for a worthy reward. On the home 45
front all was calm and the magistrates carried the same names; younger men had
been born after the victory at Actium, and even most of the older men in the midst
of the civil wars: how many were left who had seen republican government?

---

1   How is Augustus portrayed here? Is his rise depicted as carefully calculated, or
    as the result of chance?
2   What plan did Augustus develop for the succession? Is his behaviour
    consistent?
3   What steps do modern-day political regimes take to ensure that the successor
    of their choosing comes to power?
4   Look at all the references to names and titles in this section. What point is
    Tacitus trying to put across?
5   What attitude does Tacitus display towards the previous republican system of
    government? Do you think that he idealizes it?

---

paraded before all the armies   this is a slight exaggeration, as he only visited the armies
of Illyricum and Germany in this period. However, these were the key armies of the time,
and Tacitus is perhaps at pains to emphasize where power potentially lay.

Agrippa Postumus   the third son of Agrippa and Julia was born after his father's death
in 12 BC, but after his adoption by Augustus in AD 4 (together with Tiberius), he was
subsequently relegated by Augustus to Surrentum (modern Sorrento) in 6, before being
banished the following year to Planasia (a small island off Elba).

Germanicus   the son of Drusus, Tiberius' brother, and Antonia the Younger, born in 15 or
16 BC. He was adopted by Tiberius in AD 4 and given overall command in Germany in 13.

there was already a son in Tiberius' household   this Drusus was the only surviving son of
Tiberius' marriage to Vipsania, born in about 13 BC; he married Germanicus' sister Livilla.

the loss of the army with Quinctilius Varus   this is a reference to the ambush and almost
total annihilation of three legions under Publius Quinctilius Varus in AD 9 by Arminius. It
took place in the Teutoburg forest north of modern Osnabrück: the heavy defeat had put
an end to Augustus' hopes to expand the empire in Germany beyond the Rhine, and also
seems to have altered his overall vision with regard to the empire. Previously he seems to
have had an expansionist policy, but now instead adopted one of consolidation of what
was already held.

1.4   Therefore, once the system of government had been overturned, no trace of the former proper behaviour remained: after shedding political equality, all looked to the orders of the *princeps*, while Augustus in the prime of life secured himself, his house and peace. But after his old age had now advanced and become worn out by physical illness, and the end was at hand and with it **new hopes**, a few men vainly discussed the benefits of freedom, a greater number feared war, while yet others desired it. **Much the greatest number had different things to say** about their prospective masters: that Agrippa was savage, fired up by **his disgrace**, and unequal to such a great responsibility because of his youth and a lack of experience, that Tiberius Nero was mature in years, tested in war, and possessed of the ancient and innate arrogance of the Claudian family, and that many pointers to his cruelty were now coming to the surface, although they were being suppressed. **He had been raised from his earliest infancy in the ruling house**; consulships and triumphs had been heaped on him as a young man; not even in those years in which he had lived as an exile on Rhodes behind the façade of retirement did he think of anything but anger, **pretence and hidden lusts**. In addition there was his mother and her womanly lack of self-control: he would have to serve a woman and what is more **two youths** who would crush the state for a while and at some point tear it apart.

---

1 In this section Tacitus focuses closely on what people thought about Tiberius (and Agrippa), rather than giving his own opinion. Of this Goodyear says: 'To attempt to re-create the opinions current at a particular time is often a proper and necessary part of the historian's task. And, in this present instance, the state of opinion at the crucial first transition of the principate is of exceptional interest. That Tacitus tries to present it for us is admirable; the way he does so is not' (vol. 1, pp. 119–20). Do you agree with Goodyear's point of view?

2 Why do you think that women in the imperial family are so frequently portrayed as being engaged in secrecy and deception?

3 Does Tacitus' account here live up to his claim in the preface to be writing *sine ira et studio* ('without anger and partisanship')?

---

new hopes   this is the literal translation of the Latin and suits the context, as men had hopes of a new beginning with Augustus' death. However, the Latin words also suggest the meaning 'revolutionary hopes', which is picked up by the following comments, where Tacitus suggests that some men were openly hoping for the opportunities offered by renewed civil war.

Much the greatest number had different things to say   the Latin word here is ambiguous: it could mean 'spread various negative reports of'.

his disgrace   that is, his banishment, first to Surrentum and then to Planasia.

He had been raised from his earliest infancy in the ruling house   Tiberius had been three years old when his mother divorced his father and married Octavian.

pretence and hidden lusts   note the emphasis on deception and secrecy as key qualities in Tiberius.

two youths   Germanicus and Drusus. The point was that after the death of Tiberius the existence of two potential heirs offered the prospect of civil war once more.

1.5   While men had these thoughts and others like them, the health of Augustus got worse, and some people suspected a crime on the part of his wife. Indeed the rumour had spread that a few months earlier Augustus had travelled to Planasia to see Agrippa, with chosen men in the know and only **Fabius Maximus** to accompany him; at this meeting there were many tears and signs of affection 5 on both sides, and as a result hope that the young man would be restored to his grandfather's house: Maximus had revealed this to his wife Marcia, and she to Livia. This became known to Caesar; shortly afterwards when Maximus had died, perhaps by suicide, Marcia's laments could be heard at his funeral as she accused herself for having been the cause of her husband's death. **Whatever was the case** 10 **in this matter**, Tiberius, who had scarcely set foot in Illyricum, was summoned by a speedy letter from his mother; nor has it been satisfactorily resolved whether he found Augustus in **the city of Nola** still drawing breath or already dead. For Livia had sealed off the house and streets with fierce guards, and positive news was made public from time to time until, after those measures had been 15 provided for which the moment seemed to recommend, the same report brought the simultaneous news that **Augustus had died** and **Nero** had taken control of affairs.

The accession of Tiberius: 1.6–8

1.6   **The first crime of the new principate** was the murder of Agrippa Postumus: he was unsuspecting and unarmed, and it was with difficulty that the centurion brought himself to kill him, although he went about it with a determined mind. Tiberius said nothing about this matter in the Senate: he was pretending the orders were those of Augustus, in which he had instructed the tribune who was 5

Fabius Maximus   he had been consul in 11 BC and was subsequently governor of Asia.

Whatever was the case in this matter   note that Tacitus gives this whole story only as a rumour.

the city of Nola   a town in Campania, ten miles east of Naples.

Augustus had died   the date of his death was 19 August AD 14.

Nero   on the use of this name for Tiberius, see note on p. 26.

The first crime of the new principate   this is a clear anticipation of the start of Nero's principate at the opening of Book 13, which begins with the words: 'The first death during the new principate', describing that of the proconsul of Asia, which was arranged by Agrippina, the new emperor's mother, in Nero's ignorance. This echo is made all the stronger coming as it does after similar parallels (in Tacitus' account) between the ends of the previous emperors: Agrippina had poisoned Claudius, just as some suspected a crime on Livia's part; likewise Agrippina had posted guards and kept spreading reports that Claudius was recovering (12.68); Claudius' funeral was subsequently celebrated in the fashion of Augustus'; and Tacitus describes Agrippina as 'rivalling the magnificence of her great-grandmother Livia' (12.69).

in charge of Agrippa's guard not to delay in putting him to death whenever he himself had breathed his last. There is no doubt that Augustus, after making numerous fierce complaints about the young man's behaviour, had ensured that his exile was ordained by decree of the Senate: but he had never gone so far as to kill any of his relatives, nor was it believable that his grandson's murder had been 10 carried out for his stepson's safety. It is closer to the truth that Tiberius and Livia, the former out of fear and the latter from a stepmother's hatred, had hastened the slaughter of the suspect and despised young man. When the centurion, following military practice, announced that what Tiberius had ordered had been done, he replied that he had not given any orders and that the justification for the action 15 should be reported in the Senate. After **Sallustius Crispus, who was privy to state secrets**, discovered this (he was the man who had sent the note to the tribune), in fear that he would be unfairly put forward as a defendant, which would be equally dangerous whether he told lies or the truth, he advised Livia that the secrets of the house, the advice of friends and the service of soldiers should not 20 be broadcast, and that Tiberius should not weaken the power of the principate by calling everything before the Senate: **this was the condition of autocracy, namely that the accounts did not add up unless they were submitted to only one man.**

Sallustius Crispus, who was privy to state secrets   Crispus was the great-nephew and adopted son of Sallust the historian and was to die six years later. Tacitus gives him an extended obituary (3.30), in which he compares him at length to Maecenas, one of Augustus' trustiest advisers, for the way in which he preferred to operate influentially behind the scenes rather than hold open office. This is hinted at by the wording in the present passage, which suggests that he was one of the *amici* of the *princeps*, that is 'friends' who made up an unofficial but powerful group of direct advisers to the emperor.

this was the condition of autocracy … to only one man   Tacitus closes the section with a particularly striking epigram from the mouth of Crispus. Such succinct and bitingly memorable expressions are typical of Tacitus, but in this instance the need for secrecy has important implications for the historian himself. Tacitus had noted the growing ignorance of affairs of state in his preface to the *Histories*, and Dio makes the same point more explicitly (referring to the year 27 BC): 'However, what happened after this cannot be told in the same way as earlier events. For previously every matter was brought before the Senate and the people, even if it occurred somewhere distant … But from that time most things began to be concealed and unspoken' (53.19.1–3).

1 In this section the new principate has begun, but who is in charge? Augustus, Livia or Tiberius?

2 What are we to make of the parallels between Tacitus' accounts of Tiberius and Nero at the start of their reigns? (See note on p. 29.) Are we to draw any historical conclusions from them? Is there any significance in the difference of wording for Tiberius ('the first crime of the new principate') and for Nero ('the first death during the new principate')?

3 What is the effect of Tacitus beginning his account of Tiberius' reign with this notice? What opening topic might we have expected instead?

4 What does Tacitus suggest are the difficulties for a historian writing the narrative of these events?

5 Does Crispus' assertion that secrecy is key to the principate undermine Tacitus' whole project from the outset?

6 Do similar conflicts between openness and secrecy affect modern governments as well, and even democracies?

1.7 But in Rome there was a stampede towards slavery on the part of the consuls, the senators and the equestrians. The more distinguished each man was, the more false and hastier they were, and with carefully arranged expressions, so that they should not appear happy at the death of one *princeps* nor too sad at the beginning of the next, they combined tears and joy, complaints and flattery. The 5 consuls Sextus Pompeius and Sextus Appuleius were the first to swear allegiance to Tiberius Caesar, and in their presence Seius Strabo and Gaius Turranius, the former **the prefect of the praetorian cohorts**, the latter **the prefect of the grain supply**; next came **the Senate, the soldiers and the people**. For Tiberius initiated everything through the consuls as if the old constitution still existed and he was 10 uncertain about ruling: he did not even put forward the decree in which he called the senators to **the *curia*** with any title except that of **the tribunician power** which he had received under Augustus. The words of the decree were few and

---

the prefect of the praetorian cohorts the praetorian guard had become established as the military force in Rome by Augustus: previously no troops had been allowed to bear arms within the city. They were usually commanded jointly by two equestrians, called prefects. Seius Strabo was soon joined as commander of the guard by his son Seianus.

the prefect of the grain supply this was the other great equestrian office in Rome. Turranius still held this office in AD 48.

the Senate, the soldiers and the people this is an adaptation of the conventional description of the Roman state as *S.P.Q.R.* ('the Senate and people of Rome'). The insertion of the soldiers points to the army now representing a new and distinct constituency within the Roman state.

the *curia* the Senate met in the *curia Iulia* in the Forum (see photo on p. 12).

the tribunician power on this, see note on p. 24. One of its entitlements was the right to summon meetings of the Senate.

very modest in sentiment: he would seek their advice about honours for his father, **he was not going to be parted from the body**, and convening the Senate was the one public act he was carrying out. But after the death of Augustus he had given the password to the praetorian cohorts as commander; there were guards, arms and the other paraphernalia of court; soldiers were escorting him into the Forum and to the *curia*. He sent letters to the armies as if he had taken over the principate, displaying no hesitation anywhere except when he was speaking in the Senate. **The principal reason** was fear that Germanicus, who had at his disposal so many legions, a huge number of allied auxiliaries and remarkable popularity among the people, might prefer to hold power rather than wait for it. He was also making a concession towards public opinion that he should seem to have been called upon and chosen by the state rather than to have crept to power by a wife's ambition and an old man's adoption. Later it was realized that a pose of hesitation had been assumed so that he could also observe the inclinations of leading figures at close quarters: for, twisting words and looks into an offence, he filed them away.

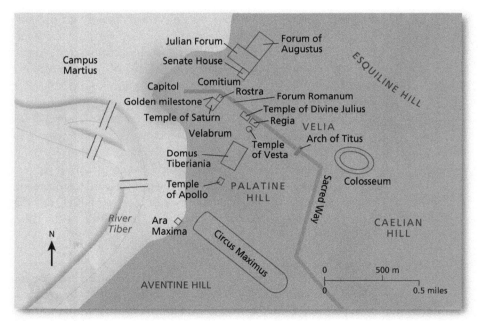

The centre of Rome.

he was not going to be parted from the body Tiberius' duty as a son (in Latin *pietas*) demanded that he should escort the body of Augustus to Rome to get there in time for the meeting of the Senate; it was from Nola that he had issued the decree.

The principal reason is this reason credible? How can anyone have known? It does prepare for the first major episode of Tiberius' reign, the mutinies in Pannonia and, especially, Germany (see Chapter 3, pp. 45–72).

1.8   On the first day of the Senate he allowed nothing to be discussed except the last rites
of Augustus, whose will, brought in by the Vestal Virgins, had Tiberius and Livia
as his heirs. Livia was adopted into the Julian family and the Augustan name. He
had included his grandsons and great-grandsons as heirs in the second instance,
and in the third leading figures of the state, the majority of whom he hated: but   5
he did it for show and glory in posterity. His legacies did not go beyond the norm
for a citizen save for the fact that he gave forty-three and a half million sesterces
to the populace and common people, a thousand sesterces to each individual
soldier of the praetorian cohorts, five hundred for each of the urban cohorts,
and three hundred to every individual who was a member of a legion or a citizen   10
cohort. Then a discussion took place about suitable honours; of these, the ones
that seemed particularly outstanding were that his funeral should be led from

---

On the first day of the Senate   the precise date is not known, but it will have been in
early September AD 14.

the Vestal Virgins   it was usual for wills and other important documents to be kept with
the Vestals.

Augustan name   henceforth she became known as Augusta or Julia Augusta.

his grandsons and great-grandsons   these were Drusus, Tiberius' son, Germanicus and
the three sons of Germanicus.

the majority of whom he hated   this contradicts Suetonius (*Augustus* 101), who says
that these men were relatives and friends.

forty-three and a half million sesterces to the populace and common people   that is 43½
times the fortune that qualified a man to be a senator. If it is assumed that this money
went to the same body of citizens who received free grain (the *plebs frumentaria*), they
numbered about 200,000 and so would have received about 200 sesterces each. The
phrase 'to the populace and common people' appears to have been a traditional formula
to refer to the citizens of Rome, who usually received such largesse.

urban cohorts   this clause is omitted in Tacitus' text as it has come down to us, but is
supplied from the parallel accounts of Suetonius and Dio. Three urban cohorts had been
established by Augustus under the control of the prefect of the city as a form of police
force.

a citizen cohort   these were volunteer units classed alongside the legionary troops, and
there seem to have been 32 or 33 of them in total.

the triumphal gate, and that the titles of the laws he had passed and the names of the peoples he had conquered should be carried before him, measures proposed by **Asinius Gallus and Lucius Arruntius** respectively. **Valerius Messala** made the additional proposal that the oath in the name of Tiberius should be renewed every year; he was asked by Tiberius whether he had tabled this motion as a result of his own instructions, and he replied that he had spoken voluntarily, and that in matters of state he would make use of no deliberations but his own, even at risk of causing offence: **this was the only form of flattery left to be used.** The senators exclaimed in unison that the body should be carried to the pyre on the shoulders of senators. **Caesar excused them this task with arrogant restraint,** and he warned the people by edict against wishing to cremate Augustus in the Forum rather than in the **Campus Martius, his appointed resting place,** in just the same way as they

15

20

---

the triumphal gate   the nature of this gate is uncertain, but it was probably a permanent structure near or in the Campus Martius and used specifically in the celebration of a triumph, i.e. a ceremony to honour a commander who had won a major victory on the battlefield. Arruntius' proposal also approximated the celebration of a triumph for Augustus' whole career, with its naming of all the peoples conquered representing the captured enemies of a conventional triumph.

Asinius Gallus and Lucius Arruntius   Gallus was the son of Asinius Pollio, the historian; he had been consul in 8 BC; he was disliked by Tiberius, arrested in AD 30 and later died of starvation. Likewise Arruntius had been consul under Augustus in AD 6, but fell from favour under Tiberius and committed suicide in 37, rather than fight trumped-up charges: even though Tiberius' death and Gaius' succession were expected soon, he felt that the change offered no prospects for improvement. Tacitus narrates the deaths of both men in the sixth book of the *Annals*: their mention by name here at the outset of the new principate is perhaps intended to foreshadow their ends in Tiberius' final years.

Valerius Messala   he had been consul in 3 BC and subsequently won triumphal decorations for his contribution in helping to put down a revolt in Illyricum in AD 6.

this was the only form of flattery left to be used   Tacitus' point is that such a show of liberty was the only form of sycophancy which was original – all the more ordinary forms had already been tried.

Caesar excused them this task with arrogant restraint   does Tacitus use the title Caesar for Tiberius purely for variety, or is he using it pointedly? This statement seems to be directly contradicted by Suetonius and Dio, who recorded that the senators did carry the body to the Campus Martius: either they are mistaken, or the senators insisted on doing it in spite of Tiberius' best efforts. The new *princeps* boasted of restraint (*moderatio*) as one of his virtues (see **3.50** with note, p. 98).

Campus Martius   the flood-plain lying to the north-west of the city (see map on p. 6).

his appointed resting place   his massive Mausoleum, whose inner drums still survive: it was under construction as early as 28 BC and was set within parkland in the northern part of the Campus Martius beside the *via Lata*. Marcellus had been the first member of the imperial family to be entombed there.

had once disrupted the funeral of divine Julius with excessive enthusiasm. On 25
the day of the funeral soldiers stood in position as if on guard duty, much to the
mockery of those who had themselves seen or heard report from their parents
of that day when slavery was still raw and freedom was sought once more, if
unsuccessfully, when the murder of the dictator Caesar seemed to some the worst
crime and to others the most beautiful: they noted that now an old *princeps* of 30
long standing sway, when even the power of his heirs towards the state had been
provided for, certainly needed to be protected by military help, so that his burial
should be peaceful.

---

1 How is the behaviour of the senators depicted in this debate?

2 Goodyear describes 'with arrogant restraint' as 'perhaps the most effective
   oxymoron in Tacitus', but goes on to say that it is a case of the historian
   attempting to 'pervert by his interpretation a virtue (that is, restraint) to
   which Tiberius could and did lay claim' (vol. 1, p. 149). Do you think that
   Tacitus is fair to Tiberius?

Tacitus has just noted that Caesar's death met with mixed reviews, and he
now expands upon this technique in offering contrasting opinions about
Augustus' rule.

Opposing assessments of Augustus: 1.9–10

1.9   After this there was a lot of talk about Augustus himself: the majority marvelled
      at empty coincidences, such as the fact that the same date which had once been
      the first occasion of his acceptance of command was also the last of his life, and
      that he had ended his life in the same house and room as his father Octavius. Also
      there was praise for the number of his consulships, with which he had matched 5

---

the funeral of divine Julius   his body and bier were burned in the Forum before they
reached the pyre that had been constructed in the Campus Martius. Augustus later built a
temple to his adoptive father on the spot in the Forum where this impromptu cremation
had occurred.

an old *princeps* of long standing sway   Augustus was 76 at the time of his death, and it
had been 44 years since Actium had left him sole ruler of the Roman world.

towards the state   I have tried to maintain Tacitus' ambiguity here. The Latin also has
the clear additional meaning of 'against the state'.

the same date   on 19 August he had been elected to his first consulship in 43 BC, and
now in AD 14 he had died on the same date.

the number of his consulships   he had been consul 13 times, Marius seven and Corvus
(in the fourth century) six.

those of Valerius Corvus and Gaius Marius put together, for his tribunician power which had been held continuously for thirty-seven years, for his winning the title of *imperator* on twenty-one occasions, and for his other honours which were held repeatedly or were innovative. But by men of intelligence his life was variously lauded or censured. The former said that as a result of his sense of duty towards **his father** and the dire need of the state, in which at that time there was no room for the laws, he had been driven to civil war, which could be neither prepared for nor conducted by honourable methods. He had made many concessions to Antony, while he was taking revenge against his father's killers, and many to **Lepidus**. After the latter grew old in idleness and the former was ruined by **his lusts**, there had been no other medicine for the strife-ridden country than for it to be ruled by one man. Nevertheless the constitution had been organized not as a kingship nor as a dictatorship, but in the name of a *princeps*; the empire had been ringed by **the Ocean or by distant rivers**; the legions, the provinces, the fleets, everything had become interconnected; the rule of law existed among the citizens, **restraint among the allies; the city itself had been finely decked out**; only a few matters had been dealt with by force so that the rest might enjoy some peace.

---

his father   this time it is his adoptive father, Julius Caesar, who is meant.

Lepidus   on the triumvirate he formed with Antony and Augustus, see p. 21.

his lusts   the reference is to his ten-year relationship with Cleopatra, with whom he had three children.

the Ocean or by distant rivers   this echoes the claims which Augustus made in his own *Res Gestae*, e.g.: 'I pacified the Gallic and Spanish provinces and Germany too, in the area which the Ocean encloses from Cadiz to the mouth of the Elbe' (26.2). The Romans considered that the known world was encircled by an all-surrounding Ocean, while the rivers meant are the Rhine, Euphrates and Danube.

restraint among the allies   the Latin can mean both 'restraint in dealing with the provincials' and 'restraint on the part of the provincials', and both are probably meant.

the city itself had been finely decked out   according to Suetonius, Augustus boasted that he had inherited a Rome made of mud-brick, but left her clad in marble (*Augustus* 28). In fact the use of marble was especially prevalent in religious buildings, such as the temple of Apollo on the Palatine, the temple of Mars Ultor (Mars the Avenger), and the *Ara Pacis* (the Altar of Peace).

Relief from the Ara Pacis *(the Altar of Peace), depicting perhaps the goddess Peace herself as the bringer of fertility.*

1.10   There was talk from the opposite point of view: his sense of duty towards his father and the crisis of the state had been used as a pretext: but it was from a lust for tyranny 25 that **veterans had been assembled by bribery**, that an army had been readied by a youth who was only a private citizen, that **the legions of the consul had been seduced**, that his support of **the Pompeian party** had been feigned; next when by senatorial decree **he had seized possession of the** *fasces* **and the status of a praetor**,

veterans had been assembled by bribery   in 44 BC Octavian had, without any official power, recruited Caesar's veterans by giving them 500 denarii each.

the legions of the consul had been seduced   in November of the same year, two legions had deserted the consul Antony.

the Pompeian party   Octavian had initially associated with the senatorial opponents of Antony, and used Caesar's veterans to fight on behalf of the 'state'. Tacitus' use of the adjective 'Pompeian' here is pointed: even the party that was notionally putting the state first was really just the power bloc of Pompey the Great, an earlier dynast.

he had seized possession of the *fasces* **and the status of a praetor**   on Cicero's motion on 1 January 43 BC, Octavian was appointed pro-praetor and given a share of the command (with the consuls) of the war against Antony, so that he might act as a counterweight to Antony in the battle for winning over Caesar's veterans. The *fasces* were the bundles of rods around an axe which symbolized the holding of *imperium* (and with it the right to mete out punishments, including the death penalty), given here because of Octavian's status as a praetor.

Hirtius and Pansa were slaughtered – whether the enemy had killed them, or 30
poison poured into a wound had done for Pansa and his own soldiers for Hirtius,
acting in concert with the trick's author, Caesar – and he had seized the forces of
both; a consulship had been twisted out of an unwilling Senate, and the arms
which he had received against Antony had been turned against the state; as for
the proscription of citizens and the allotment of land, these had been praised 35
not even by those who had carried them out. Certainly the deaths of Cassius and
Brutus could be ascribed to paternal enmities – although it was right for private
hatreds to be given up for the public good: but Pompeius had been deceived
by the appearance of peace, Lepidus by the pretence of friendship; afterwards
Antony, who had been seduced by the treaties of Tarentum and Brundisium 40
and the marriage to his sister, had paid the penalty of this deceptive marriage
tie with death.

Hirtius and Pansa were slaughtered   of the two consuls of 43 BC, Pansa was wounded
in a battle with Antony on the way to join his colleague, and subsequently died of his
wounds, while Hirtius was actually killed in the battle of Mutina against Antony. It is hard
to imagine there was any substance to these allegations, though Suetonius, *Augustus* 11
gives a full account of the conspiracy theories, which appear to have been contemporary
in origin.

a consulship had been twisted out of an unwilling Senate   following Mutina, Octavian
had marched on Rome and demanded to be made consul at the age of merely 19 (the
minimum legal age was 41), before subsequently changing allegiance and joining Antony
and Lepidus.

the allotment of land   this was land seized to redistribute among the veterans of the
armies of the various triumvirs. Such land grabs caused a great deal of resentment and
chaos in Italy, and earned Octavian huge unpopularity.

Pompeius had been deceived by the appearance of peace   this is Sextus Pompeius who
had made the treaty of Misenum with the triumvirs in 39 BC, before Octavian alleged
that it had been contravened in the following year, when hostilities resumed.

the treaties of Tarentum and Brundisium and the marriage to his sister   these were
treaties of reconciliation between Antony and Octavian in 37 and 40 BC respectively.
The chronological order has been reversed so that Tacitus can end with the marriage
between Antony and Octavian's sister, Octavia, which was one of the terms of the treaty
of Brundisium. It is not entirely fair to refer to a 'deceptive marriage tie', since Antony
had three children with Cleopatra over nine years, while still married to Octavia (with
whom he had also produced two daughters): he eventually divorced her in 32.

The *Res Gestae*

It is interesting to compare these criticisms with Augustus' own version of these same events in the first two sections of *Res Gestae Divi Augusti* ('the achievements of the god Augustus'):

> [1] At the age of nineteen I obtained by private means and at my own private expense an army, with which I delivered the state to freedom when it had been overwhelmed by the tyranny of a faction. For this purpose the Senate added me to its number with honorific decrees, when Gaius Pansa and Aulus Hirtius were consuls, giving me the right to speak my opinion among the ex-consuls, and it bestowed *imperium* on me. It ordered me as a pro-praetor together with the consuls to see to it that the state should suffer no harm. The people, moreover, in the same year elected me consul, when both consuls had fallen in war, and triumvir for the organization of the state. [2] Those who had murdered my father, I drove into exile, avenging their crime by the lawful decisions of the courts, and later I twice defeated them in battle when they waged war on the state.

- How do the two accounts portray the same events differently? Do they use the same or different language?
- Do you think that Tacitus' version is directly indebted to the *Res Gestae*, and that it is an implicit debunking of Augustus' own propaganda?

Certainly there had been peace after this, but it was bloody: there were **the Lollian and Varian disasters**, the executions of men like **Varro, Egnatius and Iullus**. And he did not escape criticism for his domestic life: **his wife had been seized from Nero** and as a mockery the priests were consulted as to whether he could marry her in a proper fashion whilst her pregnancy was still to run its course ... **and** ⁵ **the luxurious excess of Vedius Pollio**; finally Livia was a harsh mother for the

---

the Lollian and Varian disasters   Marcus Lollius had suffered a defeat in Gaul at the hands of raiding Germans in 17–16 BC, a defeat whose importance was perhaps exaggerated and did not match the scale of the one suffered by Varus (on which see note on p. 27).

Varro, Egnatius and Iullus   Varro Murena in the late 20s BC and Egnatius Rufus in 19 were executed for conspiracy against the emperor; Iullus Antonius, a son of Antony, was forced to commit suicide in 2 BC for adultery with Augustus' daughter Julia.

his wife had been seized from Nero   Livia had been married to Tiberius Claudius Nero (see p. 26).

... and the luxurious excess of Vedius Pollio   the received text is corrupt here, and the scale of what is lost is uncertain. Pollio was a friend of Augustus, known for his wealth and excess, but most notorious for feeding to lampreys those slaves he wished to be rid of (Dio 54.23).

state, and a harsh stepmother for the house of the Caesars. Nothing had been left to the honours of the gods since **he wished to be worshipped** with temples and in the likeness of gods through *flamines* and priests. He had not even adopted Tiberius to be his successor as a result of affection or a concern for the state, but, having examined this man's arrogance and cruelty, he sought glory for himself **by offering the worst comparison**. For, **a few years previously**, Augustus had again been asking the senators for tribunician power for Tiberius when – although in an honorific speech – he threw in certain remarks about his deportment, lifestyle and habits to criticize them in the pretence of excusing them. But after the burial had been carried out in customary fashion **a temple and divine rites were decreed**.

---

1 What is the effect of including these two contrasting sets of opinions about Augustus within the narrative?
2 Is greater weight given to either point of view? And if so, how?
3 What is Tacitus' point in offering these opinions as general gossip, rather than giving his own considered opinion? Is he shirking his duty as a historian, or does he have another purpose?
4 What is the tone of the final sentence of this section?

Tacitus has announced that Augustus was officially deified, following his funeral, at a meeting of the Senate which occurred on 17 September. He now goes on to give a much longer account of the rest of this meeting, which focuses on the constitutional position of Tiberius.

---

he wished to be worshipped   this is a simplification of a complicated picture, and worship of Augustus varied by region of the empire. In the East he inherited the worship of the Hellenistic kings, the rulers of the Greek kingdoms which were established following Alexander's conquests, who received personal cult. Here his worship was always linked with the worship of Rome itself (Dio 51.20.6–8), and his cult was encouraged in the West for similarly political reasons. However, in Italy direct worship was forbidden: instead his *genius* or divine entity was worshipped, which was a public form of a similar practice for the head of a family within a household.

flamines   these were a group of priests assigned to specific deities. There was no major priest for Augustus until after his death, but there were lesser ones appointed in individual Italian towns and the provinces.

by offering the worst comparison   this is hardly a fair criticism, given that Tiberius was not exactly his first choice as heir. On his problems in finding a successor, see **1.3** (pp. 25–27).

a few years previously   in AD 4. However, Suetonius, in describing these mannerisms at *Tiberius* 68, says that Augustus often excused them to the Senate. This sentence is no longer part of the reported criticisms but expressed in Tacitus' own voice.

a temple and divine rites were decreed   this was done by the Senate, but although the temple to Augustus was built by Livia and Tiberius, it was not finally dedicated until the reign of Gaius.

Senatorial debate on Tiberius' role: 1.11–13

1.11 Then prayers turned towards Tiberius. And he spoke in different ways about the scale of power and **his own self-restraint**: that only the mind of Augustus had been capable of bearing such a weight, and that after being called by the latter to a share of his concerns, he had learned by experience how strenuous and how subject to fortune was the burden of total rule. Therefore in a state supported by 5 so many distinguished men they should not refer every matter to one individual: greater numbers would more easily carry out the duties of state by sharing out the labours. In such a speech there were more fine words than credible ones; and even in the sort of matters which he was not concealing, whether by nature or by habit, Tiberius' words were always hesitant and obscure: certainly at this time, as he 10 strove to conceal his true feelings deep within himself, they were more entangled in uncertainty and ambiguity. But the senators, whose sole fear was that they should seem to understand, broke out into complaints, tears and prayers; they stretched out their hands to the gods, to the image of Augustus, and to his own knees, at which point he ordered that **the little book** should be brought forward 15 and read out. The public resources were recorded within it, the number of citizens and allies in arms, how many fleets, **client kingdoms** and provinces there were, the direct or indirect taxes, and essential expenditure and **gifts**. Augustus had detailed all these in his own hand and had added **an injunction to limit the empire within its bounds** – whether he had done this from fear or through envy 20 was uncertain.

1.12 Whilst the Senate in the face of this argument prostrated itself in the most degrading entreaties, Tiberius happened to say that as one unequal to the whole state he would take on whatever part was entrusted to him as his responsibility. Then Asinius Gallus responded: 'I ask you, Caesar, which section of the state 25

---

his own self-restraint   on his claims to the virtue of restraint, see **3.50** with note, p. 98.

the little book   this was one of three documents mentioned by Suetonius (*Augustus* 101.4) which had been entrusted to the Vestal Virgins together with Augustus' will; the other two were instructions for his funeral and a record of the achievements of his reign, his *Res Gestae*.

client kingdoms   this is the largely modern name for nominally independent kingdoms, whose rulers in fact operated under Roman patronage.

gifts   these were the acts of largesse which were expected of the emperor from time to time, such as to the people or legionaries.

an injunction to limit the empire within its bounds   this marked a significant shift from the policy in the earlier part of Augustus' reign, which seems to be reflected by the famous prophecy of Jupiter in Vergil's *Aeneid*, who said he had granted 'empire without end' (1.279). This shift was perhaps in part motivated by the Varian disaster (see note on p. 27).

would you like to be entrusted to you?' Stunned by this unforeseen question, he was silent for a short time: then after collecting his thoughts he replied that it was not at all appropriate for his modesty to choose some section, or avoid one from which he would prefer to be altogether excused. In reply Gallus (since he had guessed the offence taken by Tiberius from his expression) said that the question 30 had not been posed in order to divide up what could not be separated, but so that it could be proven by Tiberius' own admission that the body of state was a unity and needed to be ruled by the mind of one man. He added praise for Augustus and reminded Tiberius himself of his own victories and what notable achievements he had enjoyed **in the toga** over so many years. But he did not soften Tiberius' anger 35 through doing this, since he had been long hated on the grounds that after he had married Vipsania, Marcus Agrippa's daughter, **who had once been Tiberius' wife**, he aspired to be more than a citizen and had inherited the intractability of his father Asinius Pollio.

1.13   After this Lucius Arruntius, in a speech not very different from that of Gallus, 40 caused equal offence, although Tiberius had held no longstanding anger against Arruntius: but since he was wealthy, active, and a man of notable accomplishments and a matching reputation amongst the people, he mistrusted him. Indeed Augustus in his final conversations discussed those who had the capability for the role of *princeps* but would refuse it, those who were not equal to 45 it but wanted it, and those who had both the ability and the desire: he had said that **Marcus Lepidus was capable but not interested**, Asinius Gallus was eager but lacked the talent, and that Lucius Arruntius was not unworthy and would have the daring, if the chance were given him. There is agreement about the first two, but some authors have recorded **Gnaeus Piso** in place of Arruntius; and all except 50 Lepidus were subsequently trapped by various accusations of **Tiberius' design**.

---

in the toga this means in the civilian arena, in contrast with the military one, where Tiberius had certainly won his greatest renown.

who had once been Tiberius' wife Tiberius had been forced to divorce Vipsania against his will, so that he could marry, as part of Augustus' dynastic plans, his daughter Julia in 12 BC.

Marcus Lepidus was capable but not interested coming from a noble family, he had been consul in AD 6 and won triumphal decorations in AD 9 for his service under Tiberius against the revolt in Illyricum. For Tacitus he becomes a model in the Tiberian books for how to steer a middle course between flattery and open opposition (see **4.20**, p. 103).

Gnaeus Piso he had been consul in 7 BC and is a major player in Books 2 and 3 of the *Annals*, when as governor of Syria he falls out with Germanicus, and stands trial in Rome after the latter's death (see pp. 78–95).

Tiberius' design this is pushing the facts – it is hardly fair in the case of Piso, and Gallus and Arruntius fell only in the 30s AD, the latter at the hands of Macro (on whom see pp. 127–8) rather than Tiberius.

Also **Quintus Haterius and Mamercus Scaurus** grated upon his suspicious mind, the former when he had said: 'Just how long, Caesar, will you allow there to be no head of state in Rome?', Scaurus because he had said that there was hope that the Senate's prayers would not be unrealized as result of the fact that he 55 had not vetoed **the motion of the consuls** by virtue of his tribunician power. Tiberius launched an immediate attack on Haterius; he passed in silence over Scaurus, with whom he was more implacably angry. And exhausted by the uproar from everyone and by the protests of individuals **he gradually relented**, not so as to admit that power was being assumed by him, but to stop refusing and being 60 asked. It is agreed that Haterius, when he had entered the palace to apologize and was grovelling at the knees of Tiberius as he was walking along, had almost been killed by the soldiers, because Tiberius had fallen over, whether by chance or tripped by Haterius' hands. But he was not placated by the danger that such a great man faced, until Haterius entreated **Augusta** and was protected by her most 65 solicitous prayers.

---

1 How helpful is Tacitus' narrative of this meeting of the Senate? Would it have been more useful if he had given a clearer account of its agenda? Why do you think he has chosen not to do so?

2 What are the key characteristics of Tiberius that are portrayed in the debate? Is his reluctance to assume full responsibility as *princeps* genuine? What good reasons, if any, might he have for this reluctance?

3 How are the various senators who participate in the debate presented? Do they show any real independence? Why do their interventions anger Tiberius so much?

4 Why does Tacitus not include a clear conclusion to the debate? Is the implication that the whole debate is perhaps irrelevant?

5 Why do you think that Tacitus includes the final story about Haterius in the palace?

Quintus Haterius and Mamercus Scaurus   both men were notable orators. Haterius was already in his late seventies, Scaurus was subsequently to be accused of treason on two occasions, the second time in AD 34 anticipating a verdict by suicide.

the motion of the consuls   Tacitus fails to state anywhere the precise details of the consuls' proposal at this meeting of the Senate, but it must have included some formal acknowledgement of Tiberius' constitutional position. Scaurus' point is that Tiberius could have used the tribunician power he already held to veto any consular proposal: the fact that he had not chosen to do so might be seen as a tacit acceptance of it.

he gradually relented   it is not explicitly stated that any motion was passed at the end of the debate, but it seems likely that some decision must have been reached as is indicated by Suetonius at *Tiberius* 24.

Augusta   the new title of Livia, Tiberius' mother (see note on p. 33).

Tacitus then relates that Tiberius opposed various extraordinary honours that were proposed for his mother and sought proconsular command for Germanicus. The last action which he records Tiberius taking in the Senate at this time concerned the election of magistrates.

Electoral reforms: 1.15

1.15   Then for the first time elections were transferred from **the Campus Martius** to the senators: for up to that day, although **the most powerful offices** lay with the decision of the *princeps*, nevertheless certain positions were filled by **the popular voting of the tribes**. And the people did not complain about the loss of this right except in idle talk, and the Senate held it gladly, freed as it was from sordid   5
bribery and entreaties, while Tiberius limited himself to commending no more than four candidates who were to be elected without rejection and the need for campaigning.

---

1   What thinking seems to have lain behind these changes made by Tiberius?

2   Is the idea of giving the Senate more direct control over government consistent with his other words and actions following Augustus' death?

3   How significant an action was it on Tiberius' part to deprive the people of any say in the selection of magistrates?

4   In fact we know from inscriptions that the mechanism of popular elections continued to operate. What happened was that Tiberius allowed the Senate to vote in advance for a list of candidates which matched in number the total of posts to be filled: this list was then simply rubber-stamped by the people. Is Goodyear right to say of this, 'Tacitus seems, as often, to be more concerned with the realities of power than its legal formalities' (vol. 1, p. 193)?

---

the Campus Martius   this was the site of elections to the highest magistracies. In the republican period these had taken place democratically, although the votes of the richer citizens had carried a hugely disproportionate weight.

the most powerful offices   this will have certainly included the consulships and perhaps many praetorships since Tiberius promises to restrict himself to nominating only four (out of 12 available posts each year) in the future.

the popular voting of the tribes   this seems a little confused, as the ancient tribes of Rome formed the electorate for the minor magistracies such as the tribunes, aediles and quaestors, whose elections occurred in the Forum. It seems that Tacitus is recording the fact that all elections were transferred from the people to the Senate, but has become confused over some of the details, perhaps because the initial decision was taken over the praetorian elections, which happened to be the first after Tiberius came to power.

3 Mutinies in the armies of Pannonia and Germany

After one other brief report, Tacitus immediately moves the focus abroad for the first extended narrative of the work. In this he describes in succession mutinies among the legions in Pannonia (this province lay between the Austrian Alps and the Danube) and those in Germany along the Rhine. These are dealt with by Tiberius' son Drusus and his nephew Germanicus, respectively. It is significant that Tacitus chooses to devote such a lengthy account to these episodes, especially since the seriousness of the threat which they posed to Tiberius' power is doubtful. As a result it is important to ask exactly why the historian did decide to pay such attention to them, and in particular why he chose to narrate the events of both mutinies rather than focus on one to be exemplary for both.

Mutiny in Pannonia: 1.16–18, 21–5, 28–30

1.16   **This was the state of affairs in the city,** when mutiny struck the Pannonian legions, a mutiny which was motivated by no new factors, save that **the change of emperor** offered a freedom to riot and the hope of rewards stemming from civil war. **Three legions** were stationed together in their summer camp under

---

This was the state of affairs in the city   such a phrase is typical of annalistic history, marking a shift from the domestic narrative of events based in Rome (such as the passage of laws) to an account of foreign affairs: here it is noteworthy that these foreign affairs consist of internal dissent rather than glorious wars of foreign conquest (see Tacitus' digression on the disagreeable content of his work at **4. 32**, pp. 105–6).

the change of emperor   Tacitus is clear that, for all the subsequent listing of detailed grievances, this simple fact is the main motivation behind the disquiet of the soldiers.

Three legions   the three legions were VIII Augusta, XV Apollinaris, and IX Hispana. Quintus Iunius Blaesus, the commander in Pannonia, was the uncle of Seianus, who was later to rise to such prominence under Tiberius as the prefect of the praetorian guard.

---

the leadership of Iunius Blaesus, who had interrupted normal duties **for public** 5
mourning or celebration after news had arrived of the death of Augustus and the
beginning of Tiberius' principate. From this beginning the soldiers abandoned
discipline, quarrelled, and lent their ears to the words of **every scoundrel**; this
culminated in their desiring luxury and ease, and rejecting discipline and hard
work. There was in the camp a certain Percennius, who had in the past been **a** 10
professional leader of applause in the theatre, but who then became a rank-and-

A Roman camp (Housesteads on Hadrian's Wall) with its plan clearly visible from the air. Note
the barrack buildings in the top right corner and the headquarters to the right of the centre. The
legionary camp in Pannonia would have had a similar layout, although much greater in size.

for public mourning or celebration   a *iustitium* was a cessation of all judicial and public
business, which was typically held as a mark of respect for a period of mourning. Tacitus
complicates the phrase with a second alternative, namely that the relaxation of discipline
could be ascribed to celebration. This could simply mean that Blaesus intended the
soldiers to lament the passing of Augustus and celebrate Tiberius' succession. However,
a more sinister reading is possible, in which the celebration could also stem from the
passing of Augustus. Are readers meant to decide between the two, or are both readings
intentionally left possible?

every scoundrel   note that Tacitus uses very moralistic vocabulary to describe those who
wanted to campaign for better terms, and he continues to do so as the mutinies unfold.

a professional leader of applause in the theatre   there is plenty of evidence for the
existence of such claqueurs at the performances of Roman plays; they were responsible
for stirring up support for particular actors. Their actions could lead to significant
violence, such as recorded by Suetonius at *Tiberius* 37.2, when fights between the various
factions in the theatre ended in bloodshed, and Tiberius took action by exiling not only
the cheer-leaders but also the various actors involved. On Tacitus' attitude to the theatre
in general, see **14.14–15** on pp. 157–8.

file soldier, quick-tongued and with his theatrical background, clever at stirring up crowds. This man worked on the inexperienced minds of the men, minds which were uncertain what the terms of military service would be following the death of Augustus. He did so gradually in conversations held at night or as dusk 15 fell, and when the better element had dispersed he called together all the worst men.

1.17 Finally when others too were now ready to support the mutiny, **as if making a public speech**, he asked why they took orders from **a few centurions and even fewer tribunes** after the fashion of slaves. When would they dare to demand 20 improved conditions, if they would not approach the new and as yet insecure emperor with prayers or threaten him with arms? Enough mistakes had been made through inactivity over so many years, what with soldiers now old men after enduring **thirty or forty years' service**, most of them with bodies mutilated with wounds. There was no end to service even when they had been discharged, 25 but quartered under the veteran standards they endured the same tasks under a different name. And if anyone survived all these hardships, they were then dragged off to the ends of the earth, where **they were given marshy swamps or barren mountainsides**, as their so-called 'fields'. Certainly the service itself was

---

as if making a public speech   the Latin adjective used here is a compound of *contio*, the word for an official public speech. Tacitus' point is that Percennius was beginning to behave as if he held office; the mutiny is beginning to develop a structure parallel to that of Rome itself.

a few centurions and even fewer tribunes   in spite of the name, each centurion at this time commanded a group of some 80 men, rather than a hundred. As they were the disciplinarians of the Roman army, they were a particular focus for resentment among the men, and are targeted in both these mutinies. The tribunes were senior officers and there were six within each legion (which was made up of about 5,400 men).

thirty or forty years' service   the period of service had been fixed at 16 years, which were supplemented by four years as a veteran, but this had subsequently been extended to 20 years of full service. However, the treasury had been short of money to pay the lump sums to veterans on their discharge, and the 20-year term became extended by many years' service as veterans. This seems to be the most important single complaint behind both the mutinies.

they were given marshy swamps or barren mountainsides   the discharged veterans were often offered land instead of the 12,000 sesterces that they were promised, again presumably because of a shortage of money. Such land may well have been of poor quality, and Wilkes has suggested that this complaint was a particular one of the Pannonian legions who had been given an area of very poor land at Emona, near modern Ljubljana in Slovenia (pp. 270–1). If this was the case, it suggests that some important historical details are preserved in Tacitus' version of Percennius' speech (on the historicity of speeches in Tacitus, see p. 133).

burdensome and unrewarding: their lives and bodies were reckoned at **ten asses** 30
a day; from this their clothes, weapons and tents had to be paid for, from this the
cruelty of the centurions had to be bought off, and the exemption from duties
purchased. **By Hercules**, the beatings and the wounds, the harsh winters, the
arduous summers, the savagery of war and the tedium of peace were unrelenting!
There could be no alleviation unless men entered service with a fixed contract, 35
namely that they were to earn **a denarius a day**, that the sixteenth year should
mark the end of their service, that they should at this point be **discharged
unconditionally**, but that their reward should be paid out with money in the
same camp in which they served. Or do **the praetorian cohorts**, who receive two
denarii a day, who are returned to their own homes after sixteen years, face more 40
dangers? He was not disparaging the task of sentry-duty in the city; however, on
service among savage tribes, he could see the enemy from his quarters.

---

1 How persuasive do you find this speech? Is it carefully argued, or does it
   depend for its force upon rhetorical fireworks?

2 Percennius' speech focuses in several places upon the difference between
   what is said and what actually happens. Do you think that this is a concern of
   Percennius himself, or rather a reflection of the broader historical interests of
   Tacitus?

3 Tacitus gives Percennius' words as reported speech, rather than as direct
   quotation. How significant do you think that this is, and what is the effect of
   this decision?

---

ten asses a day   Julius Caesar had established this rate of pay (doubling it from its
previous level), but a substantial amount was deducted from this to pay for regular items,
including food (although this is not mentioned by Percennius). Even today, although basic
kit is provided, it has been common for troops themselves to pay for superior equipment,
as many British soldiers did in Iraq.

By Hercules   this appeal to the god is a colloquial interjection, used to express Percennius'
outrage.

a denarius a day   there were 16 asses in a denarius, so this would have meant a 60 per
cent increase in pay.

discharged unconditionally   the Latin literally says 'that they should not be held further
under the standards', meaning that they should no longer be forced to serve as veterans
for a further period before being discharged fully and receiving their reward. This phrase
recurs frequently in the account of the two mutinies, and this is how I shall translate it.

the praetorian cohorts   the praetorian guard in Rome had always enjoyed superior
conditions of service over the legionary soldiers.

1.18 The crowd applauded noisily, stirred up by different points, one group pointing indignantly to the scars caused by blows, others to their white hair, most to their ragged clothing and their exposed bodies. Finally they reached such a pitch of madness that **they considered combining the three legions into one.** Deterred by rivalry, because each man looked for the honour of primacy to be given to his 5 own legion, they turned their thoughts elsewhere and placed together the three eagles and the standards of the cohorts; at the same time they heaped up turfs and constructed a platform, so that the position of the standards should be more prominent. As they were hurrying about this work, Blaesus arrived and began rebuking and restraining individual men, crying, 'Rather stain your hands with 10 my blood: it will be a lesser crime for you to kill your commander than revolt from the emperor. Either I shall remain unharmed and maintain the loyalty of my legions, or I shall be killed and so hasten your repentance.'

> Blaesus' impassioned appeal did not have immediate success, but the mutineers did eventually abandon their plans in favour of Blaesus' advice to appoint official delegates to convey their wishes to Rome; amongst those who were sent was Blaesus' own son, who was a tribune. However, detachments sent to the nearby town of Nauportus heard of the trouble and began to turn on their centurions and their commander, Aufidienus Rufus, before their return to the camp.

1.21 At their arrival the mutiny was revived, and men roamed around and began to plunder the surrounding areas. Blaesus ordered a few who were especially weighed down by loot to be beaten and imprisoned in order to instil fear in the rest; for even at this stage the centurions and the best of the rank and file were obedient to their commander. Those who were being dragged resisted, **seized the** 5 **knees of bystanders in supplication**, called now on the names of individual men, now on the century to which each man belonged, now on the cohort, now on the legion, crying out that the threat of the same treatment hung over all of them. At the same time they heaped abuse on the commander, they called on heaven and the gods as witnesses, they left nothing untried through which they might stir up 10 indignation, pity, fear and anger. Everyone ran to their aid, and after breaking open the prison they undid the chains and now added to their ranks deserters and those condemned on capital charges.

---

they considered combining the three legions into one   throughout both mutinies, the aggrieved soldiers seek to combine units, whilst the commanders strive to maintain their separate identities. Words like 'combining' and 'mixing' carry negative associations in Tacitus' account, since such actions mark the loss of military discipline, and a total breakdown of the usual command structures, in which the distinctions of rank (with the commanders drawn from the higher social classes) were normally maintained.

seized the knees of bystanders in supplication   this was the conventional posture for someone entreating another to show pity and listen to their prayers.

1.22   Then the violence became more outrageous, and leaders for the mutiny more numerous. Vibulenus, a soldier from the ranks, was raised on the shoulders of 15 bystanders in front of Blaesus' platform and addressed the riotous crowd of men who were eager to hear what he was planning, 'You have indeed restored light and life to these most unfortunate and innocent men: but who can restore life to my brother, and who can restore my brother to me? He had been sent to you by **the army in Germany** on matters of shared interest, but last night Blaesus had 20 him killed by **his gladiators**, whom he keeps armed in order to kill off soldiers. Answer, Blaesus, and tell us where you have disposed of the corpse: not even the enemy begrudge us burials. When I have sated my grief with kisses and with tears, give orders that I too be slaughtered, provided that they bury us – men who have been put to death for no crime but because we took an interest in the good of the 25 legions.'

1.23   He added fire to these words with weeping and by striking his breast and face with his hands. Next he thrust aside those on whose shoulders he was being supported and, throwing himself head-first at the feet of individuals, stirred up so much anger and indignation that some of the soldiers arrested the gladiators 30 who were in the service of Blaesus, and others the rest of his household, while a further group flooded out to look for the body. Had it not quickly become known that there was no body to be found, that **the slaves denied the murder under torture**, and that Vibulenus had never had a brother, they would have killed their commander: indeed they came close to doing so. As it was, they did drive out 35 the tribunes and the commander of the camp, the baggage of the fugitives was looted, and the centurion Lucilius was killed: military humour had given him the nickname 'Give me another!', because after breaking **his vine-stick** on the back of a soldier he would call in a loud voice for a second and yet another. Hiding-places protected the other centurions except for one whom they held back, Iulius 40 Clemens, considering that he would be useful in presenting the demands of the

---

the army in Germany   this is the first mention of potential dissent among the German legions as well, albeit that it is made in the midst of a false claim. There would also, presumably, have been insufficient time at this stage for the news of Augustus' death to have reached Germany, for unrest to have broken out there, and for news of that unrest to have reached the soldiers in Pannonia. Are we as readers intended to see the impossibility of this claim and observe the gullibility of the riotous mob?

his gladiators   Blaesus will have kept these to provide entertainment in shows, rather than for the purpose which Vibulenus alleges.

the slaves denied the murder under torture   these would have included the gladiators as well as the rest of Blaesus' slaves who had been seized. The extraction of evidence from slaves under torture was usual in the Roman judicial system under normal circumstances, let alone in such a tumultuous situation as this.

his vine-stick   this staff was the mark of the centurion's rank, and was also used by him to administer corporal punishment.

soldiers by virtue of his quick intelligence. The eighth and fifteenth legions were actually preparing to fight against one another – with the former demanding the death of a centurion called Sirpicus, and the men of the fifteenth protecting him – and they would have fought, had the soldiers of the ninth not intervened with 45 appeals, and threats against those who ignored them.

---

1 What methods does Tacitus use in this description of the mutiny to bring the drama of the events to life?

2 Does Tacitus direct the sympathy of his readers to either side? Are we meant to feel for the grievances of the soldiers?

3 What are the key factors that caused the mutiny to founder?

4 What are we to think of the actions of Blaesus and Vibulenus? And what is the effect of Tacitus giving both men direct speech?

5 Are there any elements that we might feel are lacking from Tacitus' narrative? In particular, how much does it matter that his chronology of events seems very vague?

6 To what social class did Tacitus belong (see p. 1)? Do you think that this had any bearing on where his sympathies lay in this episode?

1.24 Although Tiberius was **inscrutable and especially secretive about the greatest crises**, the news of these events drove him to send out his son Drusus together with leading statesmen and **two praetorian cohorts**: he was given no fixed instructions, but was to take appropriate decisions on the spot. The cohorts were strengthened beyond their usual complement with the addition of picked troops. Also attached 5 were a large contingent of **the praetorian cavalry** and the pick of **the Germans**, who at that time attended the emperor as a bodyguard. Together with them travelled

---

inscrutable and especially secretive about the greatest crises   Tacitus focuses on this characteristic of Tiberius from his very first involvement in the mutinies, just as he had done in his account of the accession following Augustus' death.

two praetorian cohorts   each cohort probably consisted of 500 men (direct evidence for this period is lacking, but this was the size of cohorts in the ordinary legions). By the end of Augustus' principate there were nine praetorian cohorts in total, but they were not all based in Rome; only three were stationed in the capital itself at any one time, whilst the rest were dispersed throughout various towns in Italy. What effect might the dispatch of praetorian cohorts be expected to have, given the fact that the difference in pay between praetorians and legionaries was one of the mutineers' grievances?

the praetorian cavalry   cavalry units seem to have been attached to all the praetorian cohorts, with perhaps 90 cavalry per cohort in this period.

the Germans   the origin of foreign bodyguards lay in the period of the civil wars, when they perhaps seemed more reliable than Romans. As Octavian, Augustus had employed Spaniards initially, but after the defeat of Antony he employed Germans, except for a brief spell after the defeat of Varus in Germany in AD 9. They were maintained until the accession of Galba in 68: he dismissed them on the suspicion of disloyalty.

Mutinies in the armies of Pannonia and Germany   **51**

the praetorian prefect, Aelius Seianus, who had been appointed as a colleague to his father Strabo, and who had great influence with Tiberius: he was to serve as an adviser to the young Drusus, and to make clear to the rest the dangers and 10 rewards inherent in the situation. As if fulfilling their duty, the legions came to meet Drusus as he approached, not offering a happy welcome, as was customary, nor resplendent in their decorations, but dirtily unkempt and with expressions that feigned unhappiness but came closer to disrespect.

1.25 After he had entered the fortifications, they secured the gates with pickets and 15 ordered groups of armed men to wait at agreed points in the camp: the rest surrounded the platform in a massed formation. Drusus stood demanding silence with his hand. Whenever they turned their eyes back to the crowd, the men roared with angry voices, but when they looked on Caesar once more, they were alarmed; there were indistinct rumblings, fierce cries, and sudden silence; they 20 felt and caused fear in turn, as their emotions varied. Finally, once the uproar had abated, he read out a letter from his father: in it he stated that uppermost in his mind was concern for the bravest legions, legions with which he had endured very many wars; as soon as his mind had recovered from its grief, he would discuss their demands with the Senate; in the meantime he had sent his son to grant 25

Aelius Seianus   this is the first mention of Lucius Aelius Seianus (his name is also spelled Sejanus in English), a man who was to become a central character in Tacitus' account of the second half of Tiberius' reign, and the man who perhaps posed the single greatest threat to the security of the principate as a political system in its early years. In 2 BC Augustus had appointed two equestrians to serve as the commanders of the praetorians – two, so that no one man should be owed their loyalty, and equestrians, not senators, so that they should not pose a serious political threat to the emperor. It is striking therefore that a father and son should have been given these two powerful positions by Augustus; however, after Strabo's appointment as prefect of Egypt in AD 15, Seianus was left as the sole commander. For an account of his rise and fall, see pp. 112–27.

resplendent in their decorations   the Latin word is *insignia*, which corresponded to medals and which were awarded to individual soldiers. They would be expected to wear them on a formal parade, welcoming, as here, the arrival of an important dignitary.

with his hand   the use of gestures was an essential aspect of ancient oratory, both Roman and Greek.

Caesar   Tacitus' choice of proper names to refer to the individuals involved in his narrative is often pointed. Drusus, as the son of Tiberius, was a Caesar, as also was his nephew, Germanicus, who has to deal with the mutiny of the German legions, and at certain points in his narrative Tacitus chooses to refer to them as simply Caesar, rather than by their individual names. Julius Caesar had himself on a celebrated occasion in 47 BC put down a mutiny among his own troops in Italy during the civil wars, an incident to which Germanicus himself refers in his speech to the German legions (see **1.42**, p. 66). Why do you think that Tacitus refers to Drusus as Caesar on this occasion?

without delay those requests which could be met at once; **the remaining matters must be reserved for the Senate** – it was right to remember that this was a body not incapable of largesse as well as strictness.

> Following the reading of this letter, the centurion Iulius Clemens put the demands of the men to Drusus: a maximum period of sixteen years' service, better pay, unconditional discharge, and the payment of a lump sum on the occasion of that discharge. When Drusus urged that the Senate had to be consulted on these questions, uproar broke out. They claimed that this was purely a delaying tactic, particularly noting that the emperor never consulted the Senate on other questions, such as when to launch a war or carry out the death penalty against someone. The meeting did eventually break up, but disorder continued, on one occasion flaring up into violence. However, that night Drusus received a lucky break, of which he took full advantage.

1.28   A piece of luck brought calm on this threatening night which had looked like it was going to erupt into violence: although the sky was clear, **the moon was suddenly seen to grow faint.** The soldiers, ignorant of the reason, took it as an omen of the present situation, drawing a parallel between the moon's eclipse and their own efforts, considering that things would turn out well for their plans if **the goddess** recovered her sparkling brightness. Therefore **they made a din by striking bronze and by blowing trumpets and horns**; as it appeared brighter or

5

---

the remaining matters must be reserved for the Senate   this again fits with Tiberius' policy to involve the Senate more actively in all decision-making, but in this instance is it just an excuse to stall for time?

the moon was suddenly seen to grow faint   this lunar eclipse provides the first datable event of the mutiny (following the death of Augustus on 19 August). Miller, in her edition of *Annals* 1, on the authority of the Nautical Almanac Office (the national UK body which provides astronomical information), states that it occurred at about 5 a.m. on 27 September. This emphasizes the speed with which events moved: in fewer than 40 days, news of Augustus' death had reached Pannonia, mutiny had broken out and report of it had reached Rome, whereupon Drusus and the praetorians had been dispatched to sort it out. In his edition, Goodyear observes, on Miller's timing for the eclipse, that it occurred so late in the night that 'the mutineers seem to have waited an extraordinarily long time without starting trouble. This makes me suspect that Tacitus has attached too much importance to the eclipse' (vol. 1, p. 229). If this is the case, why might the significance of the eclipse have been exaggerated?

the goddess   Diana, the moon goddess.

they made a din by striking bronze and by blowing trumpets and horns   educated Romans were well aware of what caused lunar eclipses, but the rank-and-file soldiers clearly still regarded the moon as divine, and ascribed an eclipse to magical forces. The noise they made was intended to help the moon fight off enchantment (Pliny, *Natural History* 2.12).

dimmer, so they cheered up or grew sad; then clouds sprang up and obscured their sight, and they believed that the moon had been plunged into darkness: as minds once disturbed are susceptible to superstition, they bewailed the fact that 10 unending toil was being foretold for them, and that their crimes were turning the gods against them. Caesar thought that he had to make use of this change in mood, and that the gift of chance needed to be put to the service of good sense: he ordered a tour of the tents to be made. The centurion Clemens was sent for along with any others of good character who were popular with the ranks. These men 15 mixed with the patrols, the sentries and those guarding the gates, they offered each man hope, and they gave him reasons to fear. 'Just how far will we continue to lay siege to the son of the emperor? What will be the end of our conflict? Are we going to take oaths to Percennius and Vibulenus? Will Percennius and Vibulenus pay salaries to the soldiers, and give land to those who are discharged? To cap it 20 all, will they take charge of the empire of the Roman people in place of **the Neros and the Drususes**? Why should we not rather be the first to show repentance just as we were the last to be guilty of wrongdoing? The demands of a group are slow to be met: as an individual you would earn gratitude at once, you would receive it at once.' By disturbing their thoughts in this way and making them 25 suspicious of each other, they split the raw recruits from the veterans, and one legion from another. Then their love of discipline gradually returned: they left the gates unblocked, and they restored to their proper places the standards, which they had brought together at the onset of the mutiny.

1.29   At dawn Drusus called a meeting and, although he was not a polished speaker, 30 with a natural dignity rebuked their earlier behaviour and praised their present conduct. He said that he was not susceptible to fear and threats: if he saw them displaying discipline again, and heard them adopting a submissive tone, he would write to his father asking that he listen to the pleas of the legions with a conciliatory ear. On their earnest requests, the same Blaesus was again sent to Tiberius, and with 35 him Lucius Aponius, a Roman equestrian from Drusus' entourage, and Catonius Iustus, a senior centurion. Then there was a divergence of opinions, with some advising that they should await the return of the envoys and in the meantime calm the soldiers in a friendly way, while others recommended that there was a need for firmer remedies: they argued that there could be no half measures with 40 the rank and file; they caused fear unless they felt fear, and when they were afraid, there was no risk in treating them with contempt: while superstition restrained them, their general should heighten their fears by removing the instigators of the mutiny. Drusus was by nature inclined to the harsher course: he gave orders for

---

the Neros and the Drususes   these names were both common to the Claudian family, and Tiberius was himself called Tiberius Nero before he was adopted by Augustus.

Vibulenus and Percennius to be sent for and killed. **Most sources relate** that they 45
were buried inside the general's tent, others that their bodies were thrown outside
the fortifications for display.

1.30   Then every leading trouble-maker was hunted down, and some were killed by
        centurions or soldiers of the praetorian cohorts while they wandered around
        outside the camp: men of the rank and file took the initiative in handing over 50
        certain individuals as evidence of their own loyalty.

> The end of the mutiny was followed by the early onset of winter, and in
> particular heavy rains. This proved fortunate for Drusus, since it deterred the
> soldiers from assembling to discuss their grievances and they continued to
> link the bad weather with divine displeasure at their actions. As a result the
> various legions were all too happy to leave for their separate winter camps,
> even the ninth which had adopted the hardest line. Drusus therefore departed
> for Rome without waiting for the return of the legates who had been sent to
> the emperor.

---

1   How effectively does Tacitus convey the tensions between the mutiny's
    various participants?

2   How does he use direct speech and indirect speech to add to the effectiveness
    of the third-person narrative?

3   What picture of Drusus emerges from his handling of the situation? How
    is his speaking style contrasted with the more flamboyant and theatrical
    approach of Percennius and Vibulenus? Are his actions portrayed as
    excessively harsh or fair, given the situation that he faced? How similar is his
    portrayal to the picture we have already been given of his father?

4   How important is the role which Tacitus gives to luck within his account?

Most sources relate   this is the first occasion on which Tacitus raises the matter of sources
in his account of the Pannonian mutiny, but in doing so he implies that he referred to
multiple narratives of the events. Miller, in the introduction to her commentary on Book
1, notes that the detail of his narrative suggests that he had access to the accounts of
eye-witnesses (p. 6). A more immediate question is why Tacitus chooses this particular
point in his narrative to bring the attention of his readers to the matter of his sources. At
13.20 Tacitus states that he will only refer to individual sources where they disagree, but
will otherwise follow their authority without citation. Is that simply what the historian
is doing? Or is he raising the question of sources here to underscore the total reliability
of the rest of his account, whilst offering a macabre focus on the demise of the two
ringleaders?

Mutiny in Germany: 1.31–5, 38–43, 46–7, 49, 52

1.31   At about the same time and for the same reasons the legions in Germany mutinied, all the more violently in that they were more numerous; they did so in the confident hope that Germanicus Caesar would be unable to suffer rule by another man and would entrust himself to legions who would carry all before them with their own violence. There were two armies along the banks of the Rhine: 5 what was called the upper army was under the command of Gaius Silius, Aulus Caecina was in charge of the lower. Overall control lay with Germanicus, but he was at that time busy conducting a census in the provinces of Gaul. However, Silius' men watched with mixed feelings the fortunes of a mutiny which they did not consider their own: the soldiers of the lower army sank into madness, with 10 the impetus coming from the men of the twenty-first and fifth legions, who soon dragged in the first and the twentieth legions as well: they were being billeted in the same summer camp in the territory of the Ubii, and were idle or engaged in only light duties. As a result, once news arrived of Augustus' death, the large

---

At about the same time notice again the imprecision of Tacitus' chronology. Does it matter in this context?

Germanicus Caesar note the nomenclature which Tacitus uses in conveying the thoughts of the legionaries – why is he not simply called Germanicus? The latter provides the central focus to the account of this mutiny in a way which was not true of Drusus for events in Pannonia. It is striking that his first introduction suggests his opposition to his uncle and adoptive father, Tiberius, and that this insinuation is made through the eyes of others. It suggests that in his portrayal of Germanicus, Tacitus is just as interested in how he was perceived by others, as in what he was actually like.

the upper army the military districts of Upper and Lower Germany were defined by their relationship along the Rhine. Upper Germany lay to the south, further up-river, while Lower Germany, the main focus of the mutiny, lay closer to the North Sea around the site of modern Cologne.

Overall control lay with Germanicus Germanicus held what was called *imperium maius*, that is, a power which gave him authority over the other holders of *imperium* in the west, in this case Caecina and Silius. Such power had been the basis of Augustus' control over the provinces, and he had also given it to those whom he marked out as successors. Tiberius had shared it with him, and Germanicus had been granted it perhaps in 11 BC as another potential successor. Tiberius was recorded as confirming Germanicus in this power at 1.14.

a census provincial censuses were first conducted by the central government under Augustus (such as the one in Judaea which is described in the gospel of Luke). Their primary purpose was to produce an accurate account of possessions owned in order to calculate tax liabilities.

in the territory of the Ubii the Ubii were a German tribe, friendly to Rome, who had been resettled on the west bank of the Rhine, having originally occupied territory to the east. Their capital became a colony under Claudius (*colonia Agrippinensis*), from which the modern city of Cologne took its name (see map on p. 7).

number of city recruits, **who had been enrolled recently in Rome**, accustomed 15
as they were to licence and intolerant of hard work, filled the ignorant minds of
the rest with ideas: namely that the time had come for the veterans to demand
early discharge, the younger soldiers more generous pay, and all to demand an
end to their sufferings and to exact vengeance for the cruelty of the centurions.
It was not one man who was saying this, **as was the case with Percennius among** 20
the Pannonian legions, nor was it said in the timid ears of men who could look
to other stronger armies, but there were many faces and voices of mutiny: they
observed that Rome itself lay in their hands, that the state was being enlarged by
their victories, that **their commanders were taking their own name**.

1.32   The commander took no action against them: indeed the madness of the majority 25
had destroyed his nerve. All of a sudden crazed men attacked the centurions with
drawn swords: they provided the most traditional focus for the hatred of soldiers
and the impetus for their furious rage. They threw them to the ground and rained
blows on them, sixty for each man, to match the number of centurions. When they
were battered and mutilated, and some of them were unconscious, they threw them 30
outside the fortifications or into the river Rhine. Although Septimius had escaped
and was grovelling at the feet of Caecina, they demanded his surrender with such
force that he was eventually given up to his fate. Cassius Chaerea, **who was later**
to win lasting memory among future generations for the murder of Gaius Caesar

---

who had been enrolled recently in Rome   these recruits had been gathered quickly in Rome following Varus' disaster in Germany in AD 9 when three legions were lost, a defeat which seems to have led Augustus to abandon his expansionist foreign policy (see note on p. 27).

as was the case with Percennius among the Pannonian legions   Tacitus here explicitly contrasts the two mutinies; by doing so early in the account of the German mutiny, he encourages his readers to compare the two outbreaks more systematically.

their commanders were taking their own name   this refers not only to their current commander, Germanicus himself, but also to his father Drusus, who had been the first to earn the additional name (*cognomen*) of Germanicus for his achievements in this province: upon his death in 9 BC the Senate granted that the same name could be used by all his descendants. The German legions here are shown as confident of their own pre-eminence and, as Furneaux notes, they still seem to believe that they are engaged in a war of conquest against Germany, in spite of Varus' disastrous defeat in AD 9. After already reading Tacitus' remarks at *Annals* **1.3** (p. 27), are we intended to question these boasts as overconfident?

who was later to win lasting memory ... for the murder of Gaius Caesar   Tacitus' account of Gaius' assassination is lost, but Suetonius asserts that it stemmed from Gaius' persistent humiliation of Chaerea (*Gaius* 56–8). The present passage is an excellent example of the way in which Tacitus hints at a longer-term perspective on the principate. Gaius himself is about to be introduced to the narrative as Germanicus' son: these two men who were to clash in one of the great crises of the early principate in Rome are first introduced as bit-part players in a distant camp in Germany. Tacitus maintains a fairly rigid annalistic structure but he uses such devices to create a broader canvas: the next occasion on which Chaerea is recorded as using this sword it will have more serious consequences.

---

but at that time was a young man of fierce spirit, used his sword to open a route 35
to escape between the armed men who blocked his path. The tribunes did not
have control any more, nor did the commander of the camp: the men themselves
created rotas for patrols, sentry-duty and whatever else the immediate situation
called for. For students of military psychology the clearest indicator that this was a
serious and implacable rising was the fact that they were not disunited nor driven 40
by a few men, but were passionate as one, were silent as one, with such uniformity
and determination that you would believe that they were acting under direction.

1　What are the differences between the two mutinies in the early stages?

2　It is likely that for the German mutiny Tacitus used as a major source Pliny the
Elder, who had himself served on the Rhine in the middle of the first century
AD, and wrote an account of the wars in Germany in 20 books. Are there any
indications that Tacitus is using a source for this mutiny which is different
from the one he used for events in Pannonia?

1.33　　In the meantime, while Germanicus, as I have mentioned, was conducting a
census throughout the provinces of Gaul, it was reported to him that Augustus
had died. **He was married to Augustus' granddaughter, Agrippina,** and had
several children by her; he himself was the son of Tiberius' brother, Drusus,
and the grandson of Livia, but **he was concerned at the secret hatred of his** 5
uncle and grandmother towards him, the reasons for which were all the keener
because they were unfair. Indeed, the Roman people had strong memories
of Drusus, and it was believed that, if he had gained control of the state,

---

He was married to Augustus' granddaughter, Agrippina　Germanicus has already been
introduced through the eyes of the soldiers, but on his appearance in the narrative as
an active player, Tacitus gives a very selective biography of him. The details of his family
connections, and particularly his close ties to the newly deceased emperor Augustus,
emphasize the potential threat he poses to Tiberius. Unlike the new emperor, he has
numerous children and they are descended by blood from Augustus himself.

he was concerned at the secret hatred of his uncle and grandmother towards him　Tacitus
had already recorded Tiberius' fear of Germanicus (**1.7**, p. 32), but Goodyear calls the
second half of this sentence 'an overloaded and deadly appendage' (vol. 1, p. 250). He
notes that it includes three suppositions, that Germanicus was concerned, that Livia and
Tiberius secretly hated him, and that this hatred was all the stronger because it was
unjustified, the last of which he describes as 'particularly insidious', because it is such
a persuasive paradox. Again, Tacitus is focusing on the way in which Germanicus was
perceived by others, and just as importantly that he was concerned with what others
thought of him.

---

he would have restored political freedom; as a result of this, there was support for Germanicus and the same hope. For the young man possessed an 10 unassuming disposition and a remarkable affability, far removed from the speech and expression of Tiberius, which were arrogant and inscrutable. There were in addition female jealousies, arising from the stepmotherly barbs of Livia towards Agrippina, and Agrippina herself was a little too volatile, except for the fact that by her faithfulness and love for her husband she turned her mind, ungovernable 15 though it was, to the good.

1　How is the character of Germanicus contrasted with that of Tiberius in this section? Is he being contrasted implicitly with anyone else as well?

2　In this section of third-person narrative Tiberius is referred to as Germanicus' uncle, and this is typical of Tacitean narrative. In speeches put in the mouths of Tiberius or Germanicus, or addressed to them, reference is made to their adoptive relationship: Tiberius is referred to as father, and Germanicus as son. In making this distinction, what is Tacitus trying to suggest about their relationship?

3　Can Tacitus have had any evidence for all the claims he makes about what the various members of the imperial family thought of one another?

4　How significant is the role which Tacitus allows to the women of the imperial family in this section? What are we intended to make of his sketch of Agrippina?

5　What expectations does this digression create for Germanicus' leadership in the course of the mutiny?

he would have restored political freedom　Drusus' 'republicanism' seems to have been a widespread tradition, recorded by Suetonius as well as Tacitus; Suetonius tells how Drusus had written to Tiberius pressing the latter to support him in urging Augustus to restore the republican system (*Tiberius* 50.1). However, it is questionable how seriously this should be taken, since Augustus himself boasted at *Res Gestae* 34 that he had restored the state to the control of the Senate and people as early as 28–7 BC. Perhaps Drusus' early death and popularity had led to the spread of this belief.

the same hope　namely that Germanicus would pursue political change; however, it is questionable how many people really hoped for the restoration of the old system, as Tacitus has already made clear in **1.2** (p. 25).

stepmotherly　in fact, Livia was the stepmother of Agrippina's mother, Julia, who had been banished by her own father in 2 BC, but the relationship could be extended across subsequent generations.

1.34 But the closer Germanicus stood to the pinnacle of ambition, the more keen were his efforts on Tiberius' behalf. He bound **himself, his entourage and the communities of the Belgae** in an oath of allegiance to the new emperor. Then, when he heard about the mutiny of the legions, he set out hurriedly and met them outside the camp; their eyes were cast down towards the ground as if in 5 repentance. After he entered the fortifications, confused complaints began to be voiced. Some individuals took his hand on the pretext of covering it with kisses, and stuck his fingers in their mouths so that he could feel their missing teeth; others showed him their limbs bent with old age. He ordered the gathering which stood before him, because it appeared all jumbled up, **to separate into maniples**: their 10 reply was that they would hear better as they were; he ordered that the standards be brought forward so that this at least would separate the cohorts: slowly they obeyed. Then he began with words of respect towards Augustus, before turning to the victories and triumphs of Tiberius: he celebrated with especial praises **the very fine achievements the new emperor had enjoyed in the Germanies with** 15 **those very legions.** Then he praised **the unanimity of Italy**, and the loyalty of the

---

himself, his entourage and the communities of the Belgae   this translation follows the solution to a textual problem suggested by Haase, but differs from the Oxford text, which adopts the suggested emendation *Sequanos* as the best solution to the problem posed by the *seque* preserved in the main manuscript. However, it seems more important to the logic of the narrative that Germanicus himself swears loyalty to Tiberius rather than any particular Gallic tribe, least of all one very distant from the Belgae. The Belgae occupied an area north of the Seine and the Marne: they had initially been subdued by Julius Caesar in 57 BC, but they had remained restless for another 30 years.

to separate into maniples   the soldiers' reluctance here to assemble in their units echoes the mutiny in Pannonia, where the three legions had united their legionary standards and sought to form a single unit (see **1.18**, p. 49). Germanicus seeks to re-establish the military structure as the basis for army discipline: it is this structure which would mark out the gathering as an army, and not the revolutionary crowd of citizens which it was in danger of becoming. The Latin for 'gathering' here is *contio*, the word for an official public speech, and it was also used of Percennius' (**1.17** with note, p. 47). As there, it is inappropriate in a military context, but is Tacitus also trying to suggest a parallelism between the two meetings?

the very fine achievements ... with those very legions   Tiberius had been active on campaign beyond the Rhine and towards the Elbe from 9 to 7 BC and again from AD 4 to 6. He won a triumph after his first tour of duty, and the historian Velleius Paterculus is effusive in his praise of Tiberius' achievements, but these were interrupted by the revolt of Illyricum in AD 6; the loss of three legions under Varus in AD 9 finally put paid to Augustus' plans for expansion beyond the Rhine (see note on p. 27).

the unanimity of Italy   this slogan has echoes of Augustus' own ideology against Antony in 32 BC, as he records at *Res Gestae* 25: 'The whole of Italy of its own free will swore allegiance to me.' Dio does indeed record that an oath was taken by all of Italy towards Tiberius upon Augustus' death (57.3.2).

---

provinces of Gaul; **nowhere was there any violence or dissent**. These words were heard in silence or with limited grumbling.

1.35   When he mentioned the mutiny, asking where their good conduct as soldiers, where the glory of their traditional discipline had gone, just where they had 20 driven their tribunes, and where their centurions, they all bared their bodies, they angrily pointed to the scars from their wounds and the marks of blows; next with indistinguishable voices they railed against the costs of exemptions, the meanness of their pay, the harshness of their labours, and – identifying them specifically – the fortifications, the ditches, the collection of fodder, timber and firewood, and 25 whatever other errands men were sent on from necessity, **or to battle against idleness in a military camp. The fiercest outcry arose from the veterans** who, counting thirty years' service each, or more, begged him to offer exhausted men respite and an end to such severe military service with a comfortable retirement, so that they should not meet their deaths amid the same labours. There were 30 also those who demanded the money bequeathed by **the divine Augustus**, with favourable cries of support towards Germanicus; and if he wanted supreme power they showed themselves ready. At this, as if polluted by their crime, he leaped headlong from the platform. They blocked his way with weapons as he departed, threatening him unless he returned; but he, shouting that he would rather die 35 than give up his loyalty, snatched his sword from his side, lifted it up and was bringing it down into his chest, **had not those closest to him seized his right arm** and restrained it by force. The furthest section of the gathering, which was packed closely together and – though it is scarcely credible to say this – certain individuals came closer and urged him to strike; and a soldier called Calusidius 40 drew his sword and offered it to him, adding the comment that it was sharper. That appeared cruel and in poor taste even to the raging crowd, and there was a pause in which Caesar could be snatched away into his tent by his friends.

---

nowhere was there any violence or dissent   in the light of the mutiny in Pannonia Germanicus is here rather overstating his case, but he could not yet have known of reactions across the whole empire to the accession of Tiberius.

or to battle against idleness in a military camp   this is a typically Tacitean addition. Camp duties may have been seen as a good way of keeping troops out of trouble in peacetime, but it adds force to the protestations of the troops that many of the hardships which they underwent had no intrinsic purpose.

The fiercest outcry arose from the veterans   in the Latin, the grammar of this sentence is particularly convoluted; perhaps this is an attempt by Tacitus to mimic the confused nature of the veterans' cries.

the divine Augustus   on the various legacies he had left in his will and his deification, see **1.8**, p. 33 and **1.10**, p. 40 respectively.

had not those closest to him seized his right arm   on the style of this sentence and the passage as a whole, see Introduction, p. 5.

1. Are the mutinous legions in Germany portrayed differently from those in Pannonia? Do they make similar demands? What effect does it have on readers that we do not hear about the leaders of this mutiny, as we did with the first one?

2. How is Germanicus' behaviour portrayed? Does he show strong leadership? How does he compare with Drusus?

3. Is there any sense that we are invited to compare him with Percennius? Each is given the first extended speech of the two mutinies, and this parallel is reinforced by the use of the word *contio* of both occasions. Does Germanicus display the same theatricality as Percennius? Is this desirable in a military commander?

4. Notice that in the final sentence of this passage he is again called Caesar. Why does Tacitus use this name for him here?

5. Imagine the scene that Tacitus has described. Is it possible for a commander to calm mutinous soldiers by delivering a moving speech? Can you think of other instances where the power of words has triumphed over violence?

Following this episode, Germanicus and his advisers were alarmed by reports that the legions were set on plundering Gaul and abandoning the frontier, which might lead to an incursion by the Germans. However, since they feared civil war if they put down the mutiny by force, they decided to forge a letter from the emperor granting many concessions, including paying out and doubling Augustus' legacy to the soldiers. This deceit again suggests disconcerting parallels between Germanicus and the leaders of the Pannonian mutiny, namely Vibulenus' false story of his murdered brother. The crude ruse was quickly suspected by the soldiers, who demanded an immediate fulfilment of the letter's terms to ensure that they could not be reneged on subsequently. Germanicus was forced to scrape together the money himself, before the legions eventually allowed themselves to be led off to their various winter camps. Germanicus then departed for the still loyal upper army, to whom he granted the same concessions. Tacitus next inserts a brief digression on a unit deployed separately from the main body of the legions.

1.38   But **among the Chauci**, detachments of the seditious legions who were carrying out garrison duty began to mutiny and were suppressed for a short time by the immediate execution of two soldiers. Manius Ennius, the prefect of the camp, had given the order, setting a good example rather than adhering to his actual powers. Then as the uprising gathered momentum he turned fugitive and when he was   5
discovered, once his hiding-place proved unsafe, he relied for protection instead

---

among the Chauci   this tribe lay well beyond the Rhine and close to the Elbe, on the north coast of modern Germany.

on his boldness, saying that it was not their prefect who was being dishonoured by them, but Germanicus their commander, and Tiberius the emperor. At the same time, terrifying those who stood in his way, he seized the standard and turned back to the Rhine; shouting that anyone who departed from the column would be   10 treated as a deserter, **he led them back to winter quarters**, rebellious but without having ventured any action.

1.39   Meanwhile **the ambassadors from the Senate** approached Germanicus, who had now returned to **the altar of the Ubii**. Two legions were wintering there, the first and the twentieth, and the veterans who had recently been conditionally   15 discharged. Fear descended upon their terrified minds, frenzied as they were with a guilty conscience and a fear that the ambassadors had come on the orders of the senators to annul those concessions which they had extorted through the mutiny. And, as it is typical for a mob to bring charges, however false, against a scapegoat, they accused Munatius Plancus, who had held the consulship and was   20 leader of the embassy, of being the proposer of the senatorial decree; early in the night they began to demand **the standard which was located in Germanicus' quarters**, they made a rush for the entrance and broke down the doors, they dragged Caesar from his bed and compelled him to hand over the standard by frightening him with the threat of death. Next, while wandering through the   25 streets, they came upon the ambassadors, who were heading to see Germanicus after hearing the commotion. They hurled insults and planned murder, especially that of Plancus, whose rank had prevented him from flight; in this moment of danger there was no other help for him except the camp of the first legion. There he embraced the standards and eagle and protected himself with religion, and if   30 the standard-bearer Calpurnius had not prevented the ultimate act of violence,

---

he led them back to winter quarters   this episode offers a parallel to Tacitus' account of how the Pannonian mutiny was reignited by a detachment of troops in Nauportus (1.20): Ennius, by contrast, stamps out any potential fresh outbreak. More suggestive perhaps is the implicit contrast between Germanicus' and Ennius' responses to the mutiny.

the ambassadors from the Senate   this embassy had been sent to confirm Germanicus' command and to console him for Augustus' death. Its dispatch is recorded at 1.14.

the altar of the Ubii   this is likely to have been the same location as the main town of the Ubii, the site of the later colony, and modern Cologne. The altar will probably have been to Rome and Augustus, and served as a focus of the imperial cult for Germany, just as that at Lugdunum (Lyon) was for Gaul.

the standard which was located in Germanicus' quarters   it is not entirely clear which this standard was – it seems most likely to have been the veterans' standard, under which they were still held, although they had been discharged from full service. As Miller notes, the veterans had most to lose if the settlement were to be overturned (*Annals Book 1*, p. 160).

in an event rare even among the enemy, **an ambassador of the Roman people in a Roman camp** would have stained the altar of the gods with his own blood. At dawn finally, after the commander, the soldiers and the events were seen for what they were, Germanicus entered the camp, ordered Plancus to be brought to him, and received him onto the platform. Then, rebuking the fatal madness and saying that it was rising again **as a result of the anger not of the soldiers but of the gods,** he revealed why the ambassadors had come; he spoke about the rights of ambassadors and eloquently bewailed the serious and undeserved suffering of Plancus himself and at the same time the degree of shame that the legion had incurred. With the gathering stunned rather than pacified, he dismissed the ambassadors under the protection of some auxiliary cavalry.

1.40   In this alarming situation **all censured Germanicus** for not going to the upper army, where obedience and assistance against the rebels were to be found: enough mistakes and more had been made with the granting of discharge, the gift of money and a soft response. Or if his own safety was of no importance to him, why was he keeping **his little son,** and why his pregnant wife among men who were frenzied and violating every human right? Let him at least return them to the boy's grandfather and the state. Germanicus hesitated for a long time, but his wife was scornful, as she bore witness to **her descent from the god Augustus** and the fact that she was not weak in the face of dangers. In the end amid much lamentation he embraced his wife's belly and the son they shared, and forced her to leave. The pitiable column of women went on its way, the wife of the commander a fugitive, holding her little son to her breast. The wives of his friends who were being dragged off at the same time surrounded her, weeping – and no less sad were those who were staying behind.

---

an ambassador of the Roman people in a Roman camp   in the Latin, with its more flexible word-order, the two adjectives for 'Roman' are put right next to one another to emphasize how outrageous such behaviour was in a Roman context. In what other ways does Tacitus seek to underline the outrageousness of the soldiers' behaviour?

as a result of the anger not of the soldiers but of the gods   is there anything surprising in the way in which Germanicus absolves the soldiers of blame here? Or is he pursuing a clever psychological strategy at a time when tempers were running high?

all censured Germanicus   it is typical of Tacitus' style that he does not criticize Germanicus directly in his own narrative voice, but records the criticism of others. Are we meant to agree with these criticisms or not?

his little son   this was the future emperor Gaius. Tacitus here uses a diminutive form of the word little (*parvulum*), which is meant affectionately, but is perhaps also intended as a pun on the boy's nickname, Caligula, which is itself a diminutive, meaning 'Little Boots'. On the military connotations of this name see note on p. 65.

her descent from the god Augustus   to emphasize this was at best undiplomatic. As noted on **1.33** (p. 58), the fact that Germanicus' wife and hence his children were directly descended from Augustus made him a potential threat to Tiberius, who was unable to make the same boast.

1.41   The appearance was not that of a Caesar in his prime, nor in his own camp,
        but as if in a conquered city. The groaning and wailing attracted the ears and
        eyes of even the soldiers: they came out of their tents. What was that sound of
        weeping? What was so sad? Here were distinguished women, not a centurion to   60
        protect them, not a soldier, nothing one would expect of a general's wife or of her
        customary entourage: they were heading for **the Treveri** and foreign protection.
        Then there was shame and pity and memory of her father Agrippa, and of **her
        grandfather Augustus**, her father-in-law Drusus, and herself, **distinguished for
        her fertility** and famed for her loyalty as a wife; besides there was her child, born   65
        in the camp, brought up among the camaraderie of the legions, whom they called
        by the military nickname, **Caligula,** because he often wore this footwear to win
        the favour of the ordinary ranks. But nothing affected them as much as jealousy
        of the Treveri: they begged, they implored that Agrippina should come back and
        stay, some running to meet her, the majority returning to Germanicus. And he,   70
        fresh as he was in his grief and anger, **began to speak** in this way to them as they
        poured around him.

1.42   'Neither my wife nor son are dearer to me than my father and the state, but his own
        majesty will indeed protect the former, its other armies will protect the Roman
        empire. My wife and children whom I would willingly offer up to destruction for   75
        your glory, I am now moving far away from you madmen, so that whatever crime
        this is which threatens may be atoned for by my blood alone, and so that the
        killing of the great-grandson of Augustus and **the murder of Tiberius' daughter-
        in-law** may not make you more culpable. For what has not been dared or defiled

---

the Treveri   this tribe's territory lay in the Moselle basin around Trier, the site of a town
established under Augustus on the river.

her grandfather Augustus   the soldiers are just as aware of her distinguished ancestry
as she is.

distinguished for her fertility   she bore nine children in all to Germanicus. This large
number of children was again politically significant, and not just because Tiberius only
had one son: Augustus had passed a raft of marriage legislation beginning in 18 BC, which
had included the granting of various privileges for those with three or more children.

Caligula   the name is a diminutive of *caliga*, the name for the boot worn by Roman
soldiers. Tacitus' addition that he wore the boots 'to win the favour of the ordinary ranks'
is pointed: it suggests that Germanicus and Agrippina are self-consciously involved in a
popularity contest. The prominence of Caligula in this part of the narrative parallels the
earlier mention of Chaerea, his eventual assassin, in **1.32** (see note on p. 57).

began to speak   this is the first long set-speech of the *Annals* and indeed one of the
longest pieces of direct speech in the whole work. It is striking that Tacitus chooses to
give this 'honour' to Germanicus rather than to anyone else.

the murder of Tiberius' daughter-in-law   notice that Germanicus himself is careful to
avoid referring to his wife as the granddaughter of Augustus, but is keen to stress her
ties with the family of the new emperor Tiberius.

---

by you over the course of these days? **What name shall I give to this gathering?** 80
Am I to call you soldiers, you who have surrounded the son of your emperor
with a fortification and weapons? Or citizens, you who have so contemptuously
discarded the authority of the Senate? You have also contravened the rights
afforded to the enemy, the sanctity of an embassy and international law. **The**
divine Julius checked the mutiny of an army with one word, by calling those who 85
refused his oath Quirites; **the divine Augustus terrified the legions at Actium**
with his facial expression: though people like myself are not yet the match of
them, we are descended from them, and if the soldiers of Spain or Syria were to
reject us, **it would nonetheless be remarkable and undeserved.** Or do you, the
first and twentieth legions – the former which received its standards from Tiberius, 90
and you his partner in so many battles, rewarded with so many prizes – do you

---

What name shall I give to this gathering?   this phrase and the questions which follow
closely echo Scipio Africanus' words to his mutinous troops in 206 BC at Livy, *History*
28.27.3–4. This had occurred in Spain following false rumours that Scipio had died from
an illness, and amid general resentment at extended military service abroad during the
war with Carthage. Miller (*Annals Book 1,* pp. 163–4) rightly stresses that such an echo
does not necessarily mean that Germanicus' speech is purely invention on Tacitus' part.
However, Goodyear is surely wrong to state that 'we need hardly see in them conscious
allusions to Livy, and least of all a subtle suggestion that Germanicus and Scipio are
comparable' (vol. 1, p. 288). An allusion to such a prominent mutiny of the republican
past with clear verbal echoes precisely encourages readers to draw comparisons between
the two men and the way in which they dealt with the situations which faced them, not
least because the narrative, as we have seen, is constantly offering other figures with
whom we are encouraged to compare Germanicus. For a further comparison between
the two men, see **2.59** with note, p. 82.

The divine Julius checked the mutiny of an army with one word   this is a reference to
Julius Caesar putting down a mutiny by the tenth legion in Rome in 47 BC (Suetonius,
Iulius 70). *Quirites* was the traditional name for Roman citizens in peacetime, and by so
calling them, as well as reminding them of their duty to Rome, Caesar was making the
point that they were no longer his soldiers. He followed up this rebuke by withholding
some of the land and money which he owed them, and by refusing to take them to Africa
with him.

the divine Augustus terrified the legions at Actium with his facial expression   it is not
entirely clear to which event this refers, but Suetonius records the strict discipline which
Augustus demanded of his men on various occasions (*Augustus* 24). It is striking that
Germanicus compares himself unfavourably with two famous predecessors who dealt
with mutinies; this seems to encourage the reader even further to draw the more implicit
comparison with Scipio Africanus suggested by the verbal echoes of Livy.

it would nonetheless be remarkable and undeserved   his point is that of all the legions,
he would expect the German legions to be particularly loyal to Tiberius and himself.

Or do you   the tortured grammar of this sentence in the Latin is perhaps intended to
convey Germanicus' own heightened emotion.

repay your leader with such outstanding gratitude? Am I to bring this report to my father who is hearing entirely happy news from the other provinces? That his recruits, that his veterans have not been satisfied with the grant of discharge, nor with money; that here alone centurions are being killed, tribunes thrown out, 95 ambassadors penned in, the camp and rivers polluted with blood, and that I am drawing breath precariously amid enemies.

1.43   'Why on that first day of assembly did you pull away that sword which I was preparing to plunge into my chest, you thoughtless friends? That man who offered me his sword acted better and more lovingly. I would at least have died as yet 100 unaware of my army's countless scandalous acts; you would have chosen a leader who might indeed have left my death unpunished, but would at least have avenged **Varus and his three legions**. For may the gods not allow that this glory and fame should belong to **the Belgae** – although they are offering help – to have come to the aid of the name of Rome, and to have subdued the peoples of Germany. 105 May your mind, divine Augustus, which has been received in heaven, and your image, my father Drusus, and your memory – may these together with these same soldiers of yours, to whom a sense of shame and pride are now returning, cleanse this pollution, and turn this internecine anger to the destruction of the enemy. You also, whose expressions I now see are different, whose hearts are different, if 110 you are restoring the ambassadors to the Senate, obedience to the emperor, if you are restoring my wife and son to me, abandon the contagion and single out the mutineers: that will be a guarantee of repentance, that will be a bond of loyalty.'

> The speech was successful in bringing the troops into line, and they began to turn on those responsible for the mutiny. They brought them before the commander of the first legion who conducted what amounted to a kangaroo court, with the rank and file as a crowd allowed to pronounce on the guilt of individuals: these were killed summarily. Germanicus did not stand in the way of this 'court' since he could see that it allowed him to avoid any unpopularity that might stem from having to punish the guilty himself. A review of individual centurions was also held in which Germanicus dismissed those whom the men declared guilty of cruelty or greed.

Varus and his three legions   on this defeat of AD 9, see note on p. 27. As yet it had remained largely unavenged, though Germanicus was to take the army to visit the site of the disaster the following year (see **1.61–2**, pp. 73–5).

the Belgae   on this people, see note on p. 60. There is no evidence to suggest that this was a genuine offer, rather than something invented to stir indignation among the legionaries.

1 How does Tacitus convey the outrageous behaviour of the soldiers in this mutiny?

2 How effective a piece of rhetoric is Germanicus' speech in the circumstances? Is his style markedly different from that of Drusus in the earlier mutiny, or not?

3 Germanicus himself introduces in his speech historical parallels of generals who dealt successfully with mutinies. How far should this encourage us to draw similar comparisons, and with other characters in the narrative as well?

4 What other options were potentially available to Germanicus in dealing with the mutiny? What risks might they have carried?

5 Is Tacitus explicit in his comments about Germanicus' leadership? If not, does he expect each reader to make up his or her own mind? Does he direct the readers in any way to pass a judgement on Germanicus?

After bringing the first and twentieth legions into line, Germanicus now turned his thoughts to the fifth and twenty-first who had started the mutiny, and who were wintering about 60 miles downstream at Vetera. Meanwhile Tacitus turns briefly to Rome.

1.46   But at Rome there was not yet news of what the outcome in Illyricum had been and word had arrived of the mutiny of the German legions. **The fearful citizens blamed Tiberius** on the grounds that, at the time when he was deceiving the senators and ordinary people – who were weak and unarmed – **with feigned hesitation**, the soldiers were disaffected and could not be brought into line by the authority of 5 two youths, an authority which was not as yet fully developed. They said that he ought to have gone in person and set his imperial majesty against men who would give in when they saw their emperor with his long experience, a man supreme in severity and generosity at the same time. They wondered how Augustus, tired with

---

Illyricum   this name is perhaps used to refer to Pannonia simply for variety's sake, but Tacitus seems to reserve it for use when the mutiny is viewed from the perspective of the capital. Perhaps the name was evocative in Rome for the memories it conjured up of the serious revolt there in AD 9.

The fearful citizens blamed Tiberius   note again that Tacitus does not criticize in his own narrative voice, but refers to the criticisms of others (compare **1.40**, p. 64). In this context it is worth considering what Tacitus' source can have been for comments so critical of the emperor, and likewise how he can have known what Tiberius' own thoughts were in this situation (given in the next section).

with feigned hesitation   this is a reference to Tiberius' behaviour in **1.11–13** (pp. 41–3), where he appeared reluctant to succeed Augustus as *princeps*.

age, could visit the provinces of Germany **so often**, while Tiberius, healthy and in 10
the prime of his life, sat in the Senate criticizing the words of the senators? Enough
had been provided for the slavery of the city: dressings needed to be applied to the
minds of the soldiers so that they might be willing **to tolerate peace**.

1.47 **It was an unshakeable and fixed principle** for Tiberius in the face of this talk not
to neglect the capital of the empire nor to entrust himself and the state to chance. 15
Numerous and varied were the factors which worried him: the army in Germany
was stronger, that in Pannonia was closer; the former could rely on the resources
of the provinces of Gaul, the latter threatened Italy: to which, therefore, should he
give precedence? And he feared that those he put second would be inflamed by
the insult. However, he thought that they could be approached on equal terms by 20
means of his sons, keeping safe his own majesty, which enjoyed greater respect at a
distance. At the same time it was excusable for the young men to refer certain issues
to their father, and those who offered resistance to Germanicus or Drusus could be
pacified or broken by himself: what other recourse could there be if they had already
rejected the emperor? But **as if he was on the point of leaving at any moment**, he 25
selected travelling companions, he assembled his baggage, he equipped ships. Then
he variously offered winter or matters of business as an excuse for postponing his
departure: he deceived the quick-witted for only a short while, the ordinary people
for longer, and those in the provinces for longest of all.

---

so often   this criticism is at best unfair. Augustus' last confirmed visit to Gaul was in
13 BC when he was in his late forties, although he was perhaps there in 8 BC when he
was 55; Tiberius was himself 56 in AD 14. Modern commentators ascribe this to error or
rhetorical flourish on Tacitus' part, but is it impossible that he intends to portray Tiberius'
critics as guilty of exaggeration? Furneaux says that the absence of an indication to alert
readers suggests that Tacitus himself was misled.

to tolerate peace   this sounds a striking paradox to a modern reader, but the equation
of slavery in Rome and the lack of opportunity to win glory against a foreign enemy is
one which frequently reappears in Tacitus' portrayal of the principate, most notably at
4.32–3 (pp. 105–7).

It was an unshakeable and fixed principle   this is a verbal echo of Vergil, *Aeneid* 4.15–
16, where Dido uses a similar form of words to express her firm intention never to marry
again. Miller suggests that 'we cannot but wonder if Tiberius' purpose will prove to be as
unstable as Dido's' ('Virgil and Tacitus', p. 32).

as if he was on the point of leaving at any moment   a skill at pretence is one of the
defining characteristics of Tacitus' portrayal of Tiberius, but one that was recognized by
contemporaries according to an anecdote told by Suetonius (*Tiberius* 38). On numerous
occasions Tiberius made convincing preparations for a tour of the provinces, though he
always cancelled and stayed in Rome: this earned him the nickname of 'Callipedes', a
Greek comic actor famous for imitating a long-distance runner while remaining rooted
to the spot.

---

1 Why does Tacitus choose to digress on the situation in Rome at this point in the narrative of the German mutiny?

2 Why does he choose to report the criticisms made by others against Tiberius, rather than simply giving his own opinion of Tiberius' behaviour? Are people's perceptions of the emperor key to an understanding of the history of the period?

3 Do these criticisms of Tiberius stand up to scrutiny, or does Tiberius answer them in a satisfactory way in 1.47?

4 How far does Tiberius' character act as a foil for that of Germanicus?

Back in Germany, Germanicus had prepared a force to deal with the last two mutinous legions at Vetera. However, he sent ahead a letter to their commander, Caecina, urging the legions to sort out their problems themselves before he arrived and carried out indiscriminate punishment. Caecina assembled all the loyal men and they fixed a time to slaughter the guilty in their beds at night.

1.49 The appearance of this civil war was different from all those that had ever happened. Not in battle, not from opposing camps, but from the same sleeping-quarters, those who ate together by day and who slept together at night split into factions and thrust home their weapons. The shouting, wounds and blood were plain to see, the reasons for them lay hidden; chance governed the rest. Some 5 of the loyal men were killed, when it was understood who were the targets of the slaughter and the worst offenders had also seized their weapons. Nor was there a commander or tribune on hand to control the situation: **the licence to take revenge was given to the ordinary soldiers for as long as they wanted it.** Soon Germanicus entered the camp, and in floods of tears called the action not a 10 remedy but a disaster; he ordered the bodies to be burned.

A desire seized the soldiers' minds, which were even then pitiless, to march against the enemy, as an act of atonement for their madness; they thought that there was no other way for the spirits of their dead fellow-soldiers to be appeased than if they received honourable wounds in **their impious breasts.** 15

---

the licence to take revenge was given ... for as long as they wanted it in the Latin, Tacitus expresses this idea in three separate abstract nouns, with a literal translation running something like: 'Licence and revenge and having their fill were entrusted to the ordinary soldiers.' The effect of this is to emphasize just how much freedom of action was given to the rank and file to exact personal revenge on the mutineers.

their impious breasts the Roman concept of *pietas* involved a respectful sense of duty towards relatives, the gods and the state, but also any other individuals with whom one might have close ties: such bonds existed between messmates and fellow-soldiers of the same legion.

Caesar followed the ardent desire of the soldiers, built a bridge and sent across twelve thousand of the legionaries, **twenty-six auxiliary cohorts and eight squadrons of cavalry**, the last two of which had preserved their discipline unblemished in the mutiny.

> Tacitus then describes the swift campaign which Germanicus fought in the wooded country across the Rhine with this force. In large part they were able to kill and ravage unhindered, perhaps all the more easily since the Germans would not have been expecting an attack so late in the year. The only danger came with the return of the Romans towards the Rhine, when the Germans from surrounding areas had assembled and attacked the rearguard as they passed along the narrow passages through the forests. However, the twenty-first legion repelled the attack, an engagement which helped to restore the morale of the troops as they settled into winter quarters.

1.52 Tiberius had mixed feelings of happiness and concern at news of these events: he was delighted that the mutiny had been crushed, but was troubled that Germanicus had courted the support of the soldiers by handing out money and hastening their discharge, and also that **he had won glory in war**. However, he made report of events to the Senate and spoke at length of Germanicus' excellence, in a speech 5 **too ostentatiously rhetorical for him to be credited with real sincerity**. As for

---

Caesar followed the ardent desire of the soldiers Dio records Germanicus as the initiator of this campaign as a means of keeping the soldiers busy and so less likely to mutiny once more (57.6.1). Goodyear (vol. 1, pp. 313–14) dismisses this difference as inconsequential, but is it? Tacitus in fact seems to draw attention to Germanicus' subordinate role by putting the word for 'follows' first in the sentence to give it added emphasis. What aspect of Germanicus' leadership might Tacitus be seeking to portray here? One might compare the example of Julius Caesar which Germanicus had himself drawn attention to in his speech (**1.42**, p. 66), not least because Germanicus is again pointedly called **Caesar** in this sentence. As we have seen, after the tenth legion had mutinied in 47 BC Julius Caesar refused to take them with him to fight in Africa although they desperately wanted to go.

twenty-six auxiliary cohorts and eight squadrons of cavalry this is likely to have meant 13,000 auxiliary infantry and 4,000 cavalry. The high proportion of more lightly armed auxiliaries and cavalry would have suited the brief raiding campaign, such as it would have to have been at such a late point in the season.

he had won glory in war it seems hard to credit such envy on Tiberius' part, given his own much greater military achievements. However, as Furneaux notes, it is likely that the victories of the popular Germanicus were overrated in Rome.

too ostentatiously rhetorical for him to be credited with real sincerity Tacitus underlines his view that for a full understanding of the period it is not enough to take the actual words that are spoken at face value, especially in the case of an emperor like Tiberius.

Drusus and the way in which he had put an end to the trouble in Illyricum, he praised him more briefly but more enthusiastically and with genuine feeling. He extended also to the Pannonian troops **all those concessions which Germanicus had granted.**

1 This marks the end of Tacitus' account of the two mutinies, an account which takes up almost half of the first book of the *Annals*. Why does he give them so much emphasis in such a key position in the work?

2 Why in particular does he choose to give detailed accounts of both mutinies, where one might have been thought able to serve as an example? Is it simply because they offer some variation from the narration of the dry politics of Rome? Or is there some more significant historical purpose to Tacitus' decision?

3 Does the threat of mutiny or a military coup affect the operation of politics in heavily militarized states in the modern world?

4 What picture of Tiberius and Germanicus emerges from the narrative? Does Tacitus offer fair portrayals of them both?

5 The two men have very different approaches to their role as a Caesar. Do they offer alternative models which the principate might follow?

10

---

all those concessions which Germanicus had granted   note that Tacitus' account of the mutinies closes with a reference to the concessions which were made by Germanicus, but not by Drusus.

4 Germanicus, his death and the trial of Piso

Following his lengthy account of Germanicus' suppression of the legionary mutiny in AD 14, Tacitus returns to narrate his campaigns of the following year. He introduces his account with the notice that Germanicus had been awarded a rather premature triumph at the start of the year, before telling how he sought to profit from hostility between the rival German leaders Segestes and Arminius. Among other successes, Germanicus managed to recover the eagle of the nineteenth legion which had been lost when Varus' three legions had been ambushed and annihilated by the Germans under Arminius' leadership in AD 9. Germanicus then brought his forces into the Teutoburg forest, where this disaster had occurred and the remains of the dead had been left exposed.

The campaigns of Germanicus: 1.61–2; 2.24, 26

1.61   Therefore **Caesar** was seized by a desire to carry out a proper funeral for the soldiers and their leader; the whole army which was on the spot was moved to pity for their relatives and friends, and in short for the fortunes of war and mankind's lot. When **Caecina** was sent ahead to explore **the remote sections of the forest tracks** and construct causeways and embankments over the wet parts 5 of the marshes and the treacherous ground, the men came upon some depressing places, grim to see and grim in the memory. **The first of Varus' camps** with its extensive perimeter and clearly marked headquarters showed the handiwork of

---

Caesar i.e. Germanicus.

Caecina Aulus Caecina Severus was governor of Lower Germany, and so under Germanicus' overall command. He had not been very effective in dealing with the mutiny the previous year (see **1.32**, p. 57).

the remote sections of the forest tracks it was in just such terrain that Varus had been ambushed and met disaster.

The first of Varus' camps the Latin does not exclude the possibility that there was just one camp, and the soldiers visited two different parts of it. However, the rhetoric of the passage seems to make much more sense if we understand that there were two, the initial marching camp (i.e. one built by legions on the march for overnight shelter, rather than a permanent base) constructed by the three legions, and a second emergency refuge built by the survivors, who only had the manpower and opportunity to construct limited defences, with low ramparts and shallow ditches.

The monument to Hermann (i.e. Arminius) for his victory over Varus. It was begun in 1841 but not completed until 1875 following the unification of most of Germany under Bismarck. It stands in the southern part of Teutoburg Forest.

three legions; then from the half-collapsed rampart and shallow ditch it could be deduced that the now-weakened survivors had taken refuge there together: in the 10 middle of the plain the whitened bones lay scattered or piled up, just as the men had fled or offered resistance. Fragments of weapons and the limbs of horses lay nearby, and with them **skulls nailed to the trunks of trees**. In the neighbouring groves were barbarian altars, at which **the tribunes and senior centurions** had been sacrificed. And the survivors of this disaster, who had slipped away from 15 the battle or captivity, related that this was the place where the commanders had fallen, and that the place where **the eagles** had been seized; they indicated where Varus' first wound had been inflicted, where he found death by the blow of his own ill-starred right hand; and they revealed the platform on which Arminius delivered his harangue, how many gibbets there were for the prisoners, which 20 were **the pits**, and how in his arrogance he mocked the standards and the eagles.

---

skulls nailed to the trunks of trees   these were trophies of victory. Some archaeological sites have been discovered, such as that at Ribemont-sur-Ancre in France, which suggest that such stories of gory trophies and prisoner sacrifice may be true.

the tribunes and senior centurions   the senior officers of the legions.

the eagles   these were the insignia of the three legions, while the term 'standards' is used to refer to those of the smaller subdivisions within each legion.

the pits   these could have been used for torturing the prisoners, or even burying them alive.

1.62   And so the Roman army, in the same spot six years after the defeat, was burying the bones of the three legions and, since none of them knew whether it was the remains of strangers or of their own relatives which they were covering with earth, they were all treating them as kinsmen and blood-relatives: their anger towards 25 the enemy was increased, and they were at one and the same time mournful and furious. Caesar, a partner in grief to the men with him, laid the first turf to raise the burial mound, as the most welcome tribute to the dead. This action was not approved of by Tiberius, whether owing to his unfavourable interpretation of all Germanicus' actions, or because he believed that the army had been blunted 30 for battle and made more fearful of the enemy by the sight of slaughtered and unburied men; and that a commander endowed with **the augurate and the most ancient religious sanctity** should not have handled funerary rituals.

---

1   How does Tacitus organize his description of the scene of Varus' disaster? Why do you think he chooses to present it in this way?

2   Is Tacitus' account critical of Germanicus, Tiberius, or both men? If so, is the criticism fair?

Tacitus continues his narrative of the campaign with an account of Caecina's retreat with four of Germanicus' legions, in which he comes close to suffering the same fate as Varus had, ambushed by the Germans. At the opening of the second book, at the start of AD 16, Tacitus relates that there was trouble in the East, following the expulsion of the pro-Roman Vonones from the kingship of Parthia and subsequent problems in Armenia, which served as a buffer-state between Parthia and Rome. Tacitus recounts that these events pleased Tiberius as offering a justification for Germanicus' recall from Germany. However, the latter was set on his most ambitious campaign to date, with the plan to use a fleet to strike more swiftly at the Germans. He won two significant victories, and after the second piled up captured weapons in a trophy. On this he added an inscription which Tacitus describes as **arrogant**: 'Following the conquest in war of the tribes between the Rhine and the Elbe, the army of Tiberius Caesar devoted these memorials to Mars, Jupiter and Augustus' (2.22); we are told that Germanicus omitted to mention himself for fear of envy. However, on the return journey matters took a turn for the worse when a storm blew up, scattering his ships.

---

the augurate and the most ancient religious sanctity   the *augurs* were experts in divination and made up one of the four main priestly colleges in Rome. Of these Germanicus was probably also a *pontifex*, as well as holding other lesser priesthoods. Contact with the dead was ritually problematic for at least some Roman priests.

arrogant   the Latin word is *superbus*. This is not only the epithet given to the last of Rome's seven kings, Tarquinius, but the related noun had also been used by the survivors of the Varian disaster to describe Arminius' attitude towards the Roman standards (see **1.61**, p. 74).

2.24   Just as **the Ocean** is more violent than the rest of the sea and Germany is exceptional for the savagery of its climate, so that disaster stood out for its unprecedented scale, taking place on a sea ringed by enemy shores, and so desolate and boundless that it is believed to be the most distant, beyond all land. Some of the ships were swallowed up, a greater number thrown onto islands which lay further away; and because the 5 region was devoid of human habitation the soldiers died from starvation, except for those who had been kept alive by eating the corpses of horses which had been cast up in the same place. Germanicus' trireme alone put in to the land of **the Chauci**; throughout all those days and nights on the cliffs and headlands, when he was shouting repeatedly that he was to blame for such great destruction, his friends 10 could scarcely restrain him from perishing in the same sea.

> **1** How are the fluctuating moods of Germanicus portrayed?
> **2** This is not the first time Germanicus' friends had to restrain him. Is his behaviour here similar to that which he displayed during the mutiny?

After regrouping from the storm, Germanicus launches further punitive expeditions against the Chatti and the Marsi, from whom he recovered another of the lost legionary eagles. However, in spite of widespread confidence that final victory was imminent, Tiberius was ever more set on Germanicus' recall.

2.26   It was considered certain that the enemy were on the point of collapse and making plans for seeking peace, and that if the war could be continued into the following summer, it could be brought to completion. But in frequent letters Tiberius advised him to return for **the triumph which had been decreed to him**: there had now been **enough results, enough happenings**. He had enjoyed great 5 and successful battles: he should also remember what the winds and waves had inflicted, through no fault of the leader, but serious and terrible losses nonetheless. Tiberius noted that he had himself been sent to Germany **nine times** by the divine Augustus, and that he had achieved more by deliberation than by force. This

---

the Ocean   the Romans considered that the known world was encircled by an all-surrounding Ocean. Here it is referring to the North Sea, across which Germanicus' fleet had to make its way back to the Rhine.

the Chauci   this tribe lived along the North Sea coast between the mouths of the Ems and the Elbe, and was very powerful in this period.

the triumph which had been decreed to him   this had happened at the start of AD 15.

enough results, enough happenings   these Latin words are intentionally ambiguous, but point to the idea that Germanicus' successes have been balanced out by setbacks.

nine times   these occasions came between 9 BC and AD 13.

A relief from the Arch of Titus depicting the celebration of a triumph. Titus is shown riding through Rome in a four-horse chariot to commemorate his success in crushing the Jewish Revolt. Although damaged, a winged Victory can be seen crowning Titus with a laurel wreath.

was how **the Sugambri** had been received under terms of surrender, and how 10
the Suebi and king Maroboduus had been pledged to peace. Even **the Cherusci**
and the other tribes of rebels could be left to their internal disagreements since
the interests of Roman vengeance had been served. When Germanicus begged

the Sugambri this tribe had initially been defeated by Tiberius' brother Drusus in 12 BC, but he had himself finally suppressed them in 8 BC.

the Suebi and king Maroboduus Maroboduus was king of the Marcomanni, a tribe inhabiting an area to the north of Vienna (and here referred to loosely by the term Suebi). The Romans had been forced to agree peace with him in AD 6 following the outbreak of a rebellion in Illyricum.

the Cherusci this tribe had been responsible for Varus' disaster under its leader Arminius. However, Tacitus' narrative itself supports Tiberius' claim, with Arminius repeatedly facing opposition for his anti-Roman stance, most notably from Segestes. Indeed, Tacitus recounts Arminius' eventual death at the hands of his kinsmen in AD 19, at the very end of this second book, ironically supplanting notices of Germanicus' own death in this emphatic position.

for a year to complete what he had begun, Tiberius put **his modesty** to the test more pointedly by offering a second consulship, **whose duties he should meet 15 in person**. At the same time he added the argument that if fighting were still required, he should leave opportunity to win glory to his brother Drusus: since there was no other enemy in the field at that time, he could not **achieve the title of** *imperator* **and win his laurels** except in the Germanies. Germanicus delayed no longer, although he understood that these reasons were fabricated and that he 20 was being removed because of envy for the glory he had already won.

---

1 What are Tiberius' publicly expressed reasons for the recall of Germanicus? Are they persuasive? Do they obscure questions about Germanicus' competence as a general?

2 Did Germanicus and Tiberius have different objectives for the campaign in Germany? If so, how could this explain the tensions between the two men?

Upon Germanicus' return to Rome, he celebrated his triumph on 26 May AD 17. Tiberius made a gift of money to the people in his name and undertook to share the consulship with him the following year. However, in the light of a range of problems in the East, the most notable of which was the state of Armenia and the relationship with Parthia, Tiberius asked the Senate to give Germanicus an extraordinary command in which he held greater *imperium* than the various governors of the East in order to resolve these difficulties. The same year he appointed Gnaeus Calpurnius Piso to be governor of Syria to help Germanicus with his duties. Piso was a fiery ex-consul, the son of a prominent republican who had been reconciled to Augustus by the offer of a consulship. He seems to have misunderstood the purpose of his appointment, thinking – according to Tacitus (2.43) – that he had been appointed to curb Germanicus' intentions: indeed a tradition arose that he had been given secret instructions by the emperor himself.

---

his modesty the precise meaning here is uncertain. It could mean his obedience to military commands, but it seems more likely to refer to his ostensible reluctance to pursue personal glory.

whose duties he should meet in person there is an irony to this argument, of which the reader will only become aware subsequently. For when Germanicus does finally enter office for the second time as consul with Tiberius in AD 18, he does so abroad at Nicopolis in Greece, as Tacitus is careful to point out (**2.53**, p. 79).

achieve the title of *imperator* **and win his laurels** for the title of *imperator* see note on **1.3**, p. 26; the mention of laurel here is a reference to the winning of a triumph, during which the triumphant general wore a laurel wreath as he rode in his chariot through Rome.

So begins the story that would lead to Germanicus' demise in AD 19, the subsequent chaos in the eastern provinces, and the trial and conviction of Piso, all brought about in significant part by the animosity which developed between Piso and the emperor's adopted son. Tacitus notes that the problem arose from divisions within the imperial household between those who favoured Germanicus and Drusus' supporters – although he also records that these two men enjoyed a remarkable friendship at a personal level. However, the episode is also very important from a historiographical perspective: in the late 1980s in southern Spain various bronze fragments of a senatorial decree concerning the condemnation of Piso were discovered through the use of metal detectors. As a result, the complete decree has been pieced together, the *senatus consultum de Cn. Pisone Patre* ('Decree of the Senate concerning Cnaeus Piso Senior': abbreviated henceforth as *SCPP*), a document which invites direct comparison with Tacitus' own narrative of the same events. We pick up the story of Germanicus' command at the start of AD 18 with an account of his journey to the East.

Germanicus and Piso: 2.53, 55, 57, 59–60

2.53   The following year saw Tiberius as consul for the third time and Germanicus for the second. But Germanicus entered this office in the city of Nicopolis in Achaia, which he had reached via the coast of Illyricum, after seeing his brother Drusus who was operating in Dalmatia, and after experiencing a difficult voyage across the Adriatic and then the Ionian Sea. Therefore he took a few days to repair his 5 fleet; at the same time he visited in recollection of his own ancestors the bays made famous by the victory at Actium, the booty consecrated by Augustus and the camp of Antony. For, as I have mentioned, Augustus was his great-uncle and Antony his grandfather, and a striking vision of grim and happy events was to be found there. 10

SCPP   a full text and translation of this document is to be found in D. S. Potter and C. Damon. This appears in an issue of the *American Journal of Philology* entirely devoted to the inscription, available on-line at http://muse.jhu.edu/journals/american_journal_of_philology/toc/ajp120.1.html.

the city of Nicopolis in Achaia   Nicopolis, literally 'victory-city' in Greek, was founded by Octavian on the site of his army's encampment opposite Actium at the entrance to the Ambracian Gulf on the Ionian Sea. It was founded soon after his naval victory over Antony and Cleopatra in 31 BC to commemorate it. Achaia was the official name for the Roman province of Greece.

Drusus who was operating in Dalmatia   Drusus had been sent to Illyricum to broker a peace between Maroboduus and the Cherusci and to gain useful military experience.

The account of Germanicus' journey continues with a respectful visit to Athens and further sightseeing in various Aegean islands and cities on the coast of Asia Minor, including Troy, the home of Aeneas, Rome's legendary founder. In contrast Piso is portrayed as hastening to take up his post, in spite of finding time on the way to launch an invective against the same Athenians that Germanicus had honoured. When he caught up with the latter at Rhodes, he fell victim to a storm and had to be rescued by Germanicus' ships.

2.55   However, Piso was not appeased and, barely tolerating a day's delay, he left Germanicus and got ahead of him. And after he reached **Syria and its legions**, by generosity, courting popularity and helping the most worthless of common soldiers – since he kept removing the centurions of long standing and the strict tribunes, and offering their positions to his own dependants or to every least 5 deserving individual, and since he was allowing idleness in the camp, unruliness in the cities and licence to the soldiers to wander without restraint through the country – he reached such a pitch of corruption that in common conversation he was called **'the father of the legions'**. Nor did **Plancina** stay within the bounds of what is appropriate for women, but attended the training of cavalry and the 10 manoeuvres of the cohorts, and made insulting remarks against Agrippina and Germanicus, with even some of the good soldiers proving quick to show her a wicked allegiance, since an obscure rumour was spreading that it was not against the emperor's wishes that these events were happening. All this was known to Germanicus, but a more pressing concern was to turn his attention to the 15 Armenians.

Germanicus successfully resolved the situation in Armenia by crowning a certain Zeno as king, as well as relieving the problems in the provinces of Cappadocia and Commagene. However, his difficulties with Piso continued.

Syria and its legions   Syria, with four legions, was the key military province in the East.

'the father of the legions'   this term would suggest that he, rather than the emperor, was seen as the object of their ultimate loyalty. The *SCPP* records a similar breakdown in discipline and the fact that the legionaries became divided into two camps, with some being called 'Pisonians' and others 'Caesarians' (lines 52–7).

Plancina   Piso's wife was well-born and domineering; Goodyear describes her as 'the most unpleasant female in Tacitus' pages' (vol. 2, p. 326). However, she also acts as a foil to Agrippina, who had indulged in similarly forward behaviour in Germany, stopping a bridge across the Rhine being removed and distributing clothes and dressings to the men (1.69, for which the Elder Pliny is cited as a source).

2.57 That all the problems concerning the allies had been settled successfully did not as a result find Germanicus happy. This was due to the arrogance of Piso who, when commanded to lead a detachment of his legions into Armenia either in person or through the agency of his son, had neglected to do either. Finally they met at **Cyrrus** at the winter quarters of the tenth legion, each with a carefully 5 chosen expression, Piso steeled against fear, Germanicus so that he would not be thought to be threatening; and he was, as I have related, rather merciful. But his friends who were clever at igniting resentments exaggerated the truth, added falsehoods, and denounced the man himself, Plancina and **their sons** in various ways. Finally, in the company of a few close friends, Caesar struck up a 10 conversation of the kind that anger and hypocrisy produce, and Piso replied with defiant entreaties; they parted in open hatred. After this Piso was seldom to be seen on Germanicus' platform, and if ever he did sit with him he was bitter and open in his disagreement. At a banquet held by **the king of the Nabateans**, when gold crowns of great weight were presented to Caesar and Agrippina, and light 15 ones to Piso and the rest, his voice was also heard, to the effect that this feast was being given for the son of the Roman *princeps* and not that of **the Parthian king**; at the same time **he threw away the crown** and added numerous remarks against luxury: although these left Germanicus with a bitter taste, he nevertheless put up with them. 20

---

1 How are Piso and Plancina characterized?

2 What are the causes of the animosity between them and Germanicus?

3 Does their relationship offer a parallel to that between Germanicus and Agrippina (compare, for example, **1.40–1**, pp. 64–5)? Why do you think that Tacitus takes such an interest in the women of his narrative? Can they really have been so powerful and influential?

Cyrrus   a town north-east of Antioch on the road towards the Euphrates.

their sons   it was only Piso's younger son, Marcus, who had accompanied his father as part of his retinue; Gnaeus had remained in Rome.

the king of the Nabateans   Aretas IV Philopatris was a client king of the Romans, and his capital was Petra (in modern Jordan).

the Parthian king   this is more than just a rejection of royal power; it is also an attack, as is reinforced by Piso's subsequent comments about luxury, on what the Romans saw as Eastern decadence, which they liked to set against traditional Roman ideals of austerity. Octavian had been able to exploit this prejudice in his propaganda against Antony for the latter's close association with Cleopatra.

he threw away the crown   this echoes the more famous refusal by Julius Caesar in 44 BC, when Antony attempted to crown him at the Lupercalia (Suetonius, *Divus Iulius* 79.2); Caesar also made great play of the rejection of the hated title of king (*rex*). Therefore Piso's remark and gesture are a pointedly barbed combination.

The relationship deteriorated still further when Germanicus acceded to the Parthian king's wishes that Vonones be removed from Syria, a man who had been currying favour with Piso by making lavish gifts to Plancina: this allegation in Tacitus' account is paralleled by the Piso inscription (*SCPP*, line 45). The following year, with no interruption to the narrative of eastern events, finds Germanicus continuing his travels to Egypt. This province was governed by an equestrian, and senators were banned from entering it without the explicit permission of the emperor because it was so politically sensitive owing to its huge contribution to the capital's grain supply. The *princeps* had to guarantee that the people of Rome were fed, and it was feared that a senator so minded could occupy Egypt and bring Rome to her knees with starvation.

2.59   In the consulship of Marcus Silanus and Lucius Norbanus, Germanicus set out to Egypt to explore its antiquities. But **concern for the province was offered as a pretext**, and by opening the granaries he reduced the price of grain and adopted many habits which were pleasing to the general public: he travelled without a military escort, with bare feet and **clothing identical to that of the Greeks**, in 5 emulation of **Publius Scipio**, who we are told used to do the same in Sicily, although war with the Carthaginians was still raging. Tiberius made a passing comment, **though in mild terms**, on his dress and appearance but reproached him most keenly for having entered Alexandria without leave from the *princeps*, against the established practice of Augustus. For amongst the other secrets of his 10

---

concern for the province was offered as a pretext   Tacitus alludes to the famine, which is recorded by Suetonius (*Tiberius* 52) as the justification for Germanicus' visit. This is borne out by a papyrus containing a report of a speech Germanicus delivered in Alexandria in which he declares that he has been sent 'to set straight the provinces beyond the sea' (*Oxyrhynchus papyrus* 2435, line 10). However, his subsequent itinerary (and previous behaviour on the way out to the East) offers Tacitus the opportunity to question the real motives for his visit.

clothing identical to that of the Greeks   this means abandoning the heavy toga for a lighter cloak (*pallium*).

Publius Scipio   Livy records Scipio being criticized by opponents for this behaviour in the Senate in 204 BC (29.19), two years before his final victory over Hannibal at Zama. But was Germanicus emulating him intentionally, or was this a comment made by others?

though in mild terms   this is perhaps because Tiberius had made a similar sartorial choice when in voluntary exile on Rhodes (from 6 BC to AD 2). However, that was a decision made when he was consciously retiring from public life.

mastery, **Augustus had forbidden the entry of senators** or distinguished Roman *equites* except with permission, and had set Egypt apart so that no one could ever use food shortage to exert pressure upon Italy by occupying this province and **the keys to it by land and sea** with the weakest of garrisons against huge armies.

2.60   But since it had not yet been discovered that this expedition was being criticized,   15
Germanicus began to travel up the Nile, setting out from the **town of Canopus**.

> Tacitus goes on to give a potted account of Germanicus' sightseeing in Egypt with repeated references to the mythical period, mentioning Menelaus' helmsman (Canopus), Heracles and Memnon (which was the Greek identification of the colossal statue of Amenophis III); there are also priestly tales of the power and wealth of the Pharaoh Ramses. The whole is striking for its incongruity and it is only when the tour reaches Elephantine and the first cataract of the Nile that Germanicus and Tacitus stop, and the narrative turns pointedly to Drusus fighting the Germans. It is notable that Tacitus chose to narrate this whole episode from Actium to Elephantine without the interruption of events in any other theatre. Indeed his entire account of AD 18 was focused on Germanicus, as has been the opening of AD 19.

---

1   Why do you think that Tacitus chose to ignore all other events in this period of over a year?

2   What are we to make of Germanicus on his travels? Is he genuinely interested in history, both modern and ancient? Does he aspire to rival the heroes of the Roman republic and the legendary past?

3   Is Germanicus' incursion into Egypt purely naïve? Is he unaware of the possible interpretations which could be put on his interest in such a key civil-war battlefield as Actium, especially in view of his descent from Antony?

4   How significant is the emergence of factions within the imperial family? Is Germanicus being badly advised?

5   What are the reasons for Tiberius' explicit displeasure at Germanicus' visit to Egypt?

Augustus had forbidden the entry of senators   Dio underlines how determined Augustus was in making this decision (51.17.1). As Octavian he had experienced food riots in Rome during the triumvirate when Sextus Pompeius was blockading Rome, and Egypt was a key grain provider, thanks to the fertility of the Nile plain. Its importance was underlined in AD 69 when Vespasian's first move towards power was the seizure of Egypt.

the keys to it by land and sea   these were, respectively, the city of Pelusium in the east and Alexandria to the west, both of which were easily defensible.

town of Canopus   this lay on the mouth of the Nile closest to Alexandria.

Upon his return from Egypt, Germanicus discovered that Piso had reversed all his orders. Following a further falling-out, Piso decided to leave Syria, but delayed when Germanicus fell ill and awaited news at Seleucia, Antioch's port.

The death of Germanicus: 2.69–71, 73

2.69   His conviction that he had been administered poison by Piso was increasing the terrible virulence of the disease; and discoveries kept being made: the remains of human corpses unearthed from the floor and walls, spells, curses and the name 'Germanicus' carved on lead tablets, half-burned ashes with putrid smears, and **other signs of black magic,** by which it is believed that souls are devoted to the   5 gods of the underworld. At the same time men sent by Piso were accused of closely monitoring his sickness.

2.70   These occurrences were greeted by Germanicus in anger as much as with fear. If his doorway was to be besieged, if he was going to have to breathe his last under the watchful eyes of his enemies, what then would be the fate of his most pitiable wife,   10 of his infant children? Poisoning seemed slow: Piso was hurrying and pressing hard to have sole control of the province, of the legions. But Germanicus was not so completely dead and gone, and the rewards for the murder would not remain in the killer's hands. He composed a letter in which **he renounced his friendship**: **most sources add that Piso was ordered to leave the province.** And the latter did   15 not delay any longer, but set sail and steered a course so that his return would be from closer at hand should the death of Germanicus open Syria to him.

2.71   **Caesar** was briefly restored to hope, but then in physical exhaustion when his end was near, he addressed his friends at his bedside in this fashion: 'If I were submitting to fate, I would rightly feel indignation even against the gods that they   20 were snatching me in my youth from parents, children and country in an early death: but as it is, cut short by the crime of Piso and Plancina, I leave my final

---

other signs of black magic   one might compare the numerous lead curse tablets which have been found in Roman Bath (in Britain) and throughout the Roman world. The thought was that writing someone's name gave power over that person, a power which was maintained by rolling up the tablet and putting it somewhere safe.

he renounced his friendship   exactly the same wording is used at *SCPP*, line 29.

most sources add that Piso was ordered to leave the province   the *SCPP* supports the other view, namely that Piso left of his own accord (lines 48–9), an act that it describes as 'setting the worst precedent'. Tacitus' version seems more nuanced than either the official version or that of the majority of sources, and it is an important issue, because a governor could not simply leave his province as he wished.

Caesar   again this name is used to refer to Germanicus.

prayers in your hearts: see that you report to my father and brother with what cruelties I have been torn to pieces, with what plots I have been encircled as I have ended my most wretched life with the worst kind of death. Anyone who was ever stirred by my hopes or by their blood relationship, and even those who felt jealousy towards me in my lifetime, they will all shed tears that a man who once flourished and was survivor of so many wars should have fallen by a woman's deceit. You will have the opportunity to protest in the Senate and to invoke the laws. It is not the chief duty of friends to honour a dead man with idle mourning, but rather to remember his wishes and to carry out his instructions. Even strangers will weep for Germanicus: you will take vengeance if you supported me rather than my status. Show to the Roman people the granddaughter of the god Augustus, who is also my wife, and count out my six children. Compassion will be on the side of the prosecutors, and men will either not believe or not forgive **those who invent wicked instructions**.' Touching the dying man's right hand, his friends swore that they would give up their lives sooner than revenge.

> After offering Agrippina some final advice, Germanicus dies and his funeral is held in Antioch.

2.73   His funeral took place **without images and a procession**, but was notable for the fulsome recollection of his virtues. And there were those who equated his good looks, age and the manner of his death, because of the proximity also of the places in which they died, with **the lot of Alexander the Great**. For both were

---

those who invent wicked instructions Tacitus portrays Germanicus even in death as openly loyal to Tiberius, although he goes on to state that some authorities say that Germanicus privately warned Agrippina about the *princeps*.

without images and a procession these images were the death-masks of famous forefathers, which were usually displayed in the family home. At funerals in Rome they were worn by actors in ceremonial dress who went in procession ahead of the dead body, so re-enacting the family's history and escorting the dead into their new role as one of the family ancestors.

the lot of Alexander the Great Alexander died in 323 BC at the age of 32, Germanicus aged 33 or 34; although rumours of poison had arisen at the time of Alexander's death, numerous versions circulated. However, Alexander had conquered most of the known world, whilst Germanicus' achievements were far more modest. A more measured reaction was Julius Caesar's tearful frustration on seeing a statue of Alexander the Great, at having achieved so little in comparison at a similar age (Suetonius, *Julius Caesar* 7). Intriguingly, Germanicus himself seems to have shown some interest in Alexander's achievements, to judge by the speech he had delivered in Alexandria, in which he told of the common debt owed to Alexander by all who shared the same aspirations (*Oxyrhynchus papyrus* 2435, lines 20–1), though such a remark might be seen as a polite reference to the city's eponymous founder.

physically handsome, of distinguished family, had hardly passed thirty years of 5
age and had died among foreign nations as a result of plots made by their own
men: but Germanicus had been kind towards his friends, modest in his pleasures,
wedded to only one wife and the father of legitimate children, and he was no less
of a warrior even if he lacked the rashness and was impeded from enslaving the
Germanies which he had sent reeling with his so numerous victories. Indeed if he 10
had been the sole controller of affairs, if he had enjoyed the royal title and power,
he would have achieved military glory just as readily as he had excelled in mercy,
self-control and other fine qualities. Before his body was burned, it was stripped
in the forum of Antioch, the place which had been chosen for the cremation,
and **there was no agreement** about whether it displayed the signs of poisoning, 15
for as each individual was quicker to side with Germanicus out of pity and the
presumption of suspicion, or with Piso out of support, they reached different
conclusions.

This reported assessment of Germanicus closes Tacitus' account of the man's
life, and the positive obituary, although in this case no counter-argument is
offered, does invite reaction from the reader.

1   Why do you think that Tacitus chooses to give only the views of other people
    rather than express his own in Germanicus' obituary?

2   To what extent is the obituary supported by Tacitus' narrative of his career?
    Has his conduct always matched the claims made on his behalf?

3   How seriously are we to take the comparison between Germanicus and
    Alexander? Does it only serve to highlight how little of substance the former
    actually achieved?

4   Respect for Alexander's achievements had become fashionable in Rome
    from Pompey onwards, and Augustus had crowned Alexander's mummified
    body and used a seal marked with his head (Suetonius, *Augustus* 18 and
    50). However, is there anything sinister about the comparison here and
    Germanicus' own interest in Alexander?

5   What are we to make of Germanicus' death and his conviction that he had
    been poisoned by Piso? What of the report that there were signs of black
    magic?

6   What feelings are evoked in the reader by his speech to his friends as he lay
    dying? Does it contain any contradictions?

there was no agreement   this was inevitable given the limitations of Roman toxicology,
but it did not stop Dio recording certainty over poison being the cause of death (57.18.9).
Pliny records that the condition of Germanicus' heart was discussed at Piso's subsequent
trial, and whether it had been affected by poisoning (*Natural History* 11.187).

Whatever we are to make of Germanicus himself, his premature death was – as he predicted – lamented widely, and perhaps helped to establish an alternative model for the principate from that which Tiberius was pursuing. At the very least his supporters, whose interests were now focused around his widow and children, formed a powerful faction within the wider imperial family. In the immediate aftermath this fuelled further problems with Piso.

Reaction in the East and in Rome: 2.80; 3.2–3, 6

Following discussion among the senators in Syria, Cnaeus Sentius was given the now-vacant governorship. Agrippina set off back to Rome with Germanicus' ashes and her children, but Piso was persuaded, against the arguments of his son, to return to reclaim his province. Sentius successfully rallied the troops loyal to Germanicus in Syria, but Piso fortified a stronghold in neighbouring Cilicia. This was at Celenderis, which was on the southern coast of Asia Minor (modern Turkey), opposite Cyprus.

2.80   By distributing among their ranks deserters, recently intercepted recruits and his own and Plancina's slaves, Piso had organized the Cilician auxiliaries which the petty kings had sent into a body **numerically equal to a legion**. And he kept solemnly declaring that he, Caesar's legate, was being kept out of the province which the *princeps* had given him not by the legions (indeed he came   5 at their summons), but by Sentius, who was disguising private hatred with false accusations. Let them only stand in their lines, since the soldiers would not fight once they had seen Piso – whom they had themselves **once called 'father'** – with the greater claim, if the matter was being decided legally, and not short of strength, if by arms. Then he deployed his units in front of the fortifications of 10 the stronghold on a steep and precipitous hill; for the other sides were ringed by the sea. Against them were drawn up veterans in ranks and reserves: on one side there was the ruggedness of the troops, on the other that of the terrain, but no spirit, no hope, not even weapons, except for rustic ones or those swiftly prepared for immediate use. When they came to close quarters, any doubts were banished 15 at the point when the Roman cohorts forced their way up to the level ground: the Cilicians turned tail and shut themselves in their stronghold.

---

numerically equal to a legion   i.e. about 5,500 men.
once called 'father'   see **2.55** with note, p. 80.

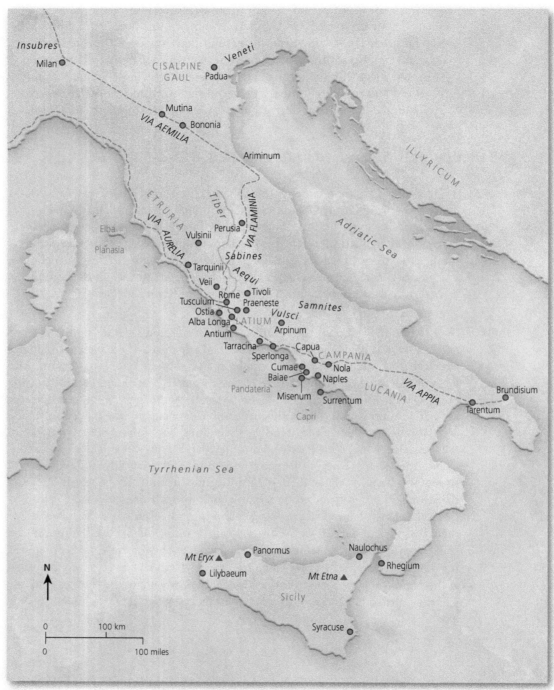

Italy.

This brief outbreak of fighting was followed by further appeals to the legions by Piso, which succeeded in causing one standard-bearer of the sixth legion to desert. However, Sentius then launched an assault on the stronghold and Piso was driven to unconditional surrender. Tacitus then turns to reaction in Rome, and the mixture of spontaneous grief and uncertainty in the capital as various contradictory reports arrived concerning Germanicus' health. There then followed the extraordinary honours granted in his memory, including statues, arches, inscriptions – again the accuracy of Tacitus' account has been confirmed by two inscriptions (the *Tabula Siarensis* and *Tabula Hebana*) which preserve even more details about these honours: indeed, Tacitus may have consulted the equivalent official records that were preserved in Rome.

The third book opens with Agrippina's arrival with Germanicus' ashes at Brundisium and her journey to Rome, accompanied by massive outpourings of grief.

3.2   Drusus advanced to Tarracina together with Germanicus' brother, Claudius, and the children who had been in the city. The consuls Marcus Valerius and Marcus Aurelius (**for they had already entered office**), the Senate and a large proportion of the people filled the road in scattered groups, each weeping as he pleased; indeed there was an absence of servile flattery, since all knew that Tiberius' pleasure at   5 the death of Germanicus was being badly concealed.

3.3   Tiberius and Augusta showed restraint in public, thinking that it was beneath their dignity if they were to weep openly, or for fear that with the eyes of all scrutinizing their expressions they would be understood to be false. Neither in the historians of this period, nor in **the daily record of events** do I find that Antonia,   10 Germanicus' mother, performed any noteworthy official duty (although in

---

the *Tabula Siarensis* and *Tabula Hebana*   these were bronze tablets, found near Seville in Spain and in Etruria respectively, preserving a record of the honours to the dead Germanicus proposed by the Senate. They are translated by R. K. Sherk (no. 36).

Tarracina   a town on the Appian Way, on the coast 65 miles south-east of Rome.

for they had already entered office   they were the consuls of AD 20. What is the effect of Tacitus not beginning the account of the year with their assuming office, but narrating Agrippina's return to Italy first? For the conventions of annalistic history, see Introduction, p. 4.

the daily record of events   this gazette, first published during Julius Caesar's first consulship in 59 BC, seems to have been a bare record of each day – of official events, ceremonies, lawsuits and even speeches. However, the *Tabula Siarensis* (1.8) does record that Antonia was invited to select appropriate honours for her son. This is not entirely at odds with the lack of evidence which Tacitus found (it does not prove she attended functions after his ashes returned to the city), but as Woodman and Martin say in their commentary (p. 92), Tacitus creates a very different impression from the inscription.

---

addition to Agrippina, Drusus and Claudius other blood-relatives were listed by name), whether because she was hampered by ill-health, or her mind, overcome by grief as it was, could not endure bearing the scale of the calamity publicly. I would more easily believe that she was restrained by Tiberius and Augusta, who did not 15 leave home, so that their grief should seem as great and that his grandmother and uncle as well should seem restrained by the example of his mother.

> Following the interment of the ashes in **Augustus' Mausoleum** and more spontaneous lament, there was open criticism that Tiberius had failed to show as much honour to Germanicus as Augustus had at the death of Germanicus' father, Drusus.

3.6   This was known to Tiberius; and in order to put an end to popular talk, he issued a reminder in an edict that many distinguished Romans had died on public service, but that none had been honoured with such ardent longing. It was fine for himself and everyone else, so long as a limit were applied. For the same behaviour was not appropriate for leading men and an imperial nation as for modest houses or 5 states. Grief and comforts drawn from sorrow had been appropriate for the pain when fresh, but now they needed to turn their thoughts back to steadfastness, just as once the divine Julius suppressed his sadness following **the loss of his only daughter**, as the divine Augustus did **when his grandsons had been snatched away**. There was no need for more ancient examples, the numerous times the 10 Roman people resolutely endured the defeats of armies, the deaths of leaders, noble families utterly lost. Leading men were mortal, the state was eternal. Accordingly they should resume their usual business, and since the celebration of the *ludi Megalenses* was at hand they should even pursue their pleasures once more. 15

Augustus' Mausoleum   see note on p. 34. It was intended by Augustus for his whole family, not just himself.

the loss of his only daughter   Julia had died in 54 BC.

when his grandsons had been snatched away   Lucius and Gaius Caesar had died in AD 2 and 4 respectively, Lucius unexpectedly in Massilia (Marseille) on his way to Spain, and Gaius while returning to Rome from a command in the East, 18 months after being seriously wounded during a siege. It was their deaths, ironically, which saw Tiberius' return to favour.

ludi Megalenses   these were celebrated in honour of Cybele on 4–10 April. They came a long time after Germanicus' death on 10 October the previous year.

1 Is Tacitus' account of Tiberius and Livia's behaviour unfairly prejudiced against them, or does he live up to his claim to be writing 'without anger and partisanship' (1.1, p. 22)? How might Tacitus have interpreted it, if they had in fact wept openly?

2 Are Tiberius' arguments against the public mourning at all persuasive from a Roman perspective?

3 What is the effect of Tacitus using reported speech for Tiberius' words rather than direct speech?

4 The reaction to Germanicus' death in Rome has been compared with that in Britain following the death of princess Diana. What parallels can you see?

The trial of Piso: 3.12, 14–16

Piso returned to Rome, visiting on the way Drusus, whose attitude towards him remained inscrutable. Upon his return to the capital, he caused resentment by celebrating his return. The very next day Piso was publicly accused before the consuls, and everyone asked that Tiberius should hear the case. However, he referred the matter to the Senate, where Piso was charged with murder and **treason**. The *princeps* opened proceedings with a speech.

3.12   On the day of the Senate's meeting Caesar delivered a speech of considered balance, saying that Piso had been **a legate and friend of his father**, and had been appointed by himself on the authority of the Senate as an assistant to Germanicus in managing the situation in the East: whether he had there exasperated the young man with his obstinacy and quarrels and rejoiced at his death, or had finished 5 him off in an actual crime, was a question that needed to be judged with impartial minds. 'For if a legate has laid aside the limits of his position and his obedience towards his commander, and has rejoiced at the same man's death and my grief, I shall hate him, banish him from my house and avenge my private enmities without recourse to the might of a *princeps*: but if a crime is revealed which 10 demands vengeance in the case of the death of any human being whatsoever, you indeed must satisfy the children of Germanicus and us, his parents, with the comforts of justice. And at the same time consider these questions: whether Piso had mutinous and revolutionary dealings with the armies, whether the support of the soldiers was sought in a spirit of ambition, whether the province had been 15 reclaimed by force of arms, or exaggerated rumours of these actions have been falsely spread by the prosecutors, at whose excessive enthusiasm I am rightly angry.

---

treason   for treason trials under Tiberius and the legal issues involved, see pp. 96–7.

a legate and friend of his father   he had been a governor in Spain in AD 9–10, and his prominence is suggested by the fact that he had served as consul together with Tiberius himself in 7 BC.

For **what was the point of stripping his body and allowing it to be exposed to the eyes of ordinary people** and of reports being spread even in front of foreigners that he had been done away with by poison, if these charges are still uncertain and 20 need investigation? I certainly mourn for my son and I always shall: but I do not prevent the defendant from putting forward all the pieces of evidence by which his innocence can be supported, or any unfairness on Germanicus' part, if there was any, can be proven, and I beg you not to accept the proffered charges as proven because the case is linked with my own grief.' 25

> Tiberius finished his speech by urging all to conduct themselves during the case **as they would in any other circumstances**, and noting that the only anomaly was that the case was being heard in the Senate rather than in the usual court where cases of poisoning were heard. Two days were allotted to the prosecution and three for the defence.

• How does Tiberius come across in this speech before the opening of the trial proper?

> After the prosecution case had been made, the defence produced strong arguments against the charge of poisoning, but they failed to answer the allegations concerning Piso's behaviour towards the troops.

3.14 For various reasons the judges could not be won over, Caesar because of the fact that war had been introduced into the province, the Senate since it never fully believed that no foul play had been involved in Germanicus' death. … **demanding what they had written**, which Tiberius no less than Piso refused. At the same time the voices of the people were heard outside the Senate House, saying that 5 they would not restrain their hands if he were to survive the judgment of the senators. They had dragged statues of Piso **to the Gemonian steps** and would

---

what was the point of stripping his body … ordinary people   this had taken place in the forum of Antioch before his cremation (**2.73**, p. 86).

as they would in any other circumstances   on Tiberius' refusal to direct the Senate towards a particular verdict here, compare his general policy of encouraging senatorial independence, see p. 101.

… demanding what they had written   some of Tacitus' words have been lost here in our manuscripts. Their content is obscure, but it perhaps involved correspondence between some of the various parties involved in the case.

to the Gemonian steps   these were located on the Aventine hill. The name literally meant 'steps of groaning', and the bodies of executed criminals were dragged down them into the Tiber (that of Seianus after his execution was abused on them for three days: Dio 58.11.5). The people's behaviour at this point is meant as a none-too-subtle hint to the Senate and the *princeps*.

---

have broken them to pieces, had it not been for the orders of the *princeps* that they should be protected and replaced. Therefore Piso was put in a litter and escorted by a tribune of the praetorian cohort, which led to contradictory rumours about whether he was accompanying him as a protective guard or as an executioner. 10

Plancina had promised to stand by her husband come what may, but once she obtained a pardon by virtue of Livia's pleas on her behalf, she started to distance herself from Piso. He decided to press on with his defence nonetheless.

3.15 And he endured the renewed charges, the hostile voices of the senators, everything cruelly ranged against him, but nothing terrified him more than the sight of Tiberius displaying no sign of pity or anger, resolute and impervious to the sway of any emotional feeling. After being carried home he committed a few thoughts to writing, as if he was pondering the future of his defence, sealed them and gave 5 them to a freedman; then he followed his usual routine of personal care. Next, after a long period of the night had passed, once his wife had left the bedroom, he gave orders for the doors to be closed; and after light had dawned he was found **with his throat punctured and a sword lying on the ground.**

3.16 I remember hearing from my elders that there was quite often to be seen in Piso's 10 hands a pamphlet, whose contents he did not personally divulge; but that his friends kept repeating that a letter from Tiberius and instructions with regards to Germanicus were contained in it, and that he had determined to produce it in front of the senators and accuse the *princeps*, and would have done so had he not been tricked by the empty promises of Seianus; and that he had not died by his 15 own hand but following the intervention of an assassin. I could affirm neither of these claims: but I should not conceal what was reported by **those who survived into my own youth.**

---

1 What inferences can be drawn from Tacitus' account of Piso's death? Does he suggest that he committed suicide or not?

2 Why do you think that Tacitus is so careful in setting out the source of his information about Piso's pamphlet?

3 What is the effect of the insertion of this digression at the very point of Piso's death?

---

with his throat punctured and a sword lying on the ground in Roman society, suicide was generally viewed positively as showing the equanimity and courage to die a death of one's choosing when the alternatives seemed worse. Cassius, Brutus and Mark Antony had all followed the example of Cato the Younger (see note on p. 19).

those who survived into my own youth it is unlikely that these conversations can have occurred before the 70s, after Tacitus' arrival in Rome, at least 50 years after the events he is here describing.

Tiberius proceeded to express regret at Piso's death, before questioning one of Piso's sons as to his father's behaviour that night. In response his son read out Piso's notes, in which he pleaded his loyalty to the emperor, while begging for the acquittal of his son Marcus, who he claimed had argued against his illegal return to Syria: he had made no reference to Plancina. A further two days were taken up with what Tacitus describes as 'a phantom of a trial', in which Tiberius declared Piso's son innocent as well as offering his mother's pleas on Plancina's behalf. Tacitus' account of the entire episode closes with a record of the decisions taken: Tiberius overruled the more severe proposals of the consul Aurelius Cotta with the result that Piso did not have his name removed retrospectively from all the official records, and Marcus was allowed to inherit his part of his father's estate. Priesthoods were granted to the prosecutors.

The official account of Piso's trial

There is not room here to give anything like a complete account of the senatorial decree concerning Piso for comparison. However, it is worth underlining one parallel and a couple of significant differences between it and Tacitus' narrative. In the first place the inscription bears out very closely Tacitus' version of events, for example in its open acknowledgement of Livia's representations on Plancina's behalf (*SCPP*, lines 113–15), but perhaps the most notable similarity between the two accounts is the emphasis laid on Piso's alleged prosecution of a civil war:

> He also tried to stir up civil war, when all the evils of civil war had long since been disposed of by the divinity of the god Augustus and the excellent qualities of Tiberius Caesar Augustus, by heading back after the death of Germanicus to the province of Syria, which he had left while the latter was alive with the worst of purposes and in the worst of precedents: and because of this Roman soldiers were forced to meet each other in battle.

> (*SCPP*, lines 45–9)

However, it is interesting to contrast the final passage translated above (**3.16**) with the Senate's gratitude for Tiberius' openness:

> The Senate and people of Rome give thanks … to Tiberius Caesar Augustus their *princeps* because he made available to the Senate a supply of all resources, which were essential for investigating the truth.

> (*SCPP*, lines 12–17)

Indeed, this contrast is key to an understanding of what Tacitus has done to the narrative of the official document. Woodman and Martin, in their commentary on Book 3, express it clearly: 'Tacitus characteristically converts the monument's monotonous self-confidence into discrepancy and doubt' (p. 17). The document nowhere suggests that Tiberius overruled some of the decisions taken by the Senate, and most strikingly there is none of the doubt evident in Tacitus' narrative as to whether Piso really had taken his own life.

- Why do you think that this decree was passed by the Senate and the decision taken to publish it on bronze tablets around the empire, in the main city of every province and the winter quarters of every legion?

- While it is perhaps not remarkable that an official document should smooth over any controversies and seem 'monotonous', is it surprising that the historian's narrative encompasses so many uncertainties?

5 Treason trials, imperial historiography and Cremutius Cordus

Throughout Tacitus' account of Tiberius' reign runs the developing theme of treason trials, a theme close to Tacitus' heart given his own participation in such trials under Domitian (see *Agricola* **45**, pp. 13–14). Interspersed within the narrative are also several digressions on the nature of writing history under the principate. These two apparently distinct strands are finally united in the person of Cremutius Cordus, who was tried for treason in AD 25 as a result of his own historical writings.

The treason trials arose from the Roman law of *maiestas*, or to give the crime its full title, 'the diminution of the majesty of the Roman people'. Its origins lay at the end of the second century BC, and the passing of the law was a populist tribunician measure aimed against the corruption of magistrates and generals and their obstruction of the people's will. There is no evidence that the actual terms of the law were reshaped under Augustus, but the existence of a *princeps* offered scope for new interpretations, as he could be seen as the personal embodiment of the people's majesty: to conspire against him or even to slander or libel him was treasonable. Those found guilty usually faced the penalty of banishment and the confiscation of their property.

The first allusion to the law in Tacitus' narrative of Tiberius' principate comes towards the end of the first book in his account of AD 15. Tiberius has just refused the title 'Father of the country', and has vetoed another senatorial proposal that everyone should swear obedience to his enactments.

Treason trials: 1.72

1.72   He did not, however, by these acts create a confident belief that he had the intention to behave in the spirit of a private citizen; for he had **reintroduced** the law of treason. This had the same name for earlier Romans, but different cases used to

---

reintroduced   this verb is perhaps unfair since the law had never been abandoned. Tiberius reintroduced it only so far as he did not let its application die away together with the deceased Augustus.

come to trial, whenever anyone had impaired the army by betrayal, the ordinary people by discord, and above all the majesty of the Roman people by conducting state affairs badly: deeds were actionable, words were exempt from punishment. Augustus was the first to conduct a judicial hearing about defamatory pamphlets on this law's pretext, provoked by the licence with which **Cassius Severus** had defamed distinguished men and women in his impudent writings; next Tiberius, when consulted by **the praetor Pompeius Macer** as to whether trials for treason should be allowed, replied that the laws must be enforced. He too had been aggrieved by poems of uncertain authorship which had been published attacking his cruelty, arrogance and quarrelsome relationship with his mother.

The law of *maiestas*

The precise application of this law had always been fluid, but a major change did take place under Augustus, and this was that cases involving this charge could now be heard in the Senate. This may have pleased the Senate initially as it finally wrested total control of such a major court from the equestrians (who had served with the senators as jurors when cases had been heard in the conventional court). However, as Levick (*Tiberius the Politician*) has noted, the change was disastrous: 'members of the Senate would not be able to keep their vote secret … it was impossible to remain uncommitted … a senator's views would become known to the *Princeps* and to lesser faction leaders; his career, even his safety, might be affected' (p. 185). The fact that such cases could be heard in the Senate meant that the charge of *maiestas* was often tacked on to other charges to ensure that the case would be heard in the Senate, where the prosecutors might have a greater opportunity to make their name and fortune in front of the *princeps*. For Rome had no public prosecution service, and so relied on individuals to bring prosecutions (see note on *Agricola* **45**, p. 13).

- Are there any modern parallels to the *maiestas* law? Is it a similar logic which leads to the punishment of sportsmen who are found guilty of 'bringing the game into disrepute'?

Cassius Severus he was an outspoken orator and wit. He initially received the mildest form of exile under Augustus, but persisted and was finally banished to the island of Seriphus in the southern Aegean under Tiberius in AD 24, when his property was confiscated.

the praetor Pompeius Macer he was consulting Tiberius because of his judicial function as a praetor, a sphere in which these magistrates retained some independence of action.

Following this decision Tacitus narrates three cases that year which were brought under the charge of treason, but all of which were thrown out on the grounds that the accusations were trivial, such as breaking an oath taken in the name of Augustus. Tacitus takes the line that these were important cases as the first indications of the way that the treason law would come to be used under Tiberius. Such cases are not totally absent from Book 2 and the start of Book 3, but as we have seen, Germanicus, his death and the subsequent trial of Piso dominate the narrative. However, from AD 21 onwards such trials begin to proliferate: indeed that year, the equestrian Clutorius Priscus was put to death for writing a poem in anticipation of the demise of Tiberius' son Drusus. He had been richly rewarded by Tiberius for a celebrated poem lamenting Germanicus' death, but had jumped the gun in the case of Drusus, recited his composition in front of many noble Roman women, and been denounced. Marcus Lepidus alone in the Senate spoke up against the death penalty.

The trials of AD 21–2: 3.50, 55, 65, 70

3.50   'But if, while outrages and crimes are limitless, with regard to punishments and cures the restraint of the *princeps* and the precedents of your ancestors and yourselves suggest moderation, and if empty gestures differ from villainies, and words from evil acts, then there is room for a proposal, through which this man's crime should not go unpunished and through which we should not have cause 5 to regret a combination of **mercy** and severity. **I have often heard our** *princeps* **complaining** whenever someone has anticipated his compassion by taking his own life. That of Clutorius remains intact: saving him will not endanger the state, nor will killing him set an example. Although his literary pursuits are insane, they are pointless and impermanent; nor would you have any weighty or substantial 10 reasons to fear a man who betrayed his very own outrages, and insinuated himself not into the minds of men, but into those of **weak women**. However, let him

---

Marcus Lepidus   for Tacitus' praise of Lepidus, see **4.20**, p. 103.

mercy   Levick notes that this virtue (*clementia*) seems to have been one of the most trumpeted by Tiberius (*Tiberius the Politician*, p. 87). An issue of coins of uncertain date from his reign celebrated mercy together with restraint (*moderatio*: also mentioned by Lepidus), and the Altar of Mercy was dedicated by the Senate in AD 28. Augustus had also celebrated this quality on the golden shield voted him by the Senate and people (*Res Gestae* 34.2).

I have often heard our *princeps* complaining   one example in Tacitus' narrative was following Libo Drusus' suicide (2.31).

weak women   Tacitus uses a diminutive, which has a dismissive sense here. The recitation of poems by their author in front of a private audience was a common practice in Rome, and women were often invited to such performances.

---

leave the city, lose his possessions and **be denied water and fire**: I propose this **as if he were liable under the law of treason.**'

> 1 In these early examples, what does Tiberius' attitude seem to have been towards the treason law? To what use was it put by the senators?
>
> 2 Can you think of any modern parallels for a law which has developed beyond its initial purpose to criminalize many other kinds of activities?

Only one of the ex-consuls agreed with Lepidus, and Priscus was quickly hurried off to be killed. Tiberius, who had left Rome for Campania in this year, reacted by criticizing the Senate's decision: he praised their devotion to avenging the *princeps*, but opposed the punishment of mere words. He also praised Lepidus.

The following year (AD 22) there was a move by some aediles to enforce the law limiting personal expenditure which they felt was being increasingly flouted. Tiberius wrote to the Senate to oppose such a move, as one which would generate a great deal of hostility. This episode leads Tacitus to a brief digression on the various factors which subsequently brought about a natural change towards greater austerity following the accession of Vespasian, who seized power in AD 69. He attributes this largely to a new wave of senators coming from the provinces with a more moral outlook on life: men, indeed, such as himself. But he concludes his digression by turning to Vespasian himself.

3.55   But the paramount instigator of restrained behaviour was Vespasian, who was himself old-fashioned in his deportment and lifestyle. There followed compliance towards the *princeps* and a passion for emulation which was stronger than legally enforced punishment and fear. Unless that is, there is perhaps in all matters something approaching circularity, so that just as the cycle of the seasons turns, so   5 too does that of behaviour; nor was everything better in earlier times, but our age too has produced many examples of artistic distinction for posterity to imitate. But may these contests with our ancestors remain honourable.

---

be denied water and fire   this was the formal expression of banishment at Rome (no one could offer the condemned man shelter), and together with the loss of property was the standard punishment for treason.

as if he were liable under the law of treason   this suggests that in this instance, for whatever reason, the Senate was technically acting outside the terms of the laws of treason. Perhaps it viewed the matter as such an outrage that it conducted the case on an ad hoc basis beyond any specific law. Tacitus typically hints at the precise legalities only in passing.

Later in the same year, Tiberius finally returned to Rome from Campania following an illness suffered by Livia. Upon her recovery the Senate voted excessive honours to thank the gods for her recovery, all of which were opposed by Tiberius as improper. This leads to another brief digression by Tacitus on the selectivity of his narrative.

3.65   I have adopted a practice of not enumerating proposals unless distinguished by their virtue or notable for their shame, because I consider it to be the primary duty of annals that examples of excellence should not be passed over in silence and that the fear of suffering infamy in posterity should attend debased words and deeds. But that period was so infected and befouled by flattery that not only   5 the leading men of the citizen body, whose own fame needed to be protected by subservience, but all ex-consuls, a great number of those who had held the praetorship, and even many junior senators, competed to stand up and make vile and excessive proposals. It has been passed down to memory that Tiberius, on every occasion that he left the Senate House, was accustomed to proclaim the   10 following in Greek: 'Men schooled for slavery!' Certainly even that man, although he did not want public freedom, was sick of such abject submissiveness on the part of the slaves.

Further trials continued for the rest of the year and in one of them Tiberius was moved to intervene personally.

3.70   Lucius Ennius, a Roman *eques*, had a case brought against him for treason on the grounds that he had melted down a silver bust of the *princeps* to put the metal to general use, but Caesar forbade the issue from coming to trial, to the open

---

Lucius Ennius   he was the son-in-law of Tiberius' astrologer, Thrasyllus.

objection of **Ateius Capito** as if in a show of freedom. For the latter claimed that the power of decision should not be removed from the senators, and that such 5 a great wrongdoing should not be left unpunished. By all means let him be slow to deal with what caused himself distress, but let him not condone injuries to the state. Tiberius understood these remarks, as they were really meant, rather than as they were spoken, and he persisted in his veto. Capito was more conspicuous in his disgrace, because although he knew human and divine law, he had brought 10 shame to **his distinguished public rank and his skilful service on the domestic front.**

- Do you think that Capito's is a genuine objection? Was it intended to embarrass Tiberius? Or draw more attention to his merciful attitude?

Early treason trials

Tiberius' general policy was to encourage senatorial independence, hence his frustration expressed at **3.65** (p. 100). Any intervention in debates on his part could only deter freely made contributions from the other senators. This is illustrated during an early treason trial in AD 15, when Tiberius became so incensed with proceedings that he broke his usual silence and stated that he would express his opinion openly on the case. This prompted a reply from Gnaeus Piso: 'In what place will you vote, Caesar? If first, I will have a precedent to follow: if last of all, I am afraid that I may be caught unawares in disagreement' (1.74). However, Tiberius was generally steadfast in his efforts to encourage the Senate to make their own decisions. In the trial of Lepida in AD 20 he even stopped Drusus from declaring his opinion in first place, as he should have done given that he was consul-designate for the following year (3.22). A year later he rebuked the Senate for failing to decide who should be appointed governor of Africa, which was a senatorial appointment: they had instead insisted that Tiberius should make the decision.

- Could Tiberius have done any more to promote senatorial independence? Or was the situation a catch-22? To stop them behaving in a servile way, did Tiberius have to curtail their freedom?

Ateius Capito   he was a notable lawyer of relatively low birth, but reached the consulship under Augustus in AD 5 and later became supervisor of the water supply, an office he still held. He died later this year and receives a brief obituary at the end of Book 3.

his distinguished public rank and his skilful service on the domestic front   the text of the first of these phrases is uncertain, but the general meaning seems clear. The second refers to his attainments as a lawyer and administrator (in contrast to the military sphere, in which he did not specialize).

After further assorted notices, the year ends with three obituaries, a common device of traditional Roman annalistic history. One of these is that of Ateius Capito, but the final notice is that of a woman, and it is given added prominence by coming at the very end of the third book, at the midpoint of Tacitus' account of Tiberius' principate.

The death of Iunia: 3.76

3.76 Also Iunia died in the sixty-fourth year after the battle of Philippi, born with Cato as her uncle, the wife of Gaius Cassius, **the sister of Marcus Brutus**. Her will was the cause of much speculation among the crowd, because despite her great wealth **she omitted to mention Caesar**, although she had named with esteem almost all the leading men. He accepted this in the manner of a fellow-citizen and did not   5 prevent her funeral being marked with the honour of an encomium delivered from the *rostra* and other formalities. **Twenty likenesses** of the most distinguished

The rostra in the Forum Romanum with the remains of the temple of Saturn and the tabularium topped by medieval buildings behind.

the sister of Marcus Brutus Iunia was his half-sister: they were both children – by separate marriages – of Servilia, the most powerful woman of her generation. At her death Iunia was over 90 years old.

she omitted to mention Caesar it was standard at this point for the *princeps* to be named as a beneficiary of any notable will.

the *rostra* this was the main speaker's platform in the Forum, so called because it was decorated with the bronze battering-rams (*rostra*) of captured ships.

Twenty likenesses for this practice at funerals, see note on that of Germanicus at **2.73**, p. 85.

families preceded her, **Manlii, Quinctii**, and other names of equivalent nobility. But Cassius and Brutus shone out most conspicuously by the very fact that their images were not to be seen.   10

---

1   Why do you think that Tacitus chose to give this notice such a prominent position?

2   If you consider who fought at the battle of Philippi, why does Tacitus choose to date Iunia's death in the way he does?

3   Effigies of Brutus and Cassius were preserved in houses and especially honoured even in the time of Pliny; why do you think that there was a reluctance to parade them in public?

Tacitus' account of AD 23 at the opening of Book 4 is dominated by the figure of Seianus and his machinations against Drusus and the family of Germanicus, and 24 sees a flurry of treason trials. In one of these Gaius Silius, who had commanded the loyal legions of Upper Germany during the mutiny in AD 14, was about to be found guilty and, though he committed suicide, he had all his property confiscated. His wife Sosia was also implicated and was exiled. There was a proposal to confiscate her property and only leave a part to her children, but this was opposed by a senator who has already figured prominently in Tacitus' narrative, Marcus Lepidus.

The trials of AD 24: 4.20, 30–1

4.20   Acting in opposition, Marcus Lepidus ensured the allocation of a quarter of her property to the prosecutors according to the demands of the law, and the rest to her children. I am finding that in those times this Lepidus was an influential and wise man: for he steered very many debates away from the cruel flattery displayed by others in a better direction. But he did not lack the ability to compromise, since   5
he enjoyed a steady authority and influence with Tiberius. As a result I am forced to doubt whether it is as a result of fate and the lottery of birth, just as in other questions, that *principes* favour some men and take against others, or whether our plans of action play a part and it is in fact possible to travel a path between sheer defiance and ugly subservience which is free from ambitious self-interest and   10
dangers.

Manlii, Quinctii these were both distinguished republican families. Although Titus Manlius Torquatus, the consul of 165 BC, was adopted into the Iunian family by Decimus Iunius Silanus, it is not entirely clear how Iunia claimed a connection to the Quinctii.

principes this is the Latin form of the plural of *princeps*.

---

1 Compare what Tacitus said about his father-in-law at *Agricola* **42** (p. 15).
   What did these two men have in common in the way in which they conducted
   themselves?

2 How is the behaviour of Lepidus to be contrasted with that of Ateius Capito
   at **3.70** (pp. 100–1)?

The litany of treason trials during the course of this year is briefly interrupted
by the news of the final defeat of the Numidian Tacfarinas in Africa: he had
served as an auxiliary but had been stirring up insurrection for seven years in
spite of repeated defeats at the hands of the Romans. After this the record of
trials continues, culminating in charges brought by Vibius Serenus against his
own father and a fellow defendant, Caecilius Cornutus, who had committed
suicide before the case had been heard.

4.30   And because Cornutus had fallen by his own hand, there was a discussion
        about taking away **the rewards of prosecutors**, whenever anyone charged with
        treason committed suicide before their trial was completed. And the meeting was
        moving in the direction of this proposal and would have done so, had Caesar not
        openly complained rather harshly and against his normal habit on behalf of the   5
        prosecutors, saying that the laws would be toothless and the state on the brink of
        disaster: let them rather overturn the laws sooner than remove their protectors.
        In this way accusers, a race of men invented for the destruction of people and
        never sufficiently suppressed even by punishments, were being encouraged by
        means of rewards.   10

4.31   Such a continuum of such depressing events was interrupted by an incident
        of moderate happiness: when Gaius Cominius, a Roman *eques*, was convicted
        of writing an abusive poem against him, Caesar gave in to the entreaties of his
        brother (who was a senator) on his behalf. Therefore it was considered all the more
        remarkable that a man who was aware of nobler actions and the reputation that   15
        was won by **mercy**, should prefer the grimmer course. For he did not do wrong
        as a result of indolence; nor is it a secret when emperors' deeds are honoured
        genuinely and when with feigned delight. Indeed Tiberius himself, who was on
        other occasions studied in his behaviour and seemed to struggle for words, used
        to speak more loosely and readily whenever he was coming to someone's aid. But   20

---

the rewards of prosecutors   in the case of *maiestas* trials, successful prosecutors were
entitled to a quarter of the condemned man's property as a reward for their service to
the state in bringing the case to court (compare **4.20**, p. 103).

mercy   as mentioned at **3.50** (p. 98), this was one of Tiberius' most keenly vaunted
qualities, but it was not unproblematic in the eyes of Romans since it was one displayed
by tyrants, in that it revealed their power over others. As such it was not a traditional
virtue in the republican period.

in the instance of **Publius Suillius**, who had once served as Germanicus' quaestor, when he was in the process of being banished from Italy on being convicted for having accepted a bribe in judging a case, he recommended with such conviction that he needed to be deported to an island that he bound himself by an oath that it was in the interests of the state. This was met with resentment at the time, but 25 subsequently there was a shift to praise after Suillius' return; the later period saw him outstandingly powerful, venal and a man who long put his friendship with the emperor Claudius to **profitable, but never good use**. The same punishment was decided for the senator **Firmius Catus**, on the grounds that he had attacked his sister with false charges of treason. Catus, as I have narrated, had enticed Libo 30 into a trap and then struck him down by turning informer. Tiberius, mindful of this service but feigning other reasons, begged exemption from exile for him: he did not stand in the way of his expulsion from the Senate.

---

1 What motivates Tiberius' interventions here?
2 Is Tiberius' behaviour in this section consistent with his portrait elsewhere in the narrative?

These trials marked the end of Tacitus' account of the year AD 24, and the subject-matter motivated him to embark on a striking digression about the style of the history he was writing, before turning to the events of 25.

Writing history: 4.32–3

4.32   The majority of those matters which I have narrated and will go on to narrate – I am well aware – may perhaps seem trivial and insignificant to relate: but let no

---

Publius Suillius he was the half-brother of Corbulo, the famous general of Nero's reign, and after his return to Rome following the death of Tiberius he was made consul. The implication here is that, as a close associate of Germanicus, he was singled out for especially harsh treatment by Tiberius.

profitable, but never good use during Claudius' principate he operated as a prosecutor, though he was again banished under Nero.

Firmius Catus as in the case of the Vibii Sereni, this accusation is a breach of the duty expected to be shown to one's family. Tacitus had already conveyed his detestable nature for the part he played in the trial of Libo Drusus (2.27–32), which he goes on to mention here. Libo had been related to the imperial family and lived a life of luxury. Catus, according to Tacitus, had encouraged him to consult astrologers over the scale of his future wealth, a treasonable act in itself as the consultation of astrologers might involve questions about the succession. Catus turned informer and the case came to trial, but Libo was another to anticipate the guilty verdict by suicide; Catus was rewarded with praetorian rank and hence membership of the Senate.

---

one compare my annals with the writing of those who told the earlier history of the Roman people. **In free digressions** they used to relate huge wars, the sackings of cities, kings routed and captured, or whenever they gave precedence to internal events, the disputes between consuls and tribunes, **agrarian and corn laws**, the conflicts between the ordinary people and the *optimates*: for me the work is tightly circumscribed and lacks glory; indeed peace was unbroken or only moderately disturbed, the business of the city was depressing and **the *princeps* was indifferent to expanding the empire**. However, it will not have been without use to examine those matters which at first sight seem trivial, but out of which the progress of great events often arises.

4.33   For over all nations and cities the people, a group of leading men or individuals rule: **the constitution which is selected and combined from all these** can be more easily praised than actually come about, or if it does come about, it cannot last for long. Therefore, when once **the ordinary people were powerful or the senators were pre-eminent**, the nature of the multitude needed to be understood

---

In free digressions   the use of the word for 'digression' here is notable, as it is being used primarily in the rhetorical sense of 'elaborate description' for earlier historians' narration of conventionally exciting material such as wars and battles, but Tacitus is making this point within a digression of his own. Similarly, the use of the word 'free' on the surface refers to the liberal choice of material available to these writers when set beside what there is for Tacitus. However, it also suggests the loss of the freedom of speech since the start of the principate.

agrarian and corn laws   these were revolutionary proposals made for the redistribution of land and the provision of cheap or free grain respectively, and were the sort made by radical tribunes towards the end of the Republic seeking to improve the living standards of the ordinary people: men such as the Gracchi brothers who died for their cause in 133 and 121 BC.

optimates   this was one of the names (meaning 'the best') which the conservative members of the Roman élite gave to themselves, using the language of morality to reinforce their status. One might compare the Greek etymology of the term 'aristocracy', which literally means 'rule by the best'.

the *princeps* was indifferent to expanding the empire   Tiberius had certainly put an end to Germanicus' ambitions in the West (see **2.26**, pp.76–8), but he had at the very least inherited this policy from that of Augustus in his later years.

the constitution which is selected and combined from all these   this is a reference to the so-called 'mixed constitution' which combined elements of monarchy, aristocracy and democracy. The Greek historian Polybius, who lived in the second century BC, had in his sixth book praised the Roman republican system for possessing elements of each in an effective balance, and this was later echoed by Romans such as Cicero. However, Tacitus suggests that the reality may not have lived up to the political theory.

the ordinary people were powerful or the senators were pre-eminent   the history of the republican period saw a series of struggles between the patrician and plebeian classes, as the latter strove to win greater rights and representation in government.

---

and the ways in which they could be managed in a restrained way, and those who had achieved the greatest understanding of the temperament of the Senate and *optimates* were considered experts and wise for the times. Just so now, with the change in constitution and **nothing left for Rome save one-man rule**, the investigation and record of these matters will have served some purpose, because few men can tell honourable and poorer qualities apart by abstract thought: the majority are taught by the experiences of others. But although they will be useful, nevertheless they bring very little pleasure. For the geography of nations, the vicissitudes of battles and the illustrious deaths of commanders hold and renew the attention of readers: in my narrative I bring together cruel orders, unremitting prosecutions, treacherous friendships, the ruin of innocent people and always the same reasons for their deaths, faced as I am with a glut of monotonous history. In addition there is the fact that early writers have few detractors, nor does anyone care **whether you praised the Carthaginian or Roman battle-lines more fulsomely**: but the descendants of many who suffered punishment or disgrace during Tiberius' reign survive. And even if the families themselves have now died out, you will find those who think that other people's wrongdoings are being imputed to themselves because of their similar behaviour. Even glory and excellence have enemies, on the grounds that they reveal their opposites from an excessive proximity. But I return to the history which I have undertaken.

> 1 What does Tacitus suggest are the disadvantages of his history when set beside republican historiography?
>
> 2 Are his complaints about his own account meant to be taken seriously?
>
> 3 How do the points which he raises in this digression tie in with the various prefaces to his works and the other passages in which he discusses the role of the historian (see Chapter 1, pp. 9–22)?

The trial of Cremutius Cordus: 4.34–5

> Immediately after this digression Tacitus moves on to his account of the year AD 25, which opens – in a striking juxtaposition – with the trial for treason of the historian Cremutius Cordus.

---

nothing left for Rome save one-man rule the Latin preserved in the manuscripts is corrupt here and the exact text is uncertain, but it means something to this effect.

whether you praised the Carthaginian or Roman battle-lines more fulsomely Tacitus uses the most extreme example possible here. Carthage had been Rome's most deadly enemy, and yet – according to Tacitus – Roman historians were allowed to admire and praise this enemy with impunity.

4.34   In the consulship of Cornelius Cossus and Asinius Agrippa, **Cremutius Cordus** was arraigned on a new and previously unheard-of charge, namely that in the annals which he had published, he had praised Marcus Brutus and called Gaius Cassius **the last of the Romans**. The accusers were Satrius Secundus and Pinarius Natta, **the clients of Seianus**. This was fatal for the defendant, as was the fact that 5
Caesar listened to his defence with a pitiless expression. Cremutius, resolved as he was that his life was over, began in this fashion: 'My words, senators, are the source of the charge: so innocent am I in my actions. But not even these were aimed at the *princeps* or the father of the *princeps*, the men protected by the law of treason: it is said that I praised Brutus and Cassius, and although numerous 10
men have written about their achievements, no one has spoken of them in dishonourable terms. Titus Livy, one of the most famed for his rhetorical style and impartiality, exalted Gnaeus Pompey with such praises that Augustus called him a Pompeian; and this did not get in the way of their friendship. He nowhere referred to **Scipio, Afranius**, this very Cassius and this Brutus as brigands and 15

Cremutius Cordus   Aulus Cremutius Cordus was a historian of the period from the civil wars up until at least 18 BC. His works were used by later writers (Suetonius refers to him as a source for the way in which Augustus conducted his review of the Senate membership: *Augustus* 35), but apart from this record of his trial in Tacitus he is otherwise not particularly significant. However, Martin and Woodman emphasize his importance in this context, by noting that his is the only speech delivered by an actual historian in all ancient historiography that survives. The novelty of the treason charge against him lay in the fact that he was a historian (others had been prosecuted previously for their work in different genres) and in that the main charge seems to have been his praise for the two killers of Julius Caesar.

the last of the Romans   Plutarch says that Brutus called Cassius this when he saw him dead after the battle of Philippi in 42 BC (*Brutus* 44.2). Shakespeare used this and makes Brutus cry, 'The last of all the Romans, fare thee well!' (*Julius Caesar* 5.3.98).

the clients of Seianus   Seianus had been upset by a remark of Cremutius three years previously, after Seianus' statue had been erected in Pompey's theatre (following its renovation after a fire), to show the Senate's gratitude for the speed with which he had brought the fire under control. Cremutius had remarked that this act was the theatre's real ruin. The patron–client relationship was one of the most important building blocks of Roman society: clients were expected to support their patrons, for example in their political careers when they were running for election, while the patrons looked after the interests of their clients, such as through offering them work or help in a legal case. However, the patron was normally the social superior, and the client his inferior – the irony here is that the equestrian Seianus is the patron of a noble such as Pinarius Natta.

Caesar   does the use of this name for Tiberius have any particular point in this context?

Scipio, Afranius   Quintus Caecilius Metellus Pius Scipio was consul with Pompey in 52 BC and his daughter married Pompey in the same year. Lucius Afranius was a *novus homo* (a man lacking senatorial ancestors) who regularly served under Pompey, and was consul in 60 BC. Both men fought and lost against Caesar at Pharsalus and Thapsus.

parricides, which are the labels now imposed on them, but often as distinguished men. The writings of **Asinius Pollio** preserve the memory of the same men as outstanding; **Messalla Corvinus** used to describe Cassius as his commander: and both these men continued to flourish in their wealth and the offices they held. As for **the book of Marcus Cicero** in which he raised Cato to the skies, what other 20 response did Caesar make to it other than in **a written reply** in the form of a speech delivered before a jury? The letters of Antony and the speeches of Brutus **contain** accusations against Augustus which are certainly false, but made with a great deal of bitterness. **The poems of Bibaculus and Catullus** which were packed with insults towards the Caesars are still read: but **the divine Julius** and the divine 25 Augustus themselves put up with them and let them be, whether as a result of

---

parricides   the point is that Julius Caesar was entitled 'father of the country' (*parens patriae*).

Asinius Pollio   the historian had first been a supporter of Caesar then Antony, serving as consul in 40 BC. His *Histories* covered the period from 60 to 42 BC, and reflected his fierce republican independence. The remark in this context is all the more striking since his grandson, Marcus Asinius Agrippa, would have been listening in the Senate as consul.

Messalla Corvinus   Marcus Valerius Messalla Corvinus was a supporter of Cassius, but after Philippi he transferred his allegiance to Antony and then Octavian, to whom he became a trusted ally, holding a series of important posts. Little is known about his history.

the book of Marcus Cicero   this was a panegyric of Marcus Porcius Cato written after his suicide at Utica in 46 BC. Soon after his death he became the idealized hero of republican Rome.

a written reply   this was the *Anticato*, written by Caesar in 45 BC.

contain   the present tense emphasizes that in Cremutius' day these letters and speeches were still available to be read. The point which he perhaps omits is that, like all the other works he mentions, they had been written long before.

The poems of Bibaculus and Catullus   Marcus Furius Bibaculus was perhaps one of the circle of 'new poets', who included Catullus and were writing around the middle of the first century BC. However, little is known of his work except that he may have written about Caesar's Gallic wars. Catullus' poems are the only works in Cremutius' list which survive (even the relevant sections of Livy are lost), and of the four poems which openly mention Julius Caesar, 29 and 57 are openly abusive attacks. Quinn notes that what is remarkable about the latter are not their accusations of sodomy, literary pretension and serial womanizing, but Catullus' 'tone of unmitigated contempt' (p. 255). An example of this is the epigrammatic poem 93:

> I am not too bothered, Caesar, about wanting to please you,
>   nor about knowing whether you are fair- or dark-skinned.

the divine Julius   Suetonius (*Divus Iulius* 73) records that Caesar accepted Catullus' apology for the poems and invited him to dinner on the very same day that he received the apology.

restraint or wisdom I could not easily say. For what is ignored dies away: if you become angry at something, it seems to be lent credence by the recognition.

4.35 'I do not mention the Greeks, among whom not only freedom but also **licence** went unpunished; or if anyone paid the words attention, he avenged them only with further words. But here one enjoyed the greatest freedom, and an absence of critics, to write about those whom death had removed from hatred or favouritism. For surely Brutus and Cassius are not now under arms and drawn up on the plains of Philippi, and I am not firing up the people with speeches in the cause of civil war? Or is it rather the case that those men, who have actually been dead for seventy years, have part of their memory preserved by writers just as naturally as they are made familiar by **their statues which not even the victor destroyed**? Posterity repays everyone the honour which is due them; and, if condemnation is almost upon me, there will be no lack of men to remember not only Cassius and Brutus but also myself.' Then Cremutius left the Senate and starved himself to death. The Senate decreed that the aediles should see to it that **his books be burned**: but they survived, **concealed and then published**. So it is all the more pleasing to laugh at the dim-wittedness of those who believe that even the memory of the following age can be extinguished by present power. For, on the contrary,

---

restraint   as noted at **3.50** (p. 98), this quality of *moderatio* was one which Tiberius claimed for himself and advertised on his coinage. Cremutius was perhaps appealing to him here.

licence   the Latin word used here is that for 'lust' and hints censoriously at the excess of freedom which Romans often felt the Greeks enjoyed in many areas of life, whether political or social.

their statues which not even the victor destroyed   as well as a general reference to surviving statues, this particularly points to the display of busts of famous ancestors in family homes. These were also displayed in funeral processions, and Cremutius' words encourage the reader to think back to the very end of Book 3 (see **3.76**, pp. 102–3), when – in contrast – these busts are all the more conspicuous by their absence. However, Plutarch does recount a story that Augustus when in Mediolanum (Milan) saw a statue of Brutus, and ordered not its destruction, but its preservation (*Comparison of Dion and Brutus* 5).

his books be burned   this was not the first such punishment under the principate. Towards the end of Augustus' reign the Senate decreed a similar fate for the books of the orator Titus Labienus.

concealed and then published   Cremutius' daughter, Marcia, was one of those who hid copies away. It was the emperor Gaius who allowed the works to be sought out and republished, along with those of Labienus, as a mark of a new enlightened age after succeeding Tiberius, 'because it was of the greatest importance to him that all facts be passed down to posterity' (Suetonius, *Gaius* 16.1).

when genius is punished, its authority grows, and neither did foreign kings nor 45
did others who employed the same brutality produce anything except shame for
themselves and glory for their opponents.

1 What modern parallels can you think of for the burning of books? Is Tacitus
   right about the futility of such acts?

2 Is Cremutius right in the arguments he uses? Or does he fail to appreciate the
   politicization of history under the principate? Are we meant to recall Iunia's
   funeral from the end of the previous book?

3 In all these trials is Tiberius any more guilty than the other senators and
   leading figures for the way in which the legal system, and in particular the
   law of treason, operated under his principate? Or does Tacitus portray a
   system in which almost every participant is equally culpable?

4 Does the trial of Cremutius give added point to the positioning of Tacitus'
   digression on the writing of imperial historiography? If so, what inferences
   are we meant to draw from this juxtaposition?

5 In Tacitus' various discussions of the historian's role, does he offer any threats
   or warnings to his own contemporaries? Do you think that such a role
   remains important for history today?

---

foreign kings it is not obvious that Tacitus has anyone specific in mind here, but the
suggestion seems to be that there is something distinctly un-Roman about Tiberius'
regime.

---

6 Tiberius and Seianus: 'partners in work'

The figure of Lucius Aelius Seianus, the commander of the praetorian guard, is present in the first three books of the Annals: he appears first when Drusus was sent to put down the mutiny in Pannonia as part of his entourage, and he also receives a passing mention when he obstructed Piso during his trial (**3.16**, p. 93). However, Tacitus has until this point largely played down his role: in particular he does not mention the decision to move all nine praetorian cohorts into one camp on the edge of the city of Rome at the point at which it occurred (dated by Dio to AD 20). Seianus receives his first significant mention at the end of Book 3, when the emperor praised him for his efforts in stopping a fire, and the Senate voted him a statue in the rebuilt Theatre of Pompey (3.72). This prepares the way for the start of Book 4, which marks the opening of the second half of the books on Tiberius' reign (Books 4–6). Here he receives an extended introduction to the narrative, but the year is already AD 23.

Seianus: 4.1–3

4.1 When Gaius Asinius and Gaius Antistius were consuls, **the year marked the ninth for Tiberius of a settled state and a thriving house** (for he counted the death of Germanicus as a favourable outcome), when all of a sudden his luck started to go awry, and he personally became cruel or began to offer opportunities to cruel men. The origin and reason for this lay in the person of Aelius Seianus, who was the prefect of the praetorian cohorts, and whose power I have mentioned above. Now I will explain his background, his character and the crime with which he came to seize absolute power. Born at **Vulsinii**, and son of **Seius Strabo, a Roman *eques*,** he was

---

the year marked the ninth for Tiberius of a settled state and a thriving house   this is the only time that Tacitus uses the years of an emperor's reign to mark a date. What effect does its juxtaposition with the use of the consular date have at this point?

Vulsinii   this lay in Etruria, to the north of Rome. Seianus' date of birth is unknown.

Seius Strabo, a Roman *eques*   he had initially shared the command of the guard with his father, becoming sole prefect on Strabo's appointment as equestrian prefect of Egypt. Although his father's family was equestrian, his mother belonged to a senatorial family, and her brother had served as consul in AD 10. The prefects commanded all the praetorians and were directly answerable to the emperor.

in his early youth a constant companion of Gaius Caesar, the grandson of the god Augustus. There were certainly rumours that **he had received payment for sex** with 10 the rich and extravagant Apicius. Next with his assorted talents he bound Tiberius to himself so tightly that he made a man who was impenetrable in his dealings with others careless and defenceless towards him alone: he achieved this not so much by his cleverness (for it was by the same talents that he was overcome) as by the anger of the gods towards the Roman state for which his period of influence and downfall 15 were equally destructive. His body could withstand **toils**, his mind was reckless; secretive about himself, he was an accuser of others; sycophancy and arrogance existed in tandem; on the surface there was a composed modesty, within there was a lust for reaching the top, and for this reason there was at times bribery and excess, but more often hard work and alertness, which are no lesser evils whenever they are 20 contrived for winning royal power.

1 Do you really believe that Tiberius considered the death of Germanicus 'a favourable outcome'? If so, why might he have thought this?

2 How effective is this character-sketch in providing a vivid image of Seianus? Does Seianus have good qualities as well as bad ones?

3 What does this brief biography of Seianus tell us about the qualities or circumstances that allowed a person to rise to the top during Tiberius' principate?

Gaius Caesar he had accompanied him on his command to the East in 1 BC.

he had received payment for sex the Latin Tacitus uses here implies that Seianus was penetrated by Apicius, which was particularly condemned by Roman writers as it implied a loss of masculinity through playing the part of the woman: compare Nero's behaviour at **15.37** (pp. 162–3). That Seianus was said to have sold himself for such sex was to be viewed as especially debased.

Apicius Marcus Gavius Apicius was the notorious epicure of the Tiberian period, though the cookbook preserved in his name is of a much later date. He was said by Seneca (*Consolatio ad Helviam* 10.8–9) to have committed suicide when he was down to his last ten million sesterces for fear that he would have to live in the grip of starvation!

toils the Latin word used here (*labor*) was also used of Tiberius' praise for Seianus at 3.72 for his efforts in stopping the spread of the fire.

4.2   He had strengthened the previously modest power of his prefectship by concentrating in one camp the cohorts which had been scattered through the city, so that they could all receive their orders at the same time, so that they should gain confidence themselves from their numbers, their strength and the sight of one another, and so that they might inspire fear in others. He used the pretext that   5
the dispersed soldiers were ill-disciplined; that if any emergency threatened, help could be brought in greater force if they were together; that they would behave more soberly if a fort was established away from the attractions of the city. **When the camp was completed**, he gradually insinuated himself into the thoughts of

---

When the camp was completed   it was built along, but outside, the wall to the north-east of the city. Its walls enclosed more than 14 acres and were more than four metres high. Its construction must have marked a striking militarization of the city. The precise date of its construction is uncertain, but Dio dated it to AD 20, and Tacitus writes as if it pre-dated 23.

the soldiers **by approaching them and calling them by name**; at the same time he 10
personally selected the centurions and tribunes. Nor did he refrain from courting
popularity in the Senate by honouring **his clients** with public offices or provinces:
Tiberius was indulgent and so accommodating that he praised him as **his partner
in work** not only in conversation, but before the Senate and people, and allowed
his likenesses to be paid honours throughout theatres and forums and **legionary** 15
headquarters.

---

1 Does Seianus display any similar qualities to Tiberius himself?

2 Why has Tacitus delayed Seianus' formal introduction until this point in
   his narrative? Is it simply that this was the moment at which he became a
   significant player?

*A relief depicting soldiers of the
praetorian guard, dating from
the Julio-Claudian period.*

---

by approaching them and calling them by name   as Martin and Woodman note, this is
behaviour appropriate to a commander before a battle.

his clients   on the striking paradox that the equestrian Seianus had senators as his
clients, see note, p. 108.

his partner in work   a similar title is given to him by Dio and Velleius, with the former
calling him 'adviser and assistant' (57.19.7) and the latter 'assistant in the burdens of the
princeps' (*Histories* 127.3). Tacitus' expression again employs the word *labor* of Seianus,
already used of him at **4.1** and 3.72 (see note, p. 113).

legionary headquarters   Suetonius (*Tiberius* 48.2) records that only the Syrian legions
refused to honour the statue of Seianus among their standards.

4.3 But the fact that the family of the Caesars was numerous, that Tiberius' son was
a young man, and that **there were grown-up grandsons** resulted in a delay to
Seianus' desires; and because it was unsafe violently to eliminate so many at the
same time, cunning demanded intervals between the crimes. Nevertheless he
decided to take a more furtive path and to begin with Drusus, by whom he had   5
been recently angered. For Drusus was impatient of a rival and rather quick to
rage: after a quarrel had happened to arise between them, he had raised his hands
against Seianus and repeatedly struck his face as he defended himself. Therefore
as Seianus was ready to try anything, it seemed most practical to turn to **Livia**,
the man's wife: she was the sister of Germanicus and, though not attractive in her   10
youth, subsequently she became exceptionally beautiful. As if he was inflamed
with love he seduced her adulterously, and after achieving this first infidelity
(and a woman, after losing her virtue, would not refuse anything else), he pushed
her to hope for marriage, a partnership in royal power and the murder of her
husband. And she, a woman whose great-uncle was Augustus, whose father-   15
in-law was Tiberius, and who had given birth to Drusus' children, disgraced
herself, her ancestors and her descendants with a small-town adulterer, **in the
hope of outrageous uncertainties** in place of what she already had with honour.
Eudemus, the doctor and friend of Livia, was taken into their confidence, a man
who could explain away his ready access to her private life by his medical skill.   20
Seianus drove from his home his wife, **Apicata**, with whom he had fathered three
children, so as not to be suspected by his mistress. But the scale of the crime led
to fear, delays and from time to time differences of opinion.

> • How does Tacitus emphasize the moral degeneracy of the characters involved
> in this episode?

there were grown-up grandsons Nero and Drusus Caesar, the two eldest sons of
Germanicus, turned 17 and 16 respectively in AD 23. There was also their brother, the
future emperor Gaius, although he was yet to turn eleven, and the twin sons of the
emperor's own son, Drusus (one of whom was to die this very year).

Livia in Suetonius and Dio she is known as Livilla (perhaps to distinguish her from Tiberius'
mother), but always by Tacitus as Livia (as she is also in inscriptions). As Germanicus' sister,
she was her husband's cousin.

in the hope of outrageous uncertainties what could Livia have hoped to gain from
Seianus, when she was already married to Tiberius' heir and had borne his sons?

Apicata Dio records that Apicata was the source of this allegation that Livia had been
part of a plot to murder her husband (68.11.6). She made it to Tiberius after the downfall
of Seianus, and on the point of her own suicide. It is an allegation likely to have been
stimulated by a desire for revenge against Livia, for whom Seianus had certainly deserted
her, but probably only after the death of Drusus had created an opening.

Tacitus himself delays the narrative of Drusus' death with a brief interlude about senatorial business and the state of the empire. He heightens the tension further by saying that this is an appropriate moment to summarize Tiberius' principate up to this point, on the grounds that everything was about to take a severe turn for the worse: thus far he has had a lot of positive things to say about the way in which Tiberius has tried to act. That is not to say that he was a personable *princeps*.

The death of Drusus: 4.7–8, 11

4.7   All these practices Tiberius maintained – albeit not in a friendly way, but grimly and for the most part frighteningly – until they were overthrown with the death of Drusus: for while he survived they remained in place, because Seianus wanted to become known for good advice while his power was still only embryonic, and he feared **a nemesis** who did not conceal his hatred, but frequently complained 5 that another was called the assistant in empire whilst the emperor's son was alive and well. **And how far off was it now that he might be called a colleague!** The initial ambitions for winning absolute power were precarious: once you had taken the first steps, devotion and accomplices were on hand. Already a camp had been constructed on the initiative of the prefect, the soldiers had been given into his 10 hands; his statue was to be seen amidst **the monuments of Gnaeus Pompey**; **his grandsons** would be shared with the family of the Drusi. After this they would have to pray for Seianus' restraint, that he should be satisfied. It was not just occasionally nor in front of only a few men that he let out such remarks, and even his remarks made in confidence were betrayed following the seduction of his wife. 15

4.8   Therefore Seianus thought that there was a need to make haste and selected a poison which, if it was introduced gradually, could create the impression of a chance illness. It was administered to Drusus through the agency of the eunuch Lygdus, **as was discovered eight years later**.

---

a nemesis   this was Drusus himself.

And how far off was it now that he might be called a colleague   this exclamation and what follows are the reported thoughts of Drusus about Seianus' rise.

the monuments of Gnaeus Pompey   this is a reference to Pompey's theatre, which Seianus had helped to save from fire (see note on p. 108).

his grandsons   these were the prospective children of the marriage to follow the engagement of Seianus' daughter and the son of the future emperor Claudius, which had taken place three years previously. In fact, Claudius' son was to die first.

as was discovered eight years later   this was following Seianus' downfall – see note on p. 116. Lygdus was perhaps the slave who tasted and checked Drusus' food before he ate it, to prevent poisoning.

Tacitus lingers no further on this version of Drusus' death, but immediately focuses on Tiberius' controlled reaction to it in the Senate, where the *princeps* also entrusted Germanicus' eldest two children, Nero and Drusus Caesar, to the care of the senators. However, Tacitus proceeds to give an alternative version of Drusus' death, according to which Tiberius was duped into poisoning his own son: he was warned that the first drink which he would be given at a banquet at his son's house was poisoned, and so handed it to his son, who was believed to have drained it from shame. Tacitus, however, goes on to reject this version of events.

4.11   This was the popular gossip, but besides the fact that it is vouched for **by no reliable author** you would quickly refute it. For what person of moderate intelligence, much less Tiberius who was practised in matters of such importance, would have administered death to his son without giving him the chance to speak for himself, and by his own hand as well and with no recourse to second thoughts? Would he   5
not rather have tortured the person who had served the poison, sought out the author of the plot, and finally used that **delay and hesitation**, which were ingrained even when dealing with outsiders, towards his only son, who had previously been found guilty of no offence? But because Seianus was considered the originator of every sort of crime as a result of Caesar's excessive devotion to him and the   10
hatred of others towards both of them, actions were credited to him, however unbelievable and monstrous they were, with rumour always more virulent when concerning the deaths of rulers. In any event the stages of Seianus' crime were betrayed by Apicata and revealed by the torture of Eudemus and Lygdus. And no writer has emerged so hostile to Tiberius as to accuse him, although they   15
rake up and level every other accusation. The reason that I related and disproved this rumour was so that, using a notable example, I might reject hearsay and ask of those into whose hands my study should come not to prefer incredible stories in popular circulation, however eagerly they may be heard, to the unromanticized truth.
                                                                                      20

---

by no reliable author   both Suetonius (*Tiberius* 62) and Dio (57.22) record that Drusus was killed by Seianus and Livia, and do not record Tacitus' second version. However, Dio does note – and reject – that some accused Tiberius of killing his own son, because he showed insufficient public grief.

delay and hesitation   delay is often imputed by the historian to Tiberius, but on many occasions, according to Tacitus, it is at least in part feigned. See, for example, his behaviour in the Senate following Augustus' death (**1.11**, p. 41).

1　Why do you think that Tacitus chooses to include a much longer account of the rejected version of Drusus' death than he did of the one he accepted? Is it simply so that he can emphasize his historical judgement as he here suggests?

2　Is it strange that he includes this digression, whilst accepting in such a seemingly unquestioning way the fact that Drusus was murdered by Seianus? Are we meant to challenge even the historicity of his main narrative?

Thucydides on writing history

The claim to truth over romantic fiction was a long-standing one in ancient historiography, and it is worth comparing the claims made in his preface by the fifth-century BC Greek historian Thucydides:

> And perhaps the absence of a romantic element may make my works appear less pleasurable to listen to. But it will be sufficient if they are judged useful by those who will wish to examine the truth of events and – such is the human condition – what is likely to happen at some point again in the future in the same or similar fashion.

(*History* 1.22)

Following the death of Drusus, Seianus begins to make moves against Germanicus' children, their supporters and other personal enemies of his own: we saw in the last chapter the moves taken by his clients against the historian Cremutius Cordus in AD 25 (p. 108). Such moves could strengthen his own position, but he sought to consolidate it still further by marriage in that same year.

Seianus and Livia: 4.39–41

4.39　But Seianus, rendered careless by his excessive good fortune and in addition **fired by a woman's ambition**, since Livia was demanding the promised marriage, wrote a letter to Caesar: it was customary even then, although he was in Rome, to approach him in writing. Its tenor was something of this sort: because of the kindness of his father Augustus and then the numerous marks of esteem from　5 Tiberius, he had as a result become accustomed to bringing his hopes and wishes not primarily to the gods but rather to the ears of the *principes*. And he had never prayed for the glitter of honours: he preferred, just as one of the soldiers, to keep

---

fired by a woman's ambition　the Latin is ambiguous here and could mean 'fired by his desire for the woman', but at **4.3** (p. 116) Tacitus had claimed that his love for Livia was feigned.

The cave by the sea at Sperlonga which was the site of an imperial dining room in the time of Tiberius. It was here that Seianus protected the principes *by shielding him from a rock-fall in AD 26.*

watch and **toil on behalf of the emperor's safety**. However, he had received the most beautiful of gifts, namely that he was considered **worthy of a marriage connection with Caesar**: this was the origin of his hope. And since he heard that Augustus in finding his daughter a husband had to some extent considered **even members of the equestrian order**, so, if a husband was being sought for Livia, he should keep in mind a friend who would enjoy only the glory of the relationship.

toil on behalf of the emperor's safety   again note the use of the Latin word *labor*, here by Seianus of himself. He was able to demonstrate his concern for the emperor's well-being the following year, after Tiberius had again left Rome, when the *princeps* was dining in the cave at Sperlonga and there was a rock-fall (4.59). Seianus was found by the soldiers who came to the rescue physically shielding Tiberius' body with his own. Apart from loyalty to his *princeps*, the point was that Tiberius' survival was essential to Seianus' own position: the next *princeps* would owe Seianus no loyalty, and might well be his enemy.

worthy of a marriage connection with Caesar   this belief stemmed from the betrothal of his daughter to Claudius' son.

even members of the equestrian order   Suetonius also suggests that Augustus considered this option (*Augustus* 63.2).

For he was not laying aside the duties that had been imposed on him: he would be 15
satisfied for the house to be secured against the hostile resentment of Agrippina,
and this **for the sake of the children**; however long a life he was to enjoy in the
company of such a *princeps* would be enough and more for himself.

> 1   What point is Seianus making in the final sentence of this letter?
> 2   Are his arguments in favour of the marriage between himself and Livia
>   persuasive?

4.40   In reply Tiberius praised Seianus' sense of duty and briefly ran through his own
acts of kindness towards him, and although he asked for time as though for a full
deliberation he added the following: for other people, plans depended on what
they thought was advantageous to themselves; the lot of *principes* was different
since they had to make the most important decisions with a view to public 5
opinion. For that reason he did not have recourse to the easy response, namely
that Livia herself could decide whether to remarry after Drusus or that she should
carry on in the same household; and that she had **a mother and grandmother**,
who were closer sources of advice. He would discuss the matter more candidly,
first regarding the hostility of Agrippina, which would burn far more fiercely if 10
Livia's marriage tore apart the house of the Caesars as if into factions. Even as
things stood, rivalry between the women was breaking out, and **his grandsons**
were being torn apart by this lack of harmony. What if the competition were to be
intensified by such a marriage? '**For you are deceived, Seianus**, if you think that
you will retain the same status, and that Livia, who has been married to **Gaius** 15
Caesar, and then Drusus, will be of such a mind as to grow old with a Roman
eques. Even supposing that I were to allow it, do you think that it will be endured
by those who have seen **her brother, her father** and our ancestors holding the
highest commands? You of course wish to remain in this present station of yours:
but those magistrates and leading figures, who burst in on you against your 20

---

for the sake of the children   Tiberius Gemellus and Julia survived from Livia and Drusus'
marriage. Tiberius' twin brother had died in AD 23.

a mother and grandmother   these were, respectively, Antonia (the younger daughter of
Mark Antony) and Livia, Tiberius' own mother.

his grandsons   this refers not only to Tiberius Gemellus, but also to Germanicus' children,
who were Tiberius' grandsons by adoption.

For you are deceived, Seianus   Tacitus here moves from indirect to direct speech in his
report of the letter's contents. On the use of direct speech by Tacitus, see p. 133.

Gaius Caesar   Augustus' grandson, with whom Seianus had been close before his early
death (see **4.1**, pp. 112–13).

her brother, her father   i.e. respectively, Germanicus and Nero Drusus, Tiberius' brother.

will and consult you on every matter, openly say that you long ago surpassed the pinnacle of the equestrian career and went far beyond **the friendships of my father**, and through their envy of you they find fault with me. But you say that Augustus deliberated about giving his own daughter to a Roman *eques* to marry. By Hercules, what a surprise if, when he was being distracted by every sort of concern and foresaw that the man whom he elevated above the rest with such a union would be raised up beyond measure, he mentioned in discussion **Gaius Proculeius** and certain men notable for the tranquillity of their lives, who were not at all involved in state business! But if we are influenced by Augustus' hesitation, how much more telling is the fact that he married her **to Marcus Agrippa** and then to me? And it is out of friendship that I have not concealed these thoughts: but I will oppose neither your nor Livia's intentions. I will omit to mention for the moment the thoughts I have pondered in my own mind and the ties with which I am planning further to connect you and me: I will reveal only this, that there is no reward so lofty that those virtues of yours and your attitude towards me do not deserve it and, given time, I shall not maintain my silence either in the Senate or in a public speech.' 25 30 35

---

1 Is Tiberius being as open and direct as he claims in this letter?

2 How successfully do you think that Tiberius answers the arguments which Seianus had made in favour of the proposed marriage?

3 What do you think might have been Tiberius' main objection to the marriage?

4 What is the effect of the change from indirect to direct speech (at line 14) in the report of this letter?

4.41   In return Seianus no longer discussed marriage, but with more deep-seated fears begged relief from the silent suspicions, popular rumour and the growing envy. And so that he should not weaken his power by stopping the frequent meetings at his house, nor offer scope to accusers by allowing them, he changed tack to push Tiberius to pursue his life in beautiful places away from Rome. He certainly foresaw many consequences: access would be in his hands and he would for the most part be the censor of letters, **since they were conveyed by soldiers**; next 5

---

the friendships of my father   Maecenas (the patron of poets such as Horace) and Sallustius Crispus are here perhaps meant in particular, men who always remained *equites* rather than be appointed senators, in spite of their closeness to Augustus. Tacitus noted their influence, in spite of their nominally lesser status, in Sallustius' obituary at 3.30.

Gaius Proculeius   he was another *eques* who enjoyed high favour with Augustus, playing an important role in Cleopatra's capture.

to Marcus Agrippa   this followed the death of her first husband, Marcellus, in 23 BC.

since they were conveyed by soldiers   Augustus had been the first person to set up a network for sending official messages by stationing carriages at frequent intervals along military roads (Suetonius, *Augustus* 49.3).

Caesar, as his old age now drew towards its end and he was softened by the seclusion of his surroundings, would more readily hand over the responsibilities of power: and envy of his own position would be reduced **once the crowd of men** 10 **paying their respects ceased to gather**, but with this removal of the trivialities there would be an increase in his real power. Therefore he gradually began to inveigh against the business of the city, the hordes of ordinary people and the numberless streams of men approaching him, instead praising to the skies peace and solitude, which were far removed from discomforts and nuisances, and where 15 the most important decisions could be pondered most fully.

---

1 In what ways do Seianus' reasoning and arguments echo the thinking of Tiberius in the previous section?

2 Were there any strong arguments for Tiberius to base himself away from Rome?

3 Given the system of government that the principate was, how effectively could Tiberius continue to rule during a prolonged absence from Rome?

The following year, these arguments prevailed on Tiberius and he left Rome for Campania, never to return. Seianus began to move more openly against Agrippina and her eldest son, Nero, even attempting to turn his brother Drusus against him. In AD 27 Tacitus records that Tiberius withdrew even further, across to the island of Capri, where he had 12 villas and was able to indulge in luxuriousness and inactivity away from the public eye: Suetonius is explicit about the forms of sexual depravity in which he is said to have indulged with young men and girls (*Tiberius* 43). In the meantime Seianus used the soldiers guarding Nero and Agrippina to record their every move and every word. He continued to move against long-standing allies of Germanicus and his family, and his most notorious act was to encourage a plot at the end of AD 29 against Titus Sabinus, an equestrian friend of Germanicus. He was induced to speak ill of Seianus and Tiberius by an ex-praetor, whilst three other men of the same status hid in the roof-space of the house to act as secret witnesses to what he said. According to Tacitus the whole episode had a terrible effect on normal interaction between citizens.

---

once the crowd of men paying their respects ceased to gather the logic of Seianus' argument here seems to be that when Tiberius was away from Rome he would no longer be seen (and envied) as controlling access to the *princeps* in the capital. While he still hoped to control whom Tiberius met and communicated with, the latter's absence would reduce the frequency with which people would bother to do so, and hence resentment towards Seianus himself would be reduced.

The ruins of the Villa Iovis, one of Tiberius' twelve villas on the island of Capri.

The plot against Titus Sabinus: 4.69–70

4.69 Then the prosecution was hastened, and his accusers sent a letter to Caesar in which they told of the stages of their deception and of their very own disgrace. At no other time was the citizen body so nervous and terrified, with men on their guard against those closest to them; meetings, conversations, familiar and unfamiliar ears were avoided; even mute and inanimate objects, roofs and walls 5 were eyed suspiciously.

4.70 But Tiberius, **after making the customary prayers for the new year by letter** on the first of January, turned to Sabinus, claiming that some of his freedmen had been bribed and that he had been under attack, and in no uncertain terms he demanded vengeance. There was no delay in the decision being taken; and as the 10 condemned man was being dragged away, he strained to shout as loudly as he could with his clothes pulled over his head and his throat being choked, that such was the start of the year and that **these victims were being sacrificed for Seianus**.

---

after making the customary prayers for the new year by letter   these prayers were for the safety of the state and made on the first day of each year. The reference to the letter, together with that of the previous section, helps to draw attention to the fact that Tiberius was no longer in Rome.

these victims were being sacrificed for Seianus   a sacrifice of bulls to Jupiter was included in the customary New Year's rituals; Sabinus' point is that he was being offered up to the real god, Seianus.

Wherever he directed his vision, wherever his words were falling, people ran away leaving the area deserted: the roads and fora were empty. And some individuals 15 returned and showed their faces again, **trembling at the very fact that they had shown fear**. For, they wondered, what day could be free from punishments when chains and nooses were being used amidst rites and prayers, **a time when it was customary to avoid even sacrilegious words**. It was felt that Tiberius was not insensitive to incurring such hatred: it had been deliberately sought, so that 20 there might be a belief that nothing could prevent the new magistrates from **throwing open the prison in just the same way as they had the shrines and altars**. A further letter followed offering thanks for their punishment of a man so hostile to the state, with the added comment that he lived in fear and suspected a plot by his enemies, although no one was accused by name; however, there was 25 no doubt that the targets were **Nero and Agrippina**.

---

1 When set beside Tiberius' attitude towards treason trials in the earlier part of his principate (see the previous chapter), how far has his approach changed here?

2 What narrative techniques does Tacitus use in this passage to heighten the empathy of the readers towards Sabinus and convey a state of universal fear?

3 Are there any modern societies where a similar climate of terror permeated or permeates everything and everyone?

Seianus was able to control Tiberius, and access to him, more easily now that he was far removed from Rome, and the Senate was left alone in the capital in a terrified limbo.

---

trembling at the very fact that they had shown fear they are concerned that their departures may have been witnessed and it may have been noted by imperial agents that they displayed fear and might therefore be suspected.

a time when it was customary to avoid even sacrilegious words there is a clear decline in religious observance since AD 25, when Salvianus was exiled after he brought a charge during a ritual (4.36). Similarly, if we assume that Sabinus was killed at once (though this is not explicitly stated), this would mark a break with the Senate's decision, after the death of Clutorius Priscus in AD 21, that nine days should elapse before any execution was carried out to allow a cooling-off period in which the decision could be overturned (3.51).

throwing open the prison in just the same way as they had the shrines and altars as Furneaux explains in his commentary (Vol. 1, p. 572), 'the prison is imagined as opened or inaugurated by the death of the first criminal, as by an act of sacrifice'.

Nero and Agrippina this pairing cannot help but echo in the reader's mind the more famous imperial mother and son of the same names (see pp. 144–54). The echo is reinforced by Tacitus referring to the marriage of the mother and father of Nero, the future *princeps*, as the very last notice of this same book (4.75).

Seianus' pre-eminence and downfall: 4.74

4.74 Domestic panic had gripped their minds, and its cure was sought in flattery. So, although they were consulted about a range of business, they voted an **Altar of Mercy**, an Altar of Friendship with statues of Caesar and Seianus on either side, and they petitioned with frequent entreaties that these two should give them the opportunity of seeing them. However, **they did not come down** to the city or its environs: it seemed sufficient to leave the island and be seen in the neighbouring area of Campania. Senators, *equites* and a large number of ordinary people assembled there, on tenterhooks with regard to Seianus: gaining a meeting with him was even harder and for that reason achieved by bribery and collusion in his plans. It was generally agreed that his arrogance was increased by witnessing that debased slavery in the forecourt; indeed at Rome bustle was customary and as a result of the size of the city it was unclear on what business each man was embarked: there, lying in the fields or on the shore, with no distinction, day and night, they endured alike the favour and disdain of the doormen, **until that too was forbidden them**: and those whom he had not deemed worthy of a conversation or an audience returned in trepidation to the city, but some were cheerful, an unfortunate state since a terrible end lay in store for their ill-starred friendship.

---

1 In what different ways does Tacitus suggest the near-divinity of Tiberius, and particularly Seianus, in this passage?

2 How effectively does this passage, which comes almost at the very end of Book 4, bring together the themes of the book as a whole?

This passage ends on a note of foreboding for those who proved unlucky enough to have won Seianus' friendship, but as yet the end was still a few years off. The fifth book of the *Annals* opens with the death of Livia, and according to Tacitus this led to even more overt attacks upon Agrippina and the eldest of Germanicus' sons. However, it is at this point that the manuscript of the work breaks off temporarily, so depriving us of Tacitus' account of Seianus reaching the pinnacle of his powers and his subsequent

---

Altar of Mercy   mercy had long been one of Tiberius' most vaunted qualities (see note on **3.50**, p. 98), but here the irony is marked, given the series of prosecutions which Seianus was encouraging.

they did not come down   the Latin verb is perhaps suggestive of gods descending from heaven to offer an epiphany.

until that too was forbidden them   the behaviour described in this sentence is a perversion of the customary Roman practice of *salutatio*, where the dependants (*clientes*) paid their respects to their patron at his house early in the morning.

downfall in AD 31. Tiberius was finally persuaded that the prefect was acting in his own interests and against the imperial family, and as a result staged an elaborate coup from Capri, using as his agent another equestrian, Quintus Naevius Cordus Sutorius Macro, who was at that time the commander of the *vigiles*: Dio provides a detailed account at 58.9–11. While Seianus was in the Senate hoping to hear of new honours, Macro used Tiberius' authority to remove the praetorians to their barracks. Since they remained loyal to the emperor, a decision helped by the promise of a generous financial reward, Seianus was left defenceless and was all too readily turned on by the Senate, condemned and executed. As he was being led off, the hatred of the people was also revealed and they started to tear down his statues; after his death they abused his body for three days before it was thrown into the Tiber; his children were also put to death, the girl being raped by the executioner first, as it was unlawful to execute a virgin.

Germanicus' eldest son, Nero, was already dead, but his mother Agrippina and younger brother Drusus still lived. The former had been exiled in AD 29 to the island of **Pandateria**, and the latter had been declared a public enemy in 30 and was confined in a dungeon on the Palatine hill. However, Seianus' death did not see their return to favour. As Levick points out, 'Seianus' technique had been to provoke acts and words of hostility; they were not obliterated by his death' (*Tiberius the Politician*, p. 173). Tacitus tells how Drusus was starved to death in 33 and Tiberius even ordered his dying words to be read out in the Senate as he denounced the *princeps* for slaughtering his own house; Agrippina starved herself to death later the same year, and died on the very same date that Seianus had been killed, 18 October. Tiberius boasted of the fact that he had not had her killed, but drew attention to the coincidence with Seianus' death: he clearly viewed the two of them as responsible for tearing apart the family with their divergent hopes for the succession.

In the meantime Book 6 recounts the vengeance exacted against Seianus' own supporters, as had been hinted at by Tacitus at the end of Book 4. Gaius, Germanicus' third son, together with Tiberius Gemellus, Drusus' son, were established as the new candidates to succeed Tiberius, with the former as the senior partner. Tacitus, however, portrays Tiberius as vacillating between the two of them and indulging in his vices with young freeborn boys in the privacy of Capri. The end came in AD 37.

---

vigiles   their primary duty was to watch out for and fight fires (on the development of their role, see note on p. 164).

Pandateria   a tiny island about 30 miles off the coast of Campania.

The death of Tiberius: 6.50–1

6.50   Now Tiberius' physical strength was deserting him, though not yet his talent for concealment: the severity of his spirit remained the same; intense in his manner of speaking and facial expression, from time to time he strove to be gracious and sought to conceal this fault, although it remained obvious. And after changing location rather a lot of times, he finally settled on **the promontory of Misenum** in 5
the villa which had once belonged to **Lucius Lucullus**. There it has been established that he approached his final hours in the following way. There was a doctor, notable for his skill, called Charicles, who was not indeed in the habit of managing the *princeps'* illnesses, but of offering him an abundance of advice. Pretending to leave on his own business, this man grasped Tiberius' hand in a gesture of respect and 10
felt the pulse of his veins. And this did not escape the latter's notice: for Tiberius – possibly offended and so concealing his anger all the more – ordered the feast to be renewed and continued to recline longer than was his usual habit, as if making a point of honouring his departing friend. Charicles, however, confirmed to **Macro** that his breathing was failing and would not last for more than two days. Then 15
all the necessary measures were hastily arranged in conversations between those present, and through messengers to the governors and the armies. On 16 March it was believed that his breathing had stopped and that he had completed his mortal span; and amidst a great gathering of men offering congratulations, Gaius Caesar was coming forward to take up the mantle of power, when it was suddenly 20
reported that the powers of speech and sight were returning to Tiberius, and men were being summoned to bring him food to relieve his indisposition. As a result everyone panicked: the rest dispersed in every direction and every man assumed an air of sadness and ignorance; **Caesar**, frozen in silence, was anticipating a complete reversal of events after having previously enjoyed the highest hopes. **Macro** 25
fearlessly gave orders for the old man to be suffocated under a great pile of clothes and for his doorway to be vacated. So Tiberius passed away in the seventy-eighth year of his life.

---

the promontory of Misenum   this lay at the western end of the bay of Naples, looking across to Vesuvius, and was the base for the western fleet.

Lucius Lucullus   after serving as consul in 74 BC he mounted a major campaign in the East against Mithradates, during which he won huge spoils. After his retirement he was noted for the luxuriousness of his lifestyle.

Macro   he had replaced Seianus as praetorian prefect after his part in the latter's demise, and was now to play a major role in Gaius' succession.

Caesar   note that it is now Gaius who is called this, rather than the departing Tiberius.

Macro fearlessly gave orders for the old man to be suffocated   Dio and Suetonius also record that Tiberius' death was unnaturally hastened, although Suetonius records other methods, such as poisoning, as well as suffocation. However, not all ancient sources agree that there was foul play – the contemporary Philo ascribed his death simply to fate (*On the Embassy to Gaius* 25) – and there has been considerable scepticism as to the truth of these allegations among modern historians.

6.51 His father was Nero and he was descended on both sides from the Claudian family, although his mother passed into the Livian and then the Julian family by adoption. From earliest infancy his fortunes had been poised on a knife-edge; for he had followed his proscribed father into exile and, when he had entered the house of Augustus as a stepson, he was beset by many rivals, while Marcellus and Agrippa, and then Gaius and Lucius Caesar flourished; even his brother Drusus was more fondly loved by the citizens. But his position was especially perilous after he married Julia, as he put up with or avoided his wife's adulterous behaviour. Then, returning from Rhodes, he secured the *princeps'* vacant home for twelve years, and next the ultimate power in Rome for nearly twenty-three. Also through the different times of his life his behaviour varied: there was an outstanding period for his life and reputation while he was a private citizen or in power under Augustus; a secretive one, cunning at feigning virtues, as long as Germanicus and Drusus survived; he was a mixture of good and bad alike, while his mother lived; unspeakable in his cruelty, though with his lusts concealed, all the time that he loved – or feared – Seianus: finally he burst out into a simultaneous spree of criminality and disgrace after all shame and fear had been removed and he was able to indulge his own undiluted nature.

Nero   his father, Tiberius Claudius Nero (not the infamous emperor Nero), had died in 33 BC.

his mother passed into the Livian and then the Julian family by adoption   her father, born Claudius, became known as Marcus Livius Drusus Claudianus after his adoption by Livius Drusus. She had been adopted into the Julian family in Augustus' will and was thereafter known as Julia Augusta (see note on p. 33).

he was beset by many rivals   on these 'rivals', see **1.3** (pp. 25–7), with notes.

as he put up with or avoided his wife's adulterous behaviour   Tiberius had been forced against his wishes to divorce his previous wife Vipsania so that he could marry Augustus' daughter in 11 BC: her many infidelities may have contributed to his decision to retire to Rhodes in 6 BC. She was herself finally banished in 2 BC when her father learned of these adulteries.

he secured the *princeps'* vacant home   after the death of Gaius Caesar in AD 4, Tiberius finally became the preferred heir, although he was made to adopt Germanicus at the same time.

though with his lusts concealed   this sentence together with the rest of this obituary is underpinned by a common ancient belief that a man's character did not really change. From this perspective Tiberius did not change for the worse – rather his true nature was revealed as he gradually stopped trying to pretend to be what he was not.

1 In the narrative of Tiberius' end, which characters other than Tiberius himself also display a talent for pretence?

2 Why might the motif of pretence as Tiberius' chief character-trait particularly suit Tacitus' overall portrayal of the principate as a political system?

3 What are the parallels and differences between this succession and that following Augustus' death at the start of the *Annals*?

4 Of Tiberius' obituary Martin says: 'despite its over-schematised framework and outmoded psychology, the obituary notice comes closer to penetrating the truth, for it seeks an answer within Tiberius' own character' (p. 42). How effective do you think it is at explaining the development and nature of the Tiberian principate?

5 Does the periodization of the obituary, with its clear temporal markers, conflict with the opening of Book 4 (translated at the start of this chapter, p. 112), where Tacitus seemed to praise the first eight years of Tiberius' rule?

6 Why do you think that in this obituary Tacitus gives so much prominence to the other people in Tiberius' life?

7 Are the qualities which Tacitus identifies here in Tiberius the same as the ones which dominate the historian's narrative of his principate?

So closes the first hexad of books with Tiberius' death, and not the end of a year (as had been traditional in republican annalistic history). Book 7 must have begun with the eventual accession of Gaius.

7 Claudius and the Senate: speeches in the historical narrative

Tacitus' whole account of the principate of Gaius 'Caligula' is lost. We are deprived of what must have been an explosive narrative, with Gaius' initial popularity swiftly followed by a return to repression and senatorial conspiracy. Since he lacked an heir, he was always exposed to assassination plots, and in January AD 41 one succeeded, leading to the eventual accession of Claudius. Tacitus' narrative is still lost at this point, so we have to depend on others for the account of how Claudius was discovered skulking in the palace, taken by praetorian soldiers to their camp, and hailed as emperor while the Senate were still debating the restoration of the republican constitution. Indeed, the narrative as it has survived does not resume until halfway through Claudius' principate (AD 47) midway through Book 11.

In his biography of Claudius, Suetonius concentrated on the surprising ascent to supreme power of a man who had been deliberately kept out of the public eye by the imperial family because of **his physical disabilities**. Suetonius describes these in some detail:

> His unsteady knees used to fail him whenever he began to walk, and whether light-hearted or involved in some serious business he had many unappealing traits: an unattractive laugh and a more disgusting temper, when he foamed at the mouth and his nostrils dribbled, and moreover stammering speech and a head that shook at all times, but especially when he was engaged in some exertion, however small.
>
> *(Claudius 30)*

---

his physical disabilities these were perhaps caused by cerebral palsy (see Levick, *Claudius*, pp. 13–14). In the ancient world there were very intolerant attitudes to physical disability – Suetonius records Antonia, Claudius' mother, describing him as a fool and 'a human monstrosity, one that nature did not complete, but only began' (*Claudius* 3).

Tacitus' portrait of Claudius in the surviving books is a complex one: although his powerlessness in the face of his freedmen and his wives is perhaps its most striking feature, it does not lack balance. As Miriam Griffin has said, 'Tacitus shows us an active, conscientious Princeps, inventive in finding tactful ways of pruning the Senate, generous towards cities in distress and noble enemies of Rome, capable of presenting his case with some elegance' ('The Lyons Tablet', p. 418). Indeed, at times Claudius seeks to involve the Senate in the decision-making process, though at others he seems to bypass them completely and run the empire from his bedroom.

It would have been easy to select a passage such as the account of Messalina's death and Claudius' subsequent remarriage to his niece Agrippina the Younger – this would have illustrated the emperor's subservience to his wives and his freedmen. However, I have chosen instead a short section of Book 11 from AD 48 in which Claudius speaks in the Senate in favour of extending the right of holding office in Rome to men from northern Gaul. This is of interest not only because of the way it portrays the emperor interacting with his Senate, but also because in addition to Tacitus' version of the speech, we also have an official version preserved in an inscription from Lyon. It therefore offers a unique insight into the historian's practice of including speeches in his work.

A relief from the Sebasteion (a temple-complex dedicated to Aphrodite and the Julio-Claudian emperors) at Aphrodisias in modern Turkey. It shows Claudius as a heroic nude, holding the hand of his wife Agrippina, and being crowned by a representation of the Roman People or Senate (now headless).

Claudius and the Senate: speeches in the historical narrative

Speeches in ancient historical texts

Ever since the Greek origins of ancient historiography with Herodotus, writing in the fifth century BC, historians had included speeches (and other records, such as letters) in their work: these purported to be the actual words spoken by the figures of history, but were not. Instead they were at the very least reworked by the historian in his own style (although he might choose to preserve elements of the original speaker's language as well), and sometimes – in the extreme – entirely fictional. A modern historian could not possibly quote anything other than the actual words if he was claiming to, but ancient historians had a much more relaxed attitude, and indeed it was only the relative few, such as the fifth-century Athenian Thucydides, who set out explicitly the practice they had adopted with regard to speeches. Even what Thucydides said about the process is obscure and highlights the ambiguities involved in the composition of such speeches. He began by saying that it was hard to remember the exact detail of what was said, and that he had made each speaker broadly say 'whatever I thought was necessary in the given situation, keeping as close as possible to the overall tenor of what was actually said' (*History* 1.22.1).

Such freedom was presumably encouraged by the fact that no system for recording the actual words spoken was in widespread use at the time. Cicero's freedman, Tiro, is said to have invented a system of shorthand, which was put to use for the first time in 63 BC to record the exact words of Cato's speech in the Senate, in which he called for the death penalty for Catiline's fellow-conspirators. However, there is no evidence to suggest that verbatim reports of Senate meetings were kept in the manner that Hansard does for debates in the British parliament: and in Britain, although parliamentary debates regularly began to be published in the early nineteenth century, a verbatim record of every speech only began to appear in 1909. Moreover, both the Greek and Roman education systems had students composing fictional speeches set in the context of important historical events (such as re-creating a particular battlefield speech of a famous general). This practice perhaps encouraged a spirit of free composition, along the lines of 'these are the likely sort of arguments which a speaker would have used in just this situation'.

Tacitus himself did at times make use of this freedom: it is hard to imagine that he had a reliable – or indeed any – source for the words of the British chieftain Calgacus, which he has him utter at some length before the decisive battle of Mons Graupius in *Agricola*. However, for other speeches, such as ones delivered in the Senate, apart from those recorded in the *Histories* which he may have heard in person, he will have had access to the official records and published collections of speeches, as well as earlier literary versions of them. The speech of Claudius in *Annals* 11.24, however, is unique in that it allows us directly to compare Tacitus' version with an official one.

Claudius speaks to the Senate: 11.23–5

11.23 In the consulship of **Aulus Vitellius** and Lucius Vipstanus, when **there was a discussion about adding members to the Senate**, and the leading men of **that part of Gaul which is known as Comata**, who had previously won ties of alliance and Roman citizenship, **were seeking the right to obtain office in the city itself**, there was a great deal of varied talk on the subject. **This was contested in front** 5
of the *princeps* **by the parties who disagreed**, with the assertion that Italy was not so sick that it could not supply the Senate for its own city: they said that **in the past true-born Romans had been adequate for their kindred peoples**, and that no one had regrets about the ancient state. Indeed, examples were still cited which the Roman character with its old-fashioned customs had handed down 10
as models of excellence and glory. Or was it not enough that **the Veneti and Insubres had burst into the Senate House**, without a mass of foreigners being introduced as if the city had been taken? What further chance of holding office would remain to what was left of the nobles, or to any poor senator from Latium? Those rich men would completely fill every office, men whose grandfathers and 15

Aulus Vitellius   this consul of AD 48 was the future emperor of 69.

there was a discussion about adding members to the Senate   Claudius was censor, an office which entailed conducting a review of the Senate's membership.

that part of Gaul which is known as Comata   the adjective itself means 'hairy', and was used in reference to the long hair preferred by its inhabitants. The term referred to the three other areas of Gaul (Aquitania, Lugdunensis and Belgica) in contrast to the more Romanized Narbonensis. Claudius himself had been born at Lugdunum (Lyon) in 10 BC.

were seeking the right to obtain office in the city itself   although it is expressed slightly differently here, it becomes clear that the point at issue is whether these men should be able to serve as senators in Rome, without which it would not be possible to hold such office. It is worth noting that it was the Gauls themselves who are described as petitioning for this right.

This was contested in front of the *princeps* by the parties who disagreed   this debate is not yet in the full Senate, but before the emperor's personal *consilium*, i.e. the close group of advisers that he consulted before putting a matter before the official body, namely the Senate itself.

in the past true-born Romans had been adequate for their kindred peoples   the objectors mean that in the distant past even men such as the other Latins (i.e. peoples closely related to the Romans themselves) had been satisfied by a state of inequality, whereby only full Romans had been allowed to serve in the Senate. This sentence and all the rest of this section are the reported arguments of those opposed to granting the wishes of the Gauls.

the Veneti and Insubres had burst into the Senate House   these were peoples from across the Po, around modern Padua and Milan, who had received the citizenship under Julius Caesar in 49 BC. This is simply a rhetorical way of expressing that it was bad enough that such peoples had been admitted to the Senate, let alone the Gauls.

great-grandfathers, as leaders of enemy peoples, had violently cut down our armies by the sword, and had besieged the divine Julius at **Alesia**. This was all recent history: what if the memory were to die of those who have had a fill of their deaths **at the hands of the same peoples beneath the Capitol and the citadel of Rome**? Certainly let them enjoy the title of citizenship: but let them not cheapen 20 the trappings of senators and the ornaments of magistrates.

---

1 How persuasive are these arguments against the Gauls being admitted to the Senate?

2 Are similar arguments used today in seeking to debar immigrants from enjoying equal rights with native citizens?

11.24   Unmoved by these arguments and others like them, the *princeps* there and then spoke in opposition, and also after calling the Senate addressed them as follows: 'My ancestors, of whom the most ancient, Clausus, **was of Sabine origin** and was admitted at one and the same time into the Roman citizenship and into the patrician families, urge the use of the same policies in the running of government, 5 namely bringing here any excellence wherever it is to be found. And I am well aware that **the Iulii are from Alba**, the Coruncanii from Camerium, and the Porcii from Tusculum, and – **so that we should not be involved in antiquarian research** – that men have been called to the Senate from Etruria, Lucania and all

---

Alesia   the Gallic chief Vercingetorix had made his last stand here against Julius Caesar in 52 BC.

at the hands of the same peoples beneath the Capitol and the citadel of Rome   the reference here is to the sack of Rome in 390 BC at the hands of the Senonian Gauls. Livy tells the story of the massacre of those too old to fight in defence of the Capitol: it was said to have begun when a Gaul was enraged at being struck over his head with an ivory staff by Marcus Papirius, after the Gaul had touched his beard (5.41.9).

was of Sabine origin   the most common tradition held that Attus (or Attius) Clausus came to Rome from Sabine territory (to the north-east of Rome) in 505 BC. Claudius' point here is that Clausus was not only admitted at once to the Senate, but also elevated to the status of one of the privileged patrician families.

the Iulii are from Alba   here and with the next two examples he is drawing attention to the fact that some of the other most prominent Roman families originated from towns outside Rome itself. The Iulii were the family of Julius Caesar and claimed descent from Aeneas' son Iulus, who according to tradition founded Alba Longa.

so that we should not be involved in antiquarian research   Claudius was himself a committed historian. As a boy he had written an Etruscan history and a Carthaginian one, and had begun a history of Rome, under Livy's encouragement. The version of the speech inscribed at Lugdunum is particularly rich in its historical digressions, a fact that Tacitus is perhaps alluding to with this remark.

---

of Italy, and that in the end **Italy herself has been extended to the Alps** so that not 10
only individuals man by man, but lands and races should be united in our name.
At that time there was stable peace at home and we flourished in our foreign
policy, when those across the Po were accepted into the citizen body and, **under
the guise that legions were being settled across the globe**, assistance was given
to our exhausted power by the addition of the strongest of the provincials. Surely 15
it causes no regret that **the Balbi** came over from Spain and no less distinguished
men from Gallia Narbonensis? **Their descendants remain and do not yield
to us in their love for this nation.** What else was the cause of destruction for
the Spartans and Athenians, in spite of their strength in arms, except the fact
that **they kept apart those they conquered as foreign-born**? But our founder 20
Romulus so excelled in wisdom that he classed very many peoples as enemies and
then fellow-citizens **on the very same day.** Immigrants ruled over us: entrusting
magistracies to the sons of freedmen is not, as most people mistakenly believe,
a recent innovation, but was made a habit of by our Roman ancestors. "But we

---

Italy herself has been extended to the Alps   this was the natural result of the grant of
citizenship to those across the River Po in 49 BC.

At that time there was stable peace at home   this was hardly the case in the immediate
aftermath of their enfranchisement. Are we meant to think of the Augustan period,
or does Tacitus intend by this statement to raise doubts in Claudius' audience (and his
readers)?

under the guise that legions were being settled across the globe   the reference here is
to the founding of colonies across the provinces, i.e. places largely peopled by legionary
veterans which served as a citizen-base in potentially hostile territory. However, Claudius'
point is that these colonies also reinvigorated the Roman citizen body by providing the
opportunity for the local élites to become citizens, through their association with the
colonies and the possibilities offered by intermarriage.

the Balbi   Lucius Cornelius Balbus had achieved citizenship through Pompey and became
consul in 40 BC; his nephew of the same name went on to win a triumph, a unique
achievement for one not born a Roman.

Their descendants remain and do not yield to us in their love for this nation   Tacitus
himself was almost certainly from Gallia Narbonensis, so the historian is perhaps not
disinterested in the arguments he gives the Lugdunum-born Claudius here.

they kept apart those they conquered as foreign-born   unlike the Romans, the Greeks
were very reluctant to make grants of citizenship to foreigners, even on an individual
basis.

on the very same day   Livy (1.13) records the tradition that on the same day that Romulus
and the Romans had fought the Sabines, and had eventually got the better of them, the
two peoples were united as one.

fought with the Senones." To be sure, **the Vulsci and the Aequi never drew up** 25
a battle-line against us. "We were captured by the Gauls." But **we also gave**
hostages to the Etruscans and went under the Samnite yoke. Nevertheless if
you review all wars, **none was completed in a shorter time** than that against the
Gauls: **since then there has been unbroken and loyal peace**. Now that they have
engaged in our customs, pursuits and relationships, let them bring in their gold 30
and wealth rather than keep them apart. Everything, **conscript fathers**, which
is now considered most ancient was new once: plebeian magistrates following
patrician ones, Latins following plebeians, those from the other races of Italy
following the Latins. This too will lose its novelty, and what we today defend with
examples will itself be reckoned among those examples.' 35

11.25 The decree of the senators followed the lead of the *princeps'* speech and the Aedui
were the first to obtain **the right of serving as senators in the city**. That privilege
was conceded owing to their long-standing treaty and because alone of the Gauls
they lay claim to the title of brotherhood with the Roman people.

---

the Vulsci and the Aequi never drew up a battle-line against us   Claudius' sarcastic
response refers to peoples to the south-east and east of Rome, whom the Romans spent
centuries fighting, according to the tradition followed in Livy's early books.

we also gave hostages to the Etruscans and went under the Samnite yoke   the first is a
reference to Rome's submission to Lars Porsenna which led to the surrender of hostages
(Livy 2.13.4); the second to Rome's defeat at the Caudine Forks in 321 BC, when the
vanquished Roman army was made to endure the humiliation of marching under the
yoke as a sign of their defeat (Livy 9.1–6).

none was completed in a shorter time   Gaul's conquest was completed in 58–50 BC, but
this was perhaps not strictly as swift as some of the eastern conquests. Indeed, in the
inscribed version of the speech, Claudius portrays Gallic resistance to Caesar as stubborn
(see p. 142).

since then there has been unbroken and loyal peace   this is very definitely not true.
Tacitus had recounted the very serious rebellion of Florus and Sacrovir of AD 21, in which
the Aedui were implicated, at 3.40–7.

conscript fathers   this was an official term for the Roman Senate, though it was probably
in origin 'fathers and conscripts', so referring to the original patrician members (*patres*)
and those subsequently added (the *conscripti*).

the right of serving as senators in the city   it is not made entirely clear whether these
Aedui were directly enrolled in the Senate or simply given the right to stand for senatorial
office.

they lay claim to the title of brotherhood with the Roman people   Braund has suggested
that the Aedui may have claimed Trojan descent, and hence a shared ancestry with
Rome. They had been allies of Rome since 121 BC, a fact to which Caesar alludes (*Gallic*
War 1.33).

The Lyon Tablet

The official version of Claudius' speech is preserved on a bronze tablet which was discovered at Lyon. It is written in two columns and the tops of both columns are missing, with the result that we do not have the entire speech, and we do not know exactly how much has been lost. The Latin is most readily accessible at E. M. Smallwood, *Documents Illustrating the Principates of Gaius Claudius and Nero*, no. 369.

'Speaking personally, I beg exemption from that first thought of all men, which I foresee will be very much the first to face me, that you should not shudder as if this is a new idea which is being put forward, but rather consider how many are the innovations that have been made in this nation, and indeed how many different types and constitutions our state has witnessed from the very foundation of our city. 5

The Lyon Tablet.

'Once kings held this city, but it was not their lot to pass it on to successors from their own house. They were succeeded by strangers and indeed foreigners, with the result that Romulus was followed by Numa who came from the Sabines, a neighbour certainly, but at that time a foreigner, and Ancus Marcius 10 by Tarquinius Priscus. When the last was rebuffed from holding office at home because of his mixed blood (he had been born to Demaratus, a Corinthian father, and a mother from Tarquinii, who was well-born but impoverished, with the result that she was obliged to submit to such a marriage), he emigrated to Rome and obtained the kingship. Servius Tullius also was king in the intervening period 15 between this Tarquinius and his son or grandson (for the sources also diverge about this). Servius was the son of the prisoner Ocresia, if we follow our own authorities; but if those of the Etruscans, he had once been the most loyal friend of Caelius Vivenna and a companion in all his adventures, and after being driven out by fluctuating fortunes he left Etruria with all that remained of Caelius' army, 20 occupied the Caelian hill and gave it its name after his own leader Caelius, and changing his name (for in Etruscan he was called Mastarna), he became known by the name I have mentioned, and gained the kingdom to the greatest advantage of the state. Then, after the conduct of Tarquinius Superbus began to be hateful to our citizen body – as much his own as that of his sons – without doubt their 25 minds became disgusted with monarchy, and the government of the state was transferred to annual magistrates, the consuls.

'Why now should I mention that the power of the dictatorship was devised by our ancestors as one more robust than this very consular power, so that they might use it in fiercer wars or during more difficult civil disturbances? Or the 30 tribunes of the people created for the protection of the ordinary people? What of the transference of power from the consuls to the decemvirs, and afterwards when the rule of the decemvirs was ended, its return again to the consuls? What of consular power spread among more men, and the military tribunes with

---

Once kings held this city   this clause is not so different from the very opening of the *Annals* themselves (**1.1**, p. 21): 'Kings held the city of Rome from the beginning' (although in Latin the word used for 'held' is different in each case). Claudius' subsequent analysis of the different offices which have held *imperium* at Rome is also not dissimilar to the opening sentences of the *Annals*.

Tarquinii   this was the leading city in Etruria; Corinth was a city in Greece.

his son or grandson   i.e. the seventh and final king of Rome, Tarquinius Superbus.

Caelius Vivenna   an Etruscan adventurer.

as much his own as that of his sons   in Livy's account it is Tarquinius' son Sextus' rape of Lucretia (1.58) which acts as a catalyst for the expulsion of the Tarquins from Rome.

the power of the dictatorship   for this and the other offices which Claudius goes on to mention, see the notes on **1.1**, p. 21.

consular power, as they were called, to be elected six and often eight at a time? 35
What, finally, of **the sharing with the ordinary people not only of the offices of** **power, but of priesthoods too**? Now, if I were to tell of the wars which marked the starting-point for our ancestors, and the point to which we have advanced, **I** **fear that I may seem to be excessively arrogant**, and to have had as my aim the glorious boast of having extended power beyond the Ocean. But I shall return to 40 my point instead. **The citizen body ...**

'Without doubt it was an innovation for both divine Augustus, my great-uncle, and my uncle Tiberius Caesar to want all the pick of the colonies and towns wherever they were – that is to say, the good and wealthy men – to be present in this Senate House. What then? Is not an Italian senator preferable to a 45 provincial? Now I will show you by my actions what I think about this matter, when I have begun to win approval for that part of my censorship. But I do not think that even provincials should be rejected so long as they are able to enhance the Senate House.

'Look at the most richly endowed and powerful colony of **Vienna**! **For how long** 50
a time now has it bestowed senators on this house? From this colony comes **Lucius Vestinus**, a jewel of the equestrian order like few others, whom I hold especially dear and today retain among my staff. I pray that his children may enjoy the very highest rank of priesthoods, as presently with the years they will proceed

---

the sharing with the ordinary people ... of priesthoods too   the consulship and priesthoods had been restricted only to the patricians initially.

I fear that I may seem to be excessively arrogant   Claudius is joking that if he responds to objections about the wars the Gauls had fought with Rome (recorded by Tacitus at **11.23**, p. 135), he may be led to describe his own conquest of Britain ('beyond the Ocean') and so be thought guilty of boastfulness.

The citizen body ...   this is the point where there is a break of uncertain length, and it comes at the start of a new section. The final word before the break (*civitas* in Latin) could also mean 'state' or 'citizenship'. This word, together with Tacitus' version of the speech, suggests that the missing section concerned the spread of Roman citizenship over the course of her history.

Vienna   this is now the French town of Vienne, on the Rhône, south of Lyon; it lay at the northern edge of the province of Narbonensis.

For how long a time now has it bestowed senators on this house   the argument from precedent was a very compelling one in Rome, where the traditions of the past were highly regarded, and 'new' often functioned as a pejorative term with revolutionary, and so dangerous, undertones.

Lucius Vestinus   he went on to become prefect of Egypt in AD 59.

The temple of Augustus and Livia in Vienne.

with the advancements in their standing. May I not mention **that frightful name** 55
of the brigand, for I despise that monster of the wrestling-ground, who brought
the consulship to his own house, before his own colony had won a universal grant
of Roman citizenship. I can say the same about his brother, who is to be pitied
and is utterly undeserving of this fate, that he is not able to serve you profitably
as a senator. 60

'Now it is time, **Tiberius Claudius Germanicus**, for you to reveal to the conscript
fathers where your speech is heading; for now you have come to the furthest
borders of Gallia Narbonensis.

'Look at all these distinguished young men that **I can see before me**! They are

---

that frightful name of the brigand Valerius Asiaticus was almost certainly the first Gallic
consul, and had indeed held the office twice (in AD 35 and 46). He had been the brother-
in-law of Gaius and initially enjoyed Claudius' favour until he fell victim to Messalina and
was driven to suicide in 47 (11.1–3); as Claudius goes on to observe, his fall encompassed
the ruin of his brother, who was also a senator. He therefore offers an example of the
power which Messalina held over her husband at this time, though her fall was to come
later this very year.

Tiberius Claudius Germanicus Claudius is here addressing himself.

I can see before me these young men were clearly part of the delegation from the Gauls
and the aspirants to senatorial membership.

no more to be regretted as senators than **Persicus**, the noblest of men and my 65
friend, regrets the fact that he reads the name of Allobrogicus among the busts of
his ancestors. But if you agree that this is the case, what more do you desire than
that I point out to you with my finger that the very soil beyond the borders of the
province of Narbonensis is already now sending you senators, **when it causes no**
regrets for us to have men of our order from Lugdunum? It is with nervousness, 70
conscript fathers, that I have left the bounds of the provinces which are familiar
and customary to you, but now the case for Gallia Comata must be made without
reservation. In this, if anyone looks to the fact that they kept divine Julius busy
with war for a period of ten years, let the same man set against this their loyalty
and obedience **unbroken over a period of a hundred years**, tested and more in 75
the many alarming crises we have faced. While my father Drusus was conquering
Germany, they provided for him, by their tranquillity, a state of peace that was
safe and secure to his rear, even indeed **in the course of the census**, when he had
been called away to war from what was at that time a new and unprecedented
procedure for the Gauls. How demanding this task is for us, at this very moment 80
now, we are discovering by too much personal experience, even though there is
no object to the enquiry other than that our resources be openly published.'

---

1 Why do you think that this version of Claudius' speech was inscribed on
   bronze and set up in Lugdunum in Gaul?

2 Can we be certain that the inscribed version is a more accurate representation
   of what Claudius actually said than Tacitus' version? Are there factors which
   could have led to its editing? Is there anything about the content of the
   inscription which might suggest that it is a fairly authentic record of what the
   princeps said?

3 How does Claudius come across in the official version of the speech? Are
   there any distinctive features to its style?

4 Do his historical digressions help to achieve the rhetorical purpose of the
   speech? Are they aimed at the same end as those in Tacitus' version of the
   speech?

Persicus   Paullus Fabius Persicus was governor of Asia in AD 48. After an ancestor had
defeated the Allobroges, he had become their patron and taken the name Allobrogicus
as a mark of his achievement.

when it causes no regrets for us to have men of our order from Lugdunum   the reference
is to Claudius himself, born in Lugdunum in 10 BC.

unbroken over a period of a hundred years   as in Tacitus' version, the revolt of AD 21
is ignored.

in the course of the census   this was started in 13 BC. Nero Drusus began his campaigns
against the Germans in the following year.

5 How different are the two versions of the speech? What has Tacitus omitted from his version? Has he added anything new (always bearing in mind that some of the official speech is missing)? How much has he changed the order of the speech's arguments?

6 In her article on the speech Griffin argued that his historical perspective and hindsight were important factors which led Tacitus to make his adaptations: whereas Claudius' speech, after its initial digression on Roman constitutional change, is very focused on Gaul, Tacitus' version has a much broader vision and sees the change as one step in a long process. Do you agree with Griffin? Or do you think that Tacitus' desire to match the style of the speech to that of his narrative was a more significant factor?

7 Has Tacitus sacrificed all traces of the real personality of Claudius by making these changes to the speech?

8 Can there be any historiographical justification for the changes which Tacitus has made? What might a modern historian have done with Claudius' speech in creating a historical narrative?

8 Nero and Agrippina

A relief from the Sebasteion in Aphrodisias with the striking image of Nero being crowned by his mother Agrippina.

Nero had succeeded Claudius, primarily owing to his mother's marriage to the old *princeps*. The younger Agrippina, the granddaughter of Germanicus, and therefore Claudius' own niece, had been chosen to replace the disgraced Messalina as his wife. Her son, Lucius Domitius Ahenobarbus, was subsequently betrothed to Octavia, Claudius and Messalina's daughter, and adopted by the *princeps*, when he took the new name Tiberius Claudius Nero Caesar. The son of Claudius and Messalina, Britannicus, was three years Nero's junior, and so on the *princeps'* death in AD 54 Nero was far better placed to succeed him. Even so, Nero was aged just 16, but **he was escorted to the praetorian camp by the prefect Burrus** and formal powers were later conferred on him by the Senate.

There is an ancient tradition that the early years of his rule were good, as he operated under the influence of Burrus and his tutor, the celebrated Stoic philosopher Seneca. The influence of his mother was certainly a visible one, as she appeared on coins together with Nero, but Tacitus suggests that her power was at best short-lived. Following the death of Britannicus in AD 55, by poison

---

he was escorted to the praetorian camp by the prefect Burrus   on the praetorian camp, see note on p. 114; prefect was the title given to their commander.

at Nero's hands according to Tacitus (13.15–16), Agrippina was moved out of the palace and her influence dwindled. However, as Nero grew up he resented the control that his mother sought to exert over him and matters came to a head in 59 concerning his affair with another woman, Poppaea Sabina. Tacitus recounts the episode at the very start of Book 14, the second Neronian book.

Silver denarius of AD 54 depicting Nero facing his mother Agrippina, bearing the legend 'Agrippina Augusta, wife of the divine Claudius, mother of Nero Caesar'.

Agrippina's downfall: 14.1–12

14.1   In the consulship of Gaius Vipstanus and Gaius Fonteius, Nero no longer postponed the crime which he had long pondered, since his brazenness had taken root with **the longevity of his power** and he was more passionately in love with **Poppaea** by the day. Since she did not hope for marriage and Nero's divorce from Octavia while Agrippina remained alive and well, she used frequent accusations 5 and at times witty remarks, reproaching the *princeps* and calling him a ward, since, answerable as he was to another's orders, he lacked not only power but even freedom. **For why was her wedding being postponed?** It must be that her looks

---

the longevity of his power   Nero had been *princeps* for just over four years and two months by the start of AD 59. He was now 21 years old.

Poppaea   Poppaea Sabina had first married Rufrius Crispinus, the praetorian prefect under Claudius, but her present husband was the future emperor Otho. Tacitus offers two versions as to how she became Nero's mistress: at *Annals* 13.45–6, he recounts that Nero began his affair with her after she had married Otho (albeit with some encouragement on Otho's part), and that Nero subsequently sent Otho off to be governor of Lusitania in Spain to get him out of the way. However, at *Histories* 1.13 he states that Poppaea had already been Nero's mistress when the *princeps* encouraged Otho to marry her so that she would be readily to hand in court. It was then only when he suspected that Otho was actually falling in love with her that he packed him off to Spain.

For why was her wedding being postponed?   from here onwards Tacitus moves into indirect speech, reporting the words of Poppaea to Nero.

dissatisfied him, and **her grandfathers who had won triumphs**. Or **her fertility** and her sincere affection? The fear was that as his wife at least she would open 10 his eyes to the instances of injustice towards the senators and the hatred of the people for the arrogance and pride of his mother. But if Agrippina could tolerate no daughter-in-law save for one hostile to her son, then she herself should be restored to her marriage with Otho: she would go anywhere on earth where she might only hear the insults directed towards the emperor, rather than witness 15 them while sharing his dangers. These and other arguments like them, which were made more persuasive by her tears and skill as a mistress, were refuted by nobody, since everyone desired the power of his mother to be broken and no one believed that her son's hatred would steel itself to her murder.

14.2   **Cluvius** relates that Agrippina was driven to such lengths by her passion for 20 retaining power that in the middle of the day, at that time when Nero was becoming heated by his wine and feasting, she offered herself on a number of occasions to her drunken son, looking her best and ready for incest; that as those closest at hand were beginning to take note of the lustful kisses and allurements which heralded disgrace, Seneca looked for assistance against her female charms 25 from a woman and sent in **the freedwoman Acte**: out of anxiety both for the danger she faced and for the disrepute threatening Nero, she was to alert him that the incest had been widely reported thanks to his mother's boasting, and that the soldiers would not stand for rule by a sacrilegious *princeps*. **Fabius Rusticus** relates that the incest was desired not by Agrippina but by Nero, and that it was 30

---

her grandfathers who had won triumphs   this is a rhetorical plural – in fact only her maternal grandfather, Poppaeus Sabinus, had won triumphal honours, for Thracian victories during Tiberius' reign. Otho is recorded as having praised his wife's good looks to the emperor at 13.46.

her fertility   she had a son by her first marriage to Crispinus, and the implicit contrast is with Octavia, who had produced no children for Nero.

Cluvius   Cluvius Rufus was a historian who lived during and wrote about the Julio-Claudian principate, although the extent of his work is unknown; he had, however, served as consul. Tacitus also referred to him at 13.20, where he remarked that he would note the versions of different sources where they diverged.

the freedwoman Acte   she claimed descent from the kings of Pergamum in Asia Minor and had possibly already been freed by Claudius. She became Nero's mistress and although subsequently supplanted by Poppaea, she was one of the few not to desert him in the course of his fall; indeed, it was she who placed Nero's remains in the family tomb of the Domitii.

Fabius Rusticus   the scope of his work is not known, but he wrote in an eloquent style according to Tacitus (*Agricola* 10.3). He was well disposed to his patron Seneca, which may have led to his hostility towards Nero.

thwarted by the cunning of the same freedwoman. But **the other authorities** have also told the same version as Cluvius, and her reputation points to this version, whether Agrippina actually conceived of such an enormity in her mind, or the consideration of a new form of lust seemed more credible in one who in her childhood had committed adultery with **Lepidus** in the hope of absolute power, 35 with an equal passion had thrown herself at **Pallas'** every whim, and practised for every outrage by her marriage to her uncle.

> 1 How persuasive are the arguments which Poppaea uses towards Nero?
>
> 2 What picture of Nero emerges in these chapters through his relations with Agrippina, Poppaea and Acte?
>
> 3 Why do you think that Tacitus chooses to report the incest only through the versions of his various sources, rather than relate it as straightforward narrative? Why does he also report contradictory versions at this point of his narrative?

14.3 As a result Nero avoided secret rendezvous with Agrippina, and praised her when she left for **her gardens or Tusculum or her estate at Antium**, on the grounds that she was enjoying her leisure. Finally he thought she was an embarrassment, wherever she kept herself, and he decided to kill her, taking advice only as to whether to use poison, the sword or some other form of violence. At first the preference 5 was for poison. But if it were administered at an imperial banquet, it could not be ascribed to chance, **since Britannicus had already met such an end**; and it seemed a daunting prospect to corrupt the agents of a woman who was alert against plots as a result of her own criminal practice; moreover she had fortified her body by taking antidotes in advance. No one could conceive of a method by which murder 10

---

the other authorities it is not known to which sources he is here referring, but Tacitus did use the Elder Pliny for the Neronian books as he reports at 13.20, as well as the memoirs of various generals for foreign affairs and, almost certainly, monographs by other authors.

Lepidus Marcus Aemilius Lepidus was Augustus' great-grandson and had been the husband of Agrippina's sister, Drusilla. He was implicated in the plot of Lentulus Gaetulicus against Caligula in AD 39, which led to his execution. Agrippina was perhaps alleged to have been involved in this plot.

Pallas he was an enormously influential freedman and the financial secretary of Claudius; he was the prime backer of Agrippina's marriage to her uncle Claudius after the removal of Messalina.

her gardens or Tusculum or her estate at Antium the first were in Rome, but the last two were country villas she owned to the south of Rome.

since Britannicus had already met such an end Nero had poisoned Claudius' natural son at a banquet in AD 55 by adding poison to some water which Britannicus asked for to cool an excessively hot drink, so circumventing his official taster.

carried out with a sword could be concealed; and he feared that anyone chosen for such a terrible crime as that would reject his orders. An ingenious suggestion was provided by the freedman Anicetus, commander of the fleet at **Misenum**, who was Nero's **childhood tutor** and enjoyed a relationship of mutual hatred and hostility with Agrippina. Therefore he explained that a ship could be constructed, a 15 part of which could be designed to collapse out at sea and catch her unawares as it threw her overboard: nothing was so prone to accidents as the sea; and if she were carried off in a shipwreck, who would be so unfair as to attribute to a crime a wrong perpetrated by the wind and waves? The *princeps* would offer in addition for the deceased a temple and altars and other displays of his filial duty. 20

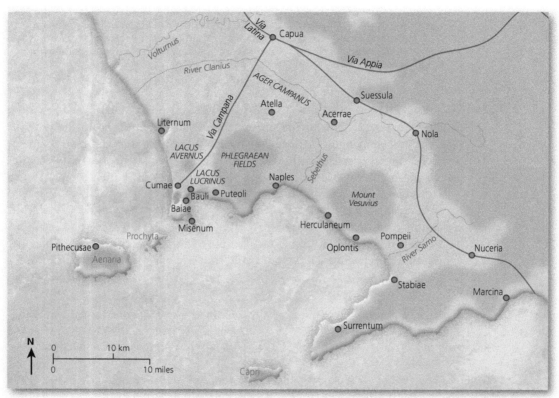

The bay of Naples and Campania.

Misenum this western promontory of the bay of Naples had become the naval base for the Tyrrhenian fleet under Augustus.

childhood tutor he had perhaps been Nero's *paedagogus*, i.e. the supervisor of his schooling and general behaviour. However, he could have been employed as a personal tutor for Nero, since it had been a long-established practice in Rome for upper-class children to receive such an education from Greek slaves or freedmen. Anicetus' role as commander of the fleet and prominence in the murder plot show that Nero remained as reliant on powerful freedmen as Claudius had been before him (see note on p. 147).

14.4   The ingenuity delighted him; the time of year was helpful too, since he was celebrating the festival of **the Quinquatrus** at **Baiae**. There he lured his mother, publicly maintaining that outbreaks of parental anger needed to be tolerated and her bad temper humoured in order to foster the rumour of a reconciliation, in the hope that Agrippina might take it at face value with the ready credulity of women 25 towards good news. Next he went to meet her as she came ashore (for she was arriving from Antium), received her into his arms with an embrace and took her to Bauli. This is the name of a villa which the sea laps up against, on the curving bay between the promontory of Misenum and the Baian lake. There stood among the ships one that was more lavishly decorated, as if this too was a gift in honour 30 of his mother: indeed she had become accustomed to travel on a trireme rowed by members of the fleet. It is generally agreed that someone came forward to betray the plot and that Agrippina after hearing of it, though doubtful whether to believe it, travelled to Baiae by the conveyance of a sedan-chair. There Nero's charming manner allayed her fear since he received her in a friendly fashion and 35 **seated her next to himself**. Now in numerous exchanges, at one moment with a youthful intimacy and then serious, as if he was consulting her on important matters, Nero prolonged the banquet to a great length; he escorted her as she left, unable to look away from her eyes and breast, whether to complete the pretence, or because the last sight of his mother on the way to her death kept a hold on his 40 mind, however wild it was.

---

1   How does Tacitus add suspense and excitement in the build-up to the attempt on Agrippina's life?

2   How is Nero characterized as the plot develops?

3   In what ways does Tacitus bring the reader's attention to the pretence involved in the plot?

14.5   The gods provided a night lit by the stars and peaceful with a calm sea, as if to expose the crime. The ship had not advanced far from the shore, with two members of her household accompanying Agrippina (of whom **Crepereius Gallus** was standing

---

the Quinquatrus   this was a festival to Minerva celebrated on 19 March (the name meant 'five days after the Ides'), but from a misunderstanding of the name it was extended to cover a period of five days. Minerva, as the equivalent of the Greek goddess Athene, could also be seen as the goddess of ingenuity.

Baiae   this resort, a favourite of upper-class Romans, lay in the bay of Naples at the northern end of the promontory of Misenum.

seated her next to himself   this was the place of honour on the same central couch as the host himself.

Crepereius Gallus   he is not mentioned elsewhere in Tacitus, but there are two inscriptions which suggest that he was from Pisidian Antioch (towards the centre of modern Turkey) and served as an equestrian official (see Levick and Jameson, pp. 98–106).

not far from the steering-oars, while Acerronia was lying across the feet of the reclining Agrippina and was joyfully recalling the son's repentance and his mother's restoration to favour), when at a given signal the roof of that section collapsed under a great weight of lead, and Crepereius was crushed and immediately killed: Agrippina and Acerronia were protected by the projecting sides of the couch, which happened to be strong enough not to give way under the weight. Nor did the disintegration of the ship ensue, since all were thrown into confusion and because the numerous people in ignorance of the plot were getting in the way even of the accomplices. Then the rowers decided to throw their weight to one side and sink the ship in this fashion: but there was no ready agreement amongst them in the sudden crisis, and others by directing their efforts against them provided the opportunity of a more gentle descent into the sea. But as Acerronia was foolishly calling out that she was Agrippina and that the emperor's mother should be helped, she was finished off with poles, oars and whatever naval weapons chance offered: Agrippina swam in silence and so was less recognized (though she received one wound on her shoulder), and then, after coming upon some small boats, **was brought to the Lucrine lake and was carried to her house.**

14.6   There she reflected that it was for this purpose that she had been summoned by a treacherous letter and held in especial honour, and noted the fact that the ship had been next to the shore, neither driven by the winds, nor dashed against rocks, when it had collapsed in its upper section **just like a land-based mechanism**; taking note also of Acerronia's murder and at the same time looking to her own wound, she realized that the only remedy for the plot was for it not to be understood as such; and she sent a freedman, Agerinus, to report to her son that by the kindness of the gods and his own good luck she had escaped a serious accident: and to add her entreaty that, however frightened he was by the danger to his mother, he should postpone the trouble of visiting her; she needed rest for the moment. And meanwhile, in a pretence of showing no concern, she applied remedies to her wound and dressings to her body; she ordered the will of Acerronia to be looked for and her possessions to be sealed up – this alone was done without pretence.

Acerronia   she was probably the daughter of Gnaeus Acerronius Proculus, who had been consul in the final year of Tiberius' principate. Her brother served as the governor of the Roman province of Achaia (Greece).

was brought to the Lucrine lake and was carried to her house   the Lucrine lake lay just behind the shore to the north of Baiae. Agrippina perhaps struck off north to get away from the danger before returning south past Baiae to her villa at Bauli by land. However, the geography of Tacitus' account is not very clear.

just like a land-based mechanism   the main point is that she realized that the sea had nothing to do with it. However, in the light of the theatricality of Nero's reign in Tacitus' account, it is also interesting to note that such mechanisms were often used in the theatre.

1   In his narrative of the murder attempt, how does Tacitus achieve a vivid description of events?

2   In the narrative of this episode, which details might Tacitus have been able to discover from reliable sources? Which can only be ascribed to his inventive reconstruction of events?

3   Does he successfully convey the psychology of the various parties involved in the action?

4   What effect does the pervasive use of irony have in these two chapters?

14.7   But as Nero waited for messengers to bring news that the crime had been accomplished, it was reported to him that she had escaped with merely a slight wound and had come only so close to danger as to be certain of its author. Then, faint with panic, he declared that she would arrive at any moment now, eager for vengeance: if she were to arm her slaves or stir up the soldiers, or if instead she ⁵ went straight to the Senate and people, in charging him with the shipwreck, the wound and the deaths of her friends, he asked what recourse he would have to combat her – unless Burrus and Seneca might think of something. He immediately had these men woken and summoned (**it is uncertain whether they had been aware of the plot even before this**). There followed a long silence from both of ¹⁰ them in case they might prove unsuccessful in their efforts to dissuade him – or they believed that such depths had been plumbed that, unless Agrippina were to be forestalled, Nero had to die. After this Seneca was the first to act: he looked at Burrus and asked whether her murder could be demanded of the soldiers. The latter replied that the praetorians were attached to the whole house of the Caesars ¹⁵ and in memory of Germanicus would venture no outrage against his flesh and blood: he said that Anicetus should fulfil his promises. With no hesitation the latter demanded the opportunity to complete the crime. At this offer, Nero declared that to be the day on which he was given true power and noted that the author of this considerable gift was a freedman: he should go swiftly and ²⁰ take the men who were most obedient to his orders. The *princeps* himself, after hearing that Agerinus had arrived as messenger sent by Agrippina, prepared the staging of an accusation on his own initiative: while Agerinus was carrying out his instructions, Nero threw down a sword between his feet, and then he ordered him

---

it is uncertain whether they had been aware of the plot even before this   as men who originally owed their position to Agrippina's influence, it seems unlikely that they would have been party to the assassination attempt from the start, even if they had wished to weaken her influence over him (as in **14.1**, p. 146), and they had already achieved one reconciliation between Nero and his mother in AD 55. On the other hand, it could be argued that such a grandiose scheme could not have been devised without the knowledge of two such powerful men.

to be thrown in chains, as if he had been caught red-handed, in order to create the pretence that his mother had attempted the murder of the *princeps* and through shame at the detection of the crime had voluntarily taken her own life.

14.8   Meanwhile, the danger which had befallen Agrippina had become common knowledge, although it was believed that it had happened by accident: as soon as each person heard about it, they ran down to the shore. Some mounted the embankments and breakwaters, others the nearest boats; others waded into the sea as far as their height allowed; some stretched out their hands; the whole shore was filled with laments, prayers and the shouting of men asking various questions and of others giving uncertain answers; a huge crowd poured down with torches, and when it became known that she was safe, they got ready to congratulate her, until they were scattered by the sight of an armed and threatening column of men. Anicetus surrounded her house with pickets, broke down the door and carried off any slaves who met him, until he came to the doors of her bedroom; few stood by it, since the rest had been alarmed in their terror at the men bursting in. In the bedroom there was a dim light, a single slave-girl, and Agrippina becoming more and more concerned since no one had come from her son, not even Agerinus: she felt that happy circumstances would wear a different expression; as it was there was solitude, sudden outbursts of noise and signs of a final disaster. Then as the slave-girl left, Agrippina addressed her, 'Do you also abandon me?', and turned to see Anicetus **accompanied by the captain Herculeius and Obaritus, a centurion**: she told them that if he had come to see her, he should report that she was recovered, but if to commit a crime, that she could not believe it was on her son's command: he would never have given the order for matricide. The assassins stood around the couch and the captain was the first to strike her head with his club. Now as the centurion drew his sword for the fatal blow, she offered him her stomach and cried, 'Strike the belly!', and she was finished off with numerous wounds.

14.9   All accounts agree on these events. As to whether Nero looked upon his dead mother and praised the beauty of her body, some writers say he did, but others deny it. She was cremated that very night **on a banqueting couch** and with humble obsequies; and, as long as Nero controlled affairs, her grave was not enclosed or heaped up with earth. Later, through the concern of her household staff, it received a slight burial mound, next to the Misenum road and the house of the dictator Caesar, which looks out from a lofty height over the bay stretching

---

accompanied by the captain Herculeius and Obaritus, a centurion i.e. both men were from the fleet and so loyal to Anicetus; Obaritus would have been a centurion of the marines.

on a banqueting couch i.e. she was deprived of even the dignity of a proper bier.

below. Once the pyre had been lit, a freedman by the name of Mnester stabbed 60
himself with a sword – it is uncertain whether this was out of affection towards
his patron or from fear of his own death. Many years earlier Agrippina had
believed that this would be her end and had thought nothing of it. For **when she
consulted astrologers about Nero**, they replied that he would rule and would kill
his mother; and she said, 'Let him kill, as long as he rules!'   65

---

1 How successfully does Tacitus cope with the swift changes of scene and
   narrative focus in his account of Agrippina's murder?

2 Is it surprising that freedmen play such a prominent part in events? Why do
   you think that they do so?

3 What is the significance of Agrippina's dying words? Are we encouraged to
   feel any pity for Agrippina as she is killed?

4 Does she have similar traits to the other powerful women that we have
   already met in the *Annals*?

5 Is there any conflict between the popularity of her public persona, as
   demonstrated by the outpouring of concern by ordinary people, and the
   reality of her private behaviour?

6 Is there a sense in which Tacitus' account of her death is theatrical?

14.10   But only when the crime had finally been carried out was its scale fully understood
by **Caesar**. For the rest of the night, sometimes rooted to the spot in silence, more
often getting up in panic and devoid of reason, he awaited dawn as if it were
going to bring his end. And it was at Burrus' instigation that the initial fawning
of centurions and tribunes gave him the strength to hope, as they took his hand 5
and congratulated him for having survived the unforeseen peril presented by his
mother's crime. Next his friends visited the temples and, after the example had
been set, the nearest towns in Campania bore witness to their joy with sacrificial
victims and deputations: the man himself, with the opposite pretence, was sad,
and behaved as if enraged at his own deliverance and weeping at his mother's   10
death. However, since the appearance of places cannot be changed in the same
way as the expressions of people, and the view of that sea and coastline offered an
oppressive sight (and there were those who believed that the sound of a trumpet
could be heard from the elevated hills around, as well as wailing at his mother's

---

when she consulted astrologers about Nero according to 6.22, she received this
prediction from the son of Tiberius' astrologer, Thrasyllus.

Caesar why do you think that Tacitus chooses to use this name for Nero here, for the
first time in this book?

tomb), **he withdrew to Naples** and sent a letter to the Senate, the key point of 15
which was that the assassin Agerinus had been discovered with a sword, one of the
freedmen closest to Agrippina, and that she had paid the penalty out of remorse
for having arranged the crime.

14.11   He added accusations recalled from the more distant past, that **she had hoped
for a partnership in power** and that the praetorian cohorts would take an oath 20
of allegiance to a woman, with the same dishonour to be visited on the Senate
and people; and that after she had been frustrated, she had, out of hostility to the
soldiers, Senate and people, advised against doles, both military and civic, and had
devised dangers for distinguished men. He boasted about the great effort that it
had taken on his part to stop her from **bursting into the Senate House, and giving** 25
replies to foreign peoples. Also, in an indirect attack on the Claudian age, he
transferred responsibility for all the crimes of that rule onto his mother, ascribing
her death to the state's fortune. Indeed he also told of the shipwreck – yet who
could be found so dull-witted as to believe that this had been an accident? Or that
one man sent with a weapon by a shipwrecked woman could break through the 30
cohorts and fleet of the emperor? Therefore, it was no longer Nero, whose brutality
surpassed all criticism, but Seneca who suffered damage to his reputation, on the
grounds that with such a speech **he had composed a confession.**

---

he withdrew to Naples   this had been founded as a Greek colony, and was one of many
such Greek cities in Campania and the rest of southern Italy. Griffin notes that Nero
seems to have found Naples a particularly comfortable place to be: 'There he gave his
first public performance, there he sought solace after the death of Poppaea, there he
brought Tiridates [who was seeking Roman approval for his elevation to the Armenian
throne] before escorting him to Rome. Naples was the scene of his triumphal return to
Italy from Greece, and the place where he lingered after hearing the news of the Vindex
rising [a revolt in Gaul which eventually led to the fall of Nero]' (*Nero*, p. 209). His love
of all things Greek became more public with his desire to perform on stage with the lyre
(see **14.15**, p. 158), and culminated in his grand tour of Greece in AD 66–7, where he
performed in all the Greek games.

she had hoped for a partnership in power   beyond Tacitus' own narrative (in particular,
see **14.1**, pp. 145–6), one may compare the coins on which her bust is depicted alongside
that of Nero.

bursting into the Senate House, and giving replies to foreign peoples   some support is
given to these and other arguments by Tacitus' own narrative. For example, at 13.5 he
records how she used to listen to meetings of the Senate from behind a screen, and had to
be dissuaded by Seneca from meeting Armenian ambassadors on the official platform.

he had composed a confession   Tacitus had already alluded to contemporary criticism of
Nero for relying on Seneca as his speech-writer, following his delivery of Claudius' funeral
eulogy, which had been written by his tutor (13.3.2). Rhetorical ability had been seen as
an essential skill for a politician during the Republic, and remained so under the *principes*,
even if the requirements and nature of oratory had perhaps changed. It may be significant
that alone of all the *principes* whom Tacitus writes about, Nero is never given any direct
speech in what survives of the *Annals*.

1 How does Tacitus focus the reader's attention on the widespread pretence following the murder of Agrippina?

2 How far are Seneca and Burrus implicated in Nero's wrongdoings?

3 What is it about Nero's letter which leads Tacitus to brand it as a confession?

14.12   However, amidst remarkable competitiveness among the leading men, it was decreed that **acts of thanksgiving should be offered at all the shrines**, that **the Quinquatrus**, on which the plot had been revealed, should be marked with annual games; that a gold statue of Minerva should be erected in the Senate House and next to it a likeness of the *princeps*; that Agrippina's birthday should be counted **among** 5 **the ill-omened days**. **Thrasea Paetus**, who had been accustomed to let previous bouts of adulation pass in silence or with brief assent, at that time walked out of the Senate and created a cause of danger for himself, without providing the beginnings of freedom for everyone else. Numerous and meaningless **prodigies** also intervened: one woman gave birth to a snake and another died after a lightning strike during 10 intercourse with her husband; now **the sun was suddenly eclipsed** and **the fourteen regions of the city** were all struck by lightning. These events took place with so little concern on the part of the gods that Nero prolonged his power and his crimes for many years afterwards. Moreover, in order to increase hatred for his mother and to bear witness to his own increased mildness following her removal, he restored 15

---

acts of thanksgiving should be offered at all the shrines   this is a reference to a ritual called *lectisternium*, where an image of the god was placed on a couch at the shrine and a table of food was laid before it.

the Quinquatrus   on this festival of Minerva, see note on **14.4**, p. 149.

among the ill-omened days   these *dies nefasti* were days on which it was considered ill-omened for the *praetor* or judge to pronounce judgments in the law-courts.

Thrasea Paetus   he was an influential Stoic senator, who became a prominent opponent to Nero: this is the first act of opposition which Tacitus records during Nero's principate. He was finally driven to commit suicide in AD 66 (see note on *Agricola* **2**, p. 10). Compare Tacitus' criticism of the futility of Thrasea's action with the praise which he offers to Agricola (see *Agricola* **42**, p. 15) and Lepidus (*Annals* **4.20**, p. 103).

prodigies   a record of unusual events that were seen as omens was traditional in republican annalistic history, but they were usually listed at the end of a year.

the sun was suddenly eclipsed   this did indeed take place shortly after noon on 30 April AD 59.

the fourteen regions of the city   Augustus had divided Rome up into 14 regions for administrative purposes.

the distinguished women **Iunia and Calpurnia** to their ancestral homes, as well as the ex-praetors Valerius Capito and Licinius Gabolus, all of whom had at some point been banished by Agrippina. He even allowed the ashes of **Lollia Paulina** to be repatriated and a tomb to be built; he also released from their sentence Iturius and Calvisius, men whom he had himself recently banished. For **Silana** had met   20
her end, after returning from distant exile to Tarentum, with Agrippina (as a result of whose enmity she had fallen) already weakened, or pacified.

Nero enjoys his new-found freedom: 14.13–16

14.13   However, he lingered in Campania, anxious as to how he should enter the city, and whether he would find the Senate obedient and the people supportive: against this every most despicable hanger-on – of which no other court has proved more fertile – argued that the very name of Agrippina was hated and that the people's favour had been fired by her death: he should go fearlessly and make trial of their   5
adoration of him in person; at the same time they demanded to precede him. And they found the situation in Rome better disposed than they had promised, with **the tribes** coming out to meet him, the Senate in festive attire, columns of wives and children arranged by gender and age, and tiers of seats constructed along the route he was to travel, after the fashion in which triumphs are viewed.   10
As a result he approached the Capitol as **the proud victor over a servile public**, offered thanks and immersed himself in every kind of lust which, though hardly restrained, had been checked by his respect for his mother – such as it was.

Iunia and Calpurnia   Iunia Calvina was the sister of Silanus, who was betrothed to Claudius' daughter Octavia. Since Agrippina wanted her to marry Nero, Silanus was ruined, and his sister was implicated and so exiled. She had ensured Calpurnia was exiled after Claudius praised her beauty. The two ex-praetors are not otherwise mentioned by Tacitus.

Lollia Paulina   she had been a rival of Agrippina for the hand of Claudius following the fall of Messalina, and so driven into exile and subsequently forced to kill herself.

Silana   Iunia Silana was an enemy of Agrippina who had used her clients, Iturius and Calvisius, to accuse her of treason in AD 55. However, on the collapse of the charge his mother had secured from Nero the punishment of all three of them.

the tribes   these were the 35 ancient tribes into which all the population of Rome was divided.

the proud victor over a servile public   this striking expression is made more notable by the use of the Latin word *superbus* ('proud' or 'arrogant'), which had been given as a sobriquet to the last king of Rome, Tarquinius (on whom see p. 139). For a similar use of *superbus* concerning Germanicus at **2.22**, see note on p. 75.

1 Why do you think that Tacitus chose to include a list of portents following the murder of Agrippina?

2 How does Tacitus manage to show the abasement of the whole of Roman society after the crime?

3 In what ways does Tacitus portray Nero as a perverse *triumphator* (a general who wins a triumph for his military successes) in this section?

14.14   He had a long-standing desire to drive a four-horse chariot and **a no less despicable passion** to sing to the lyre as a theatrical performer. He recalled that competing with horses was a royal hobby and a regular pursuit for ancient leaders, and that it was an activity **celebrated by the praise of poets and offered as an honour to the gods**. What is more, he noted that singing was sacred to Apollo, and that it was in the guise of such a performer that a powerful and prophetic deity stood not only in Greek cities but also in Roman temples. When he could be stopped no longer, Seneca and Burrus decided to grant him one desire so that he would not get his way with both. There was **an enclosed area in the Vatican valley** in which he could drive his horses without becoming a public spectacle: next the Roman people actually began to be invited and began to exalt him with praise, just as the crowd is desirous of its pleasures and happy if the *princeps* draws them in the same direction. But the public disgrace did not satisfy his desires, as they thought it would, but rather gave him encouragement. And thinking that the dishonour would be reduced, if he brought shame to more people, he put on stage the descendants of noble families, who had been made corruptible through poverty; since they have died, I think that it is owed to their ancestors that I should not mention them by name. For the disgrace belongs also to the man who gave money for the committing of wrong rather than to prevent it. In addition he drove famous Roman *equites* to promise their services to the arena with huge gifts, although in reality wages from a man who can give orders carry the force of necessity.

5

10

15

20

a no less despicable passion   Tacitus shared the traditional senatorial Roman point of view – which was the opposite to the Greek – that music had no place in the education of the upper classes. As to chariot-racing, the drivers in Rome were usually slaves, and even in Greece it was the owners who received the prize at the Olympics, not the driver; one may compare the difference in social status between owners and riders in modern horse-racing.

celebrated by the praise of poets and offered as an honour to the gods   this is a reference to the fact that chariot victors had hymns composed in their honour by Greek poets such as Pindar and Bacchylides (both of whom were writing in the first half of the fifth century BC), and to the fact that chariot-racing was an integral part of Greek religious festivals such as the Pythian and Olympic games.

an enclosed area in the Vatican valley   this became known as the Circus of Gaius and Nero, and was on the site where St Peter's Basilica now stands.

A statue of Apollo with his lyre.

However, in order that he should not yet disgrace himself in the public theatre, he instituted the games known as **the** 25 **Iuvenalia**, for which names were registered from throughout society. Neither nobility, nor age, nor honours held were an impediment to anyone practising the art of a Greek or Latin actor, even employing 30 gestures and rhythms that were unmanly. No, even notable women were involved in shameful acts; in the grove which Augustus had planted around **his naval lake** were constructed inns and places for rendezvous, 35 and stimulants to excess were put on sale. Doles were distributed which good men spent under compulsion, and the profligate with pride. After this the outrages and disgrace grew, and no generation imported 40 more depravities to a society whose morals had already been corrupted than that scum. There is scarcely any vestige of respect left for honourable pursuits, still less was there then a sense of shame or propriety or any 45 positive value preserved in competitions of vice. Finally the man himself went on stage, tuning his lyre with great attention and warming up his voice while his singing teachers stood by. In attendance were a cohort of soldiers, centurions and tribunes, 50 and Burrus mourning and offering his praise. Then for the first time Roman *equites* were enlisted under the title of *Augustiani*, notable by their age and physique, some shameless by nature, and others out of a hope for power. **For days and nights on end they rang out with applause**, ascribing to the beauty and voice of the *princeps* epithets belonging to the gods; they conducted themselves as if they were famous 55 and as if it was because of their virtue that they were honoured.

---

the Iuvenalia   the first shaving of a young Roman's beard had always been celebrated in the family, but Nero used the occasion of his own to set up a state festival.

his naval lake   this was constructed by Augustus across the Tiber for the staging of mass naval battles to celebrate the dedication of the temple of Mars Ultor in 2 BC.

For days and nights on end they rang out with applause   Suetonius describes the support these men gave Nero on his return from Greece (*Nero* 20.3); compare the figure of Percennius (**1.16–17**, pp. 46–8).

A mosaic (from the Bardo Museum, Tunis) depicting chariot racing.

14.16   However, so that the theatrical talents of the emperor should not be alone in receiving renown, he also laid claim to the study of poetry, by assembling men who had some skill at composition, **though not yet famous**. They sat together after dinner, joined verses which they had brought with them or thought of on 60 the spot, and completed his words in whatever fashion they had been composed: the very appearance of his poems betrays this, as **they lack force and inspiration and do not flow with one voice**. He also shared his time after banquets with the

---

though not yet famous   Lucan (some of whose poetry survives) was one of these, but he later fell out with Nero to such an extent that he was forbidden from giving any public recitations: according to the sources this was due to the *princeps'* jealousy of his superior poetic renown.

they lack force and inspiration and do not flow with one voice   Suetonius, who had access to the imperial archive in his administrative roles under Trajan and Hadrian, is more generous in his assessment of Nero's poetry: 'Therefore, with a poetic bent, he composed poems enthusiastically and without effort nor, as some think, did he publish the work of others as his own. There have come into my hands writing-tablets and manuscripts containing some very famous poems of his written in his own handwriting' (*Nero* 52).

teachers of philosophy in order to enjoy argument between **those defending opposite points of view**. And there was no shortage of those who desired to be 65 seen with gloomy features and expressions among the amusements of the court.

1 Nero's involvement in chariot-racing and musical performance follow closely after Tacitus' description of his mother's death. Is there a connection between the two?

2 Does Tacitus' own narrative in this section become more rhetorical in parallel with the excesses of behaviour which it describes?

3 Other emperors, including those such as Augustus who received a much more positive press than Nero, instituted games and encouraged people to participate. Why do you think that Nero receives so much criticism for doing so?

4 Is Nero's progression into actual theatre an inevitable step given his previous portrayal in Tacitus' narrative?

5 In light of the fact that, uniquely of the emperors he writes about, Tacitus never gives Nero any direct speech in the surviving books, is it significant that he accuses him of not even writing his own poetry?

This marks the end of the long section focusing on Nero in the planning, execution and aftermath of his mother's murder: given the *princeps'* recently publicized interests, it is pointed that Tacitus moves on immediately to record a crowd riot at a gladiatorial show in Pompeii. Over the following few years, events at Rome remain the focus, both in Book 14 and at the start of the next, though there are long digressions detailing the general Corbulo's activities in the East and Boudicca's revolt in Britain. Throughout, Nero's theatricality remains prominent, whether in his eventual divorce from Octavia, or in his grand gesture of throwing away rotten grain in AD 62 to reassure the people that Rome was well supplied. However, his desire to perform on stage proper remained strong, and he finally realized this ambition in Naples in 64 (15.33–4).

---

those defending opposite points of view   this might include divergent opinions within a single school, or philosophers from different schools, such as Stoics and Epicureans.

9 The Great Fire of Rome

In Book 15 Tacitus describes Nero's pursuit of his theatrical career, which attained new levels with his appearance on stage in Naples. However, although he wished to go to Greece and perform there, he postponed this trip for two years (until AD 66). Instead, he returned to Rome and, after abandoning a further planned visit to the eastern provinces, made great show to the ordinary people of his love for the capital: as we shall see, this led to him putting on parties throughout Rome. One of these marks, for Tacitus, the climax of Nero's moral degeneracy, as he publicly consummates a homosexual 'marriage' with a Greek called Pythagoras. This is perhaps the most notable example in Tacitus' writings of the power of selectivity and juxtaposition. For, without any explicit comment, the historian proceeds directly to a description of the Great Fire.

The fire broke out on 19 July AD 64: the narration of the fire's progress and its human cost is one of the most striking descriptive passages in the work. Tacitus follows it with an account of the measures taken by Nero following the fire. The most famous of these are the building of his Golden House and the first persecution of Christians, who are made scapegoats for the fire. However, Tacitus also records the sensible measures taken by Nero to alleviate the immediate effects of the disaster and those aimed at reducing the likely incidence of fire in Rome for the future. The comparison with other accounts, most notably that of Suetonius, is revealing of Tacitus' qualities: in particular Tacitus acknowledges the uncertainty of the cause of the fire, whereas other sources baldly assert that it was started by Nero.

The burning of Rome: 15.37–41

15.37   Nero himself, to make people believe that he was nowhere more happy than at Rome, set up banquets in public places and made use of the whole city **as if it were his own house**. The banquet that was the most notorious for its extravagance and

---

as if it were his own house   this remark anticipates Nero's decision to build the Golden House after the fire and suggests that he already saw the city as a space for his own personal use.

reputation was the one organized by Tigellinus, which I will recount **as a notable example** so that I need not tell of the same sort of monstrosities on any further occasions. He constructed a raft on **Agrippa's lake**, on top of which he arranged the banquet so that it could be drawn along by other boats. **The boats were embellished with gold and ivory, the degenerate rowers arranged according to their years and their expertise in vice.** He had sought out birds and wild animals from remote lands, and sea-creatures all the way from the **Ocean**. On the banks of the lake stood brothels, **filled with distinguished ladies**, and whores were on display across the water, naked: there were obscene gestures and gyrations. And after darkness fell, all the neighbouring woodland and surrounding houses rang with singing and blazed with lights. **The emperor himself**, defiled by every legal and illegal act, had left untried no depravity by which he might debase himself

5

10

15

Tigellinus   Ofonius Tigellinus had been appointed commander of the praetorian guard in AD 62. On these troops, see note on p. 31.

as a notable example   for narrative economy Tacitus makes this one example stand for all the others, but he has selected an event noteworthy for its excess.

Agrippa's lake   this was a reservoir of water for Agrippa's baths in the Campus Martius, also used as an open-air swimming pool.

The boats were embellished … expertise in vice   this banquet was notorious for its lavishness, and is described in even more detail by Dio (62.15). What is particularly striking about this sentence is the way in which it moves away from physical description to comment on the general degeneracy of all those involved. The sting is all the stronger for coming unexpectedly: the reader is perhaps not surprised to find that the rowers are arranged according to age, but then discovers that they have also been categorized by their knowledge of vice.

Ocean   this was considered to be a great sea that encompassed all the lands of the world. By bringing sea-creatures from it for the banquet, Tigellinus was underlining the way in which Rome now controlled most of the known world. Rome had long been an importer of exotic animals to be used in various public shows put on by the upper classes to impress the city population with the diversity and strangeness of the empire's fauna. When Cicero had been governor of the province of Cilicia in southern Asia Minor in 51 BC, his protégé Caelius had asked him (and others) to provide leopards for the games he was putting on as aedile (Cicero, *Ad Familiares* 8.9.3).

filled with distinguished ladies   the decline of Roman morals is emphasized by the fact that the well-born are not only to be found in brothels but actually staffing them.

The emperor himself   Miller describes how Nero now becomes the centre of attention: 'the scene, presented so far kaleidoscopically and impressionistically, is now focused sharply on Nero's activities. After a general introduction, one scandalous incident is described in detail, with the technical vocabulary of the formal marriage ceremony adding to the outrage of this perversion of it' (p. 87). This perversion is later emphasized by the juxtaposition of the word for emperor (*imperator*) with the word for veil (*flammeum*), so drawing attention to the fact that in this ceremony Nero was demeaning his position by playing the woman's role in his 'marriage' to his Greek hanger-on.

A mosaic (from the Villa Casale in Sicily) showing captured animals being loaded onto a boat to be transported to Rome for use in shows.

further, except that a few days later he had married one of that flock of perverted followers (his name was Pythagoras) in the manner of a solemn union. The emperor was decked out with a veil, soothsayers were summoned, there was a dowry, a marriage bed and wedding torches. To cap it all, everything was open to view, **which night shrouds even in the case of a woman.**

20

15.38 There ensued disaster – it is uncertain whether it was as a result of chance or the treachery of the emperor (for authors have related both versions). But it was

---

which night shrouds even in the case of a woman the conclusion to a Roman marriage came at night when, after the wedding-feast, the bride was escorted to the bridegroom's house, where she was taken to the bedchamber and undressed by women who had only known one husband (*univirae*), before the bridegroom was admitted and the marriage consummated in private, while friends sang marriage hymns outside.

There ensued disaster ... (for authors have related both versions) Tacitus does not make an explicit causal link between Nero's disgraceful behaviour and the start of the fire, and is very careful to emphasize the uncertainty over the cause of the latter. All other surviving accounts (Dio, Suetonius and Pliny the Elder) are explicit in making Nero responsible, and were it not for Tacitus we would be unaware of the divergent tradition. His wording does of course insinuate that Nero may in fact have been responsible, giving this alternative weight by putting it in the emphatic second position. But for Tacitus the observation that this is what people said and believed is as significant a historical fact as the actual truth behind the fire.

more serious and terrible than all others which have befallen this city **through the destructiveness of fire**. Its outbreak occurred in that section of **the circus** which adjoins the Palatine and Caelian hills. There the fire, as soon as it began in **shops** 25 which contained highly flammable goods, at once became fierce and, fanned by the wind, took hold along the length of the circus. For no mansions surrounded with boundary walls stood in its way, nor temples ringed with enclosures, nor any other structure that might delay its progress. **At its onset** the fire rampaged at first across the level parts of the city, then spread to higher ground and in 30 turn to the lower areas in its devastating progress. It outstripped any counter-measures by the speed of its destructiveness and because the city was vulnerable with its narrow streets, which turned this way and that, and its irregular blocks **(for this was how Rome used to be at that time)**. **In the face of the fire** laments broke out from terrified women, those wearied with age, and helplessly ignorant 35 children; there were some who looked to their own needs and some who showed

---

through the destructiveness of fire   fires had been a constant threat to the city of Rome, with its buildings closely packed together and often constructed with a wooden frame (the *opus craticum* style). In the late Republic the wealthy triumvir Marcus Licinius Crassus had engaged in the profitable scam of buying burning buildings from their owners at knock-down prices before sending in his slaves to act as firefighters. In Augustus' time the aedile of 22 BC, Marcus Egnatius Rufus, had organized a body of men at his own expense to fight fires as a public service, and as a long-term response Augustus had established groups of watchmen (the *vigiles*) to act as round-the-clock firemen in each of the 14 regions of the city. The Great Fire was remarkable not for its occurrence but for its sheer scale.

the circus   this is the Circus Maximus, where chariot racing took place, which occupied the low ground between the Palatine and Aventine hills.

shops   these occupied the arches supporting the tiered seating for spectators.

At its onset   the Latin word used here is *impetus*, meaning 'attack', which is the word regularly used in military contexts. This is one of several ways in which Tacitus seeks to describe the fire and its effects in the manner of a city's fall to armed attack. Compare Tacitus' complaints at **4.33** (p. 107), where he laments the absence from his account of geographical descriptions, exciting battle narratives and the deaths of commanders to stimulate his audience. A big set-piece like the fire allows Tacitus to engage his readers in the excitement of the event, but the implicit comparison with a sacked city also raises questions about how far Rome had sunk under Nero's principate.

for this was how Rome used to be at that time   this comment reflects the fact that by Tacitus' own day, and in part following the measures taken by Nero after the fire, there had been a move towards a more regimented layout of streets. The style of buildings had also moved away from the wooden-frame (*opus craticum*) method to the use of brick and concrete. Trajan's markets and Ostia give a good idea of what large areas of second-century Rome may have begun to look like.

In the face of the fire   the Latin syntax of this and the next two sentences is complex and difficult, but this is perhaps not without point.

concern for others: while they hauled out those who were incapacitated, or waited for them, some by their hesitation, others by their haste – in short everything – caused an obstruction. And often while people looked to their backs, they were trapped with the fire at their sides or in front of them; or if they had escaped to 40 a neighbouring area, they discovered, when this part too was in the grip of fire, that the same fate had befallen even those regions which they had considered distant. Finally, uncertain what to avoid or where to head, they filled the streets and threw themselves down in the fields; certain individuals perished after losing all their possessions and even their food for that day, others because of their love 45 for relatives whom they had tried in vain to save, even though the means of escape lay open to them. No one dared to fight the fire owing to the repeated threats of numerous people preventing them from extinguishing it, and because others were openly throwing torches and were shouting that they had authority for their actions, whether this was so that they could loot more freely, **or because they** 50 **really did have orders.**

---

1 Why does Tacitus choose to place his description of Tigellinus' banquet immediately before his description of the fire? What effect might this placement have upon readers?

2 What style does Tacitus use in his narration of the fire? In what ways does his choice of vocabulary and sentence-structure reflect the confused scene which he is describing?

3 How does this exciting passage fit with the claims he made at **4.32–3** (pp. 105–7) that he had nothing interesting to write about? Are those claims exposed as hollow and rhetorical, or is it significant that he is here describing an internal disaster, whereas there he was lamenting the absence of any excitement in foreign affairs?

15.39 At that time Nero was staying at **Antium** and did not return to the city until the fire approached **his own house**, with which he had linked the Palatine and the gardens of Maecenas. However, it could not be stopped before the Palatine, the house and everything around it were consumed. But, as a relief for the people who had been

---

or because they really did have orders   again Tacitus does not explicitly support the view that the emperor exploited the situation created by the fire. He admits the possibility that the cause of such behaviour was a widespread desire to facilitate looting, but he allows the more sinister alternative to linger in the readers' minds.

Antium   this town (modern Anzio) lay on the coast about 35 miles south of Rome. It was Nero's birthplace and had become a fashionable resort with an imperial villa.

his own house   this was the *Domus Transitoria*, which Suetonius (*Nero* 31.1) describes as stretching from the Palatine hill across to the Esquiline, so linking the traditional imperial residence on the former, which had developed around Augustus' original house, to the gardens of Maecenas on the latter.

uprooted and were now refugees, he opened **the Campus Martius and Agrippa's** 5
public buildings, indeed even his own gardens, and he constructed emergency
accommodation to house the large numbers of the destitute. Necessary supplies
were brought up from Ostia and the neighbouring towns, and **the price of corn
was reduced to three sesterces a modius.** Although these measures were popular,
they failed to achieve their purpose, because **the rumour had spread** that, at the 10
very time when the city was ablaze, Nero had mounted the stage in his house
and sung of **the destruction of Troy,** drawing comparisons between the present
calamity and the ancient disaster.

15.40   Finally on the sixth day the fire was extinguished at the foot of the Esquiline by
demolishing buildings over a vast area, so its relentless fury might meet open 15
ground and thin air, as it were. The people had not yet laid aside their fear and
regained a sense of hope, when **the fire broke out again** and raged in the more
open areas of the city. This resulted in less loss of life, but the temples of the

---

the Campus Martius ... even his own gardens   in the Republic the Campus Martius had
been the place where the citizen army had mustered and trained, since it lay outside
the sacred boundary of the city (which men were prohibited from entering under arms).
Over time important facilities and imperial monuments had been constructed here, and
Agrippa, Augustus' friend and right-hand man, had been particularly active, building not
only the first public baths, but also the original Pantheon, the *saepta Iulia* (the voting
enclosure) and athletic facilities. Furneaux (vol. 2, p. 365) identifies the gardens Tacitus
mentions here as those on the Vatican, previously mentioned at **14.14** (p. 157).

the price of corn was reduced to three sesterces a modius   a modius was a dry measure,
slightly smaller than a peck, i.e. 16 pints. This was clearly meant to be a significant drop in
price, perhaps to almost half the normal cost (Miller, p. 90). It was unusual for emperors
at this time to fix a maximum price for grain as it could discourage suppliers by removing
their profit margin, and so is a clear sign of a genuine emergency.

the rumour had spread   it is again a striking contrast that Dio (62.18.1) and Suetonius
(*Nero* 38) simply relate this rumour as being factually true.

the destruction of Troy   this stood as the archetypal city-sacking for Romans, particularly
after the publication of Vergil's *Aeneid*, in the second book of which Aeneas describes
to Dido the fall of the city. This alleged behaviour on Nero's part reinforces his portrayal
as an artist-emperor, but is particularly inappropriate in the light of the suffering of his
fellow Roman citizens. In the early fifth century BC the Athenians dealt severely with a
playwright in a similar case: soon after the fall of Miletus, an allied city, to the Persians,
Phrynichus produced a play called *The Capture of Miletus*, which upset the audience so
much that the playwright was fined for reminding them of their troubles (Herodotus
6.21). Are there any modern parallels for leaders being seen to behave inappropriately
during major crises?

the fire broke out again   this second outbreak seems to have lasted for a further three
days to judge from a surviving inscription from the Quirinal hill, 'when the city burnt in
the reign of Nero for nine days' (*CIL* VI.1826).

gods and the colonnades which beautified the city were destroyed in bigger numbers. This outbreak caused greater consternation because it had occurred on 20 **Tigellinus' Aemilian estate**, and because it appeared that Nero was aiming to win glory by founding a new city and **naming it after himself**. Rome is divided into **fourteen regions**: of these four remained undamaged, three were razed to the ground; in the remaining seven a few traces of buildings survived, mangled and half-burnt. 25

15.41   It would be hard to identify the number of mansions, blocks of flats and temples which were destroyed. **Some buildings of the most ancient sanctity were burnt down**: Servius Tullius' temple to Luna, the shrine and Great Altar which the

---

Tigellinus' Aemilian estate   the location of this is uncertain, but seems to have lain to the north of the Capitoline hill. However, it appears unlikely that this outbreak spread as far as the Campus Martius, since that is where many of the homeless had taken refuge.

naming it after himself   Tacitus does not say what this new name was, and is indeed careful to avoid corroborating the story of the renaming ('it appeared that'). However, Suetonius gives it as Neropolis (*Nero* 55), a Greek name, and therefore another indication, perhaps, of the emperor's philhellenism.

fourteen regions   Augustus had divided the city into these regions for administrative purposes. However, it is likely that this sentence is an explanatory gloss added by copyists of the text, since as Miller (p. 91) points out, Tacitus' readers knew this and he had already referred to the regions at **14.12** (see p. 155). The four regions which remained undamaged were among those which lay furthest from the centre (and certainly included region XIV, the part of the city which lay across the Tiber); the three that Tacitus describes as razed included the Palatine and the Circus Maximus. However, this is an exaggeration, since several buildings in these areas were left largely undamaged.

Some buildings of the most ancient sanctity were burnt down   the buildings which Tacitus lists were revered since they were believed to be among the most ancient of the city, dating back to the period of the kings (traditionally 753–510 BC) and even beyond. Their destruction could be seen to symbolize the present corruption of Rome and how far it had become detached from its roots. A parallel for this can be found, albeit on a greater scale, with the burning of the Capitoline Temple in AD 69 in the fighting between the Vitellians and Flavians, which Tacitus describes at *Histories* 3.71–2.

Servius Tullius' temple to Luna   Servius was traditionally the sixth king of Rome, and this temple seems to have been associated with (or identical to) a temple to Diana which he was said to have built on the Aventine (Livy 1.45). Livy's account gives the building of this temple added importance by making it symbolic of Rome's dominance over her Latin neighbours.

the shrine and Great Altar   this is the *Ara Maxima*, lying near the Tiber to the west of the Circus Maximus, which Evander, a pre-Roman inhabitant of the future site of Rome, in one version of the myth was supposed to have dedicated to Hercules out of gratitude for the latter's killing of the monster Cacus. This aetiology of the altar is related at Vergil, *Aeneid* 8.184–279.

Arcadian Evander had consecrated to Hercules when he visited the place, **the temple of Jupiter Stator** vowed by Romulus, **the palace of Numa**, and **the shrine of Vesta** containing the Penates of the Roman people. Besides this there were the treasures won in the course of so many victories and the ornaments of Greek art, then **the ancient and authentic records of genius**. As a result, despite the incredible beauty of the renascent city, its older inhabitants remembered many objects which could not be restored. There were some who noted that this fire had started on 19 July, the same date on which **the Senonian Gauls** had captured and burnt the city. Others went to such lengths of ingenuity that they calculated that **between the two fires an equal number of years, months and days had passed.**

the temple of Jupiter Stator   according to tradition, this had been dedicated by Rome's founder, Romulus, after he had promised Jupiter such a temple if he were to stop the Romans from their flight whilst fighting against the Sabines – hence the dedication to Jupiter Stator, or Jupiter 'the Stayer'. The story is told by Livy at 1.12.4–7. The temple was situated at the top of the *Sacra Via*, near the site of the later arch of Titus.

the palace of Numa   Numa Pompilius was the second king of Rome, to whom many of the religious traditions of Rome were ascribed (on which see Livy 1.19). The *Regia* ('Palace') had been the official residence of the *pontifex maximus* before the Principate and lay in the Forum behind the Temple of Vesta. It was supposed to date back to Numa.

the shrine of Vesta   this was a circular building at the eastern end of the Forum, where the Vestal Virgins maintained the sacred fire. The Penates also were kept there, literally objects which were concerned with the 'inner part of the house' (Latin: *penus*): they were probably the sacred objects said to have been brought by Aeneas from Troy. As a result its destruction was particularly ill-omened for the city.

the ancient and authentic records of genius   these are the early and hence more reliable copies of the works of great Roman authors. They were probably those belonging to individual families, destroyed in their houses, rather than those of the Palatine Library, which is not otherwise known to have been damaged before AD 363 (Furneaux, vol. 2, p. 368).

the Senonian Gauls   the Gauls had burned Rome, according to tradition, on this very day in 390 BC, an event narrated by Livy at 5.39–43. This event was seen as one of the lowest points in Rome's history, and the connection with it that was made by people at the time of the fire shows how desperately they viewed the situation.

between the two fires an equal number of years, months and days had passed   since the Gallic sack 454 years had elapsed according to Roman reckoning. This could be expressed as 418 years, 418 months, and 418 days. Fascination with numbers and numerology was typical of Romans in this period, as is revealed by the popularity of astrology, but Tacitus makes very clear what he thinks of such calculations.

The shrine of Vesta in the Forum Romanum.

Nero rebuilds the city: 15.42–4

15.42 But Nero put the ruin of his country to good use, and **built a house** whose use of jewels and gold was not so remarkable – these ornaments of extravagance have long been customary and are commonplace – as the fields and pools, in the fashion of a wilderness, with woods on one side, and open spaces and views on the other. The architects and engineers were Severus and Celer, who possessed the ability 5 and boldness to attempt to create by their skill even those effects which nature

---

built a house this was the famous Golden House (*Domus Aurea*), the building of which probably helped to establish the rumour that Nero had himself started the fire, since he was seen to benefit from it personally. The house was really an estate, stretching from the Palatine across to the Esquiline, and from the Velia to the Caelian. There was a lake where the Colosseum was later built, a monumental entrance at the top of the *Sacra Via*, and two main residential wings, on the Palatine and the Esquiline. The latter survives below Trajan's Baths and gives some idea of the opulence of the whole. In fact, much of the land already belonged to Nero and had formed the earlier *Domus Transitoria* and a great part of the estate may well have been open to the public. Tacitus emphasizes Nero's desire to create an artificial world of the countryside within the city (in Latin, *rus in urbe*), just as he goes on to describe his attempt to build a canal through impossible barriers. Romans had already built villas in the bay of Naples out over the sea, and later Hadrian was to attempt the opposite of Nero, by re-creating the city and his court in the countryside at his villa in Tivoli (*urbs in rure*). However, Nero's attempt at such artifice must have outraged previous inhabitants of the area, some of whom will have been influential nobles.

---

had refused, and to fool away the emperor's resources. For they had undertaken to dig a canal from Lake Avernus right to the mouth of the Tiber, through arid coastal regions and over mountain barriers. For apart from the Pomptine Marshes there was no water along the planned course to supply the canal: the rest of the 10 route was hilly or dry and, even if the channel could be dug, the magnitude of the task was intolerable and unjustifiable. Nero, however, as a man who loved the impossible, strove to dig through the ridges nearest to Lake Avernus: the traces of his vain hope remain.

Suetonius on Nero's Golden House

Tacitus' account of the Golden House is much shorter than that of the imperial biographer Suetonius, who concentrates in much greater detail on its opulence:

> However, in no other area was he more damaging than in his building projects: he built a house which stretched from the Palatine hill right across to the Esquiline. This he at first called the Domus Transitoria, then, after it was consumed by fire and rebuilt, he named it the Golden House. It will suffice to say the following about its size and ornamentation. Its entrance-hall was of such a scale that a colossal statue of the emperor's likeness stood in it, 120 feet high; it was so spacious that it contained triple colonnades a mile in length; similarly its lake was like a sea, ringed with buildings constructed in the form of cities; in addition there was a variety of parkland, consisting of fields, vineyards, pastures and woods, stocked with large numbers of every kind of domestic and wild beast. In its other areas everything was overlaid with gold, embellished with jewels and mother-of-pearl; the dining-rooms had ceilings constructed of revolving ivory panels and with sprinklers, designed so that flowers and perfumes could be scattered on those below; the main dining-room was circular, able to revolve continually, day and night, in time with the heavens; the baths flowed with water from the sea and from sulphur springs. When Nero was opening the house, after it had been completed in this style, he approved of it to such an extent that he said that he was now at last able to begin to live like a human being.
>
> *(Nero 31)*

---

a canal   this project is also recorded by Suetonius, who tells how prisoners were brought to Italy from all over the empire to provide a workforce (*Nero* 31.3). As noted above, the scheme was another attempt to triumph over nature, but was not without some sense. The coast between Lake Avernus in the bay of Naples and the mouth of the Tiber at Ostia was very dangerous for shipping, and the canal would have further secured the grain supply to Rome. Ships loaded with grain put into Puteoli and their cargo was then brought up the coast in other boats: in AD 62 200 of these had been wrecked off Ostia, causing great fears of shortage in Rome (Tacitus, *Annals* 15.18). The canal project was abandoned after Nero's death; its traces are still visible.

A striking domed room from the Esquiline wing of the Golden House, which survived under the platform that was built later to support Trajan's Baths.

- Why do you think that Tacitus passes over the details of the house's ornaments so rapidly in comparison with Suetonius?

- Why does Tacitus focus the reader's attention on the scale of the house's open spaces?

- Can you think of any modern examples of artificial worlds to parallel Nero's attempt to create the impression of the countryside within the city?

- Suetonius, in ascribing his final remark to Nero, presents the house as a private indulgence, but what other purpose might it have held for the emperor?

15.43   But **the parts of the city which survived his house** were not rebuilt indiscriminately or without a general plan, as had been the case after the Gallic sack. Instead, the rows of blocks were set out regularly, broad streets were laid out, the height of buildings was limited, open spaces were created, and colonnades were added to protect the façades of the flats. Nero promised to build 5 these colonnades at his own expense and to clear individual sites before handing them over to their owners. He offered inducements according to each man's rank and the size of his fortune, and set the date by which they had to complete

---

the parts of the city which survived his house   one might compare an anonymous epigram which circulated at the same time: 'Rome will become one house; leave for Veii, citizens, unless that house takes over Veii too' (preserved at Suetonius, *Nero* 39.2). Veii is a town of Etruscan origin, ten miles north of Rome.

the mansions or flats in order to win them. He decided to use the marshy land
at Ostia to receive the debris, and that the ships which had brought grain up 10
the Tiber should be loaded with this rubble and carry it away; he decreed that a
fixed proportion of the buildings themselves should be constructed from **Gabian
or Alban stone** (since this material is fireproof) and avoid the use of wooden
beams. Furthermore, **he appointed guards** to cut down the extensive use of water
by private citizens and to ensure that it was available for public use in greater 15
quantities and in more locations; he also ensured that everyone kept firefighting
equipment in their porches and that buildings should not have shared walls,
but must all be fully detached. These measures which were made for utilitarian
purposes also **contributed to the beauty of the new city.** However, **there were
some who believed** that its previous appearance had been more conducive to 20
good health, on the grounds that the narrow streets and high buildings had
offered more cover against the heat of the sun: now, by contrast, the generously
wide streets offered no protecting shade and blazed with fiercer heat.

Gabian or Alban stone   these were both types of *peperino*, i.e. a sort of tufa, a volcanic
rock. Therefore, although they were better in quality than Roman tufa, they did not
lend themselves to carving and decoration. However, the architect Vitruvius had already
noted their fireproof qualities, and tufa had been used in the *forum Augustum* to create
a massive firewall to protect it from the area of housing to the north. The Alban stone
was quarried 15 miles south-east of Rome; Gabii lay about ten miles east of Rome, on the
road to Praeneste – the quarries are still visible.

he appointed guards   these guards were to police the lines of the aqueducts, in order to
prevent private citizens from illegally siphoning off water from them.

contributed to the beauty of the new city   it is striking how explicit Tacitus is in stating
that Nero's measures not only were practical, but also made Rome a finer environment.
The contrast with Suetonius' entirely negative account is again notable. Since Augustus,
it had been seen as one of the roles of the emperor to improve the appearance of the
city, and Suetonius records that the first emperor boasted that he had inherited a Rome
made of mud-brick, but left her clad in marble (*Augustus* 28). One might compare the
way in which Mussolini removed many of the buildings of medieval Rome in order to
expose the classical monuments, perhaps most notably along the *via dei Fori Imperiali*, so
that his troops should have a suitable backdrop to march past in military parades.

there were some who believed   Tacitus typically closes this section, which is essentially
very positive about the measures Nero took, with a negative twist. This serves to
underline Nero's unpopularity: even when he did good there were people who could
only see the bad in any of his actions. However, in his preface Tacitus had promised
to write 'without anger and partisanship' (*sine ira et studio*) (**1.1**, p. 22) and perhaps
wishes to contrast himself with these men: they refused to accept the truth, whereas he,
as the self-proclaimed historian of the truth, was prepared to relate the commendable
achievements of the tyrannical emperor. Does Tacitus live up to these claims? What does
he do to convince his readers of his own reliability?

15.44 These precautions were taken on the human plane. Next there was an attempt to appease the gods and **the Sibylline Books were consulted**. As a result, public 25 prayers were offered to Vulcan, Ceres and Proserpina, and Juno was propitiated by married women, first on the Capitol and then in the sea at its nearest point: from here water was collected and ritually sprinkled on the temple and statue of the goddess. Women who had living husbands celebrated ritual banquets and all-night vigils. But neither human measures, nor the generosity of the emperor, 30 nor attempts to placate the gods succeeded in diminishing his notoriety: it was believed that the fire had been started on his orders. Therefore to eliminate this rumour Nero offered other culprits and punished in the most exquisite manner those hated for their crimes, who were beginning to be known popularly as **Christians**. The originator of this name, Christ, had been put to death during the 35 principate of Tiberius on the order of the procurator Pontius Pilate; **the deadly superstition** which had been temporarily suppressed burst out again, not only in Judaea, the origin of this evil, but even throughout this city, where all outrageous and shameful practices are collected from every direction and celebrated. Therefore, first those who confessed were arrested, then on their information a 40 huge number were convicted, not so much on the charge of arson as for hatred of the human race. They were also humiliated in the mocking manner of their deaths: they died wearing the skins of wild beasts and torn apart by dogs, by being crucified or burnt alive, and when it became dark their flames served as

---

the Sibylline Books were consulted these were written collections of prophecies traditionally consulted for religious advice by the Romans in times of national crisis. They were supposedly derived from a divinely inspired prophetess, a Sibyl. There were many collections of Sibylline writings current in the Roman world and stories evolved about many different Sibyls. The national collection at Rome was derived, according to tradition, from the Cumaean Sibyl (whom Vergil makes Aeneas visit in the *Aeneid*), with three books bought from her by Rome's fifth king, Tarquinius Priscus. However, these had been destroyed by fire in 83 BC. The Senate had commissioned three men to establish a new collection, and these had been transferred by Augustus to his new Temple of Apollo on the Palatine. It is these which Nero would have consulted on this occasion.

Christians Suetonius (*Nero* 16) also describes Nero's persecution of the Christians, but Tacitus alone links it with the aftermath of the fire. As a biographer, Suetonius had much less interest in making connections between different historical events, but if Tacitus makes such an explicit link as he does here, it is highly likely, as Miller notes (p. xxix), that he had very good evidence to do so. The following sentence, if it is genuine, is the earliest reference to the death of Christ in a non-Christian writer.

the deadly superstition the Latin word *superstitio* was reserved for foreign or unorthodox religious practices (whereas *religio* was reserved for Roman or Greek cults). However, Roman religion was normally tolerant of other cults and even embraced many: Christians were viewed with suspicion because of their unwillingness to recognize and sacrifice to the official gods, and especially the emperor himself in the form of the imperial cult.

night-time illumination. Nero had offered his own gardens for **this spectacle** and
put on games at the circus, mixing with the crowd in the dress of a charioteer or
riding in a chariot. As a result, **pity arose despite the fact that it was being shown
to men who were guilty and deserving of the most extreme punishments**: it
arose on the grounds that they were not being so treated for the public benefit,
but to satisfy the savagery of one man.

45

50

---

1 What image of Nero emerges from Tacitus' account of the fire and its
   aftermath? Is it possible to reconcile the positive and negative aspects of his
   actions?

2 How influential is the first Christian persecution in shaping our responses
   to Nero? Does Tacitus live up to his claim to be writing 'without anger and
   partisanship' (*Annals* **1.1**) in the attitude he displays towards the Christians?

3 Nero is often seen as a showman-emperor. Is this a consistent trait of his
   behaviour in AD 64? Does this help to explain why he was so popular with
   ordinary Romans and so hated by the upper classes?

4 Does Tacitus' account of the fire come across as clear and factual, or is it
   obscured by the theatricality of the narrative and its moralizing tone?

---

this spectacle   the Romans had long turned their punishments into a spectacle, and the
public degradation was intended to be part of the punishment. This practice had evolved
in such a way that criminals in their deaths imitated myths, and Martial records the re-
enactment of several stories in *On the Spectacles* (6, Pasiphae mating with a bull; 9,
Laureolus being punished by flaying like Marsyas by Apollo). However, the idea that
burning was an appropriate punishment for arsonists was a long-established one at
Rome, supposedly dating back to the Law of the Twelve Tables of the fifth century BC.

pity arose despite the fact … the most extreme punishments   this is the first recorded
persecution of the Christians at Rome, but in Tacitus' account it is very clearly motivated
by Nero's desire to identify scapegoats rather than for any clear ideological purpose.
As a result it is not at all obvious whether the remark that Christians 'were guilty and
deserving of the most extreme punishments' refers to contemporary feeling or is an
authorial comment. In Tacitus' own time, Pliny (*Letters* 10.96–7) provides evidence for
greater hostility towards, and a more organized policing of the religion, at least in some
areas of the empire. Even then, Trajan's reply to Pliny argues for tolerance, although
Pliny did execute those who failed to renounce their Christianity. It is also worth asking
what evidence Tacitus had for contemporary sympathy for the Christians, and – if it was
genuine – whether this was widespread sympathy or came just from those members of
the upper classes who were so hostile to Nero.

Tacitus proceeds to describe how Nero, in order to meet the expenses caused by the fire, went on to seek funds from across the empire in various illegal ways, including the looting of shrines. He closes the year with an account of **various bad omens** including two-headed births and a calf born beside the road with its head attached to one of its legs. These lead directly on to a narration of the conspiracy of Gaius Calpurnius Piso against the emperor, with which Tacitus begins his account of AD 65. This was a major plot by several important nobles who had become disillusioned with Nero. It ultimately failed, but was indicative of significant hostility towards the emperor on the part of the senatorial and equestrian classes following the fire and the beginnings of the Golden House. It was not, however, matched by any dip in Nero's popularity with the lower classes of Rome, which outlasted even his downfall and death in AD 68.

various bad omens compare Tacitus' reference to similar portents following Nero's murder of his mother (see **14.12**, p. 155).

10 The *Histories*: making new emperors

As we have seen, Tacitus' first major historical work had actually narrated a later period of history, from AD 69 to 96, years with which he had a much closer personal involvement. As though the republican magistracies still mattered (see Introduction, p. 4), he began with 1 January in 69, with Servius Sulpicius Galba recently installed after the removal and death of Nero. The fall of Nero was narrated in the lost final books of the *Annals* (assuming that Tacitus completed the work): the *princeps*' relationship with the Senate had broken down after his execution of three senatorial commanders, and his position was fatally weakened by the unsuccessful revolt of the governor of Gallia Lugdunensis, Iulius Vindex, in March 68. Nero's failure to act convincingly against Vindex had encouraged Galba in Spain to proclaim himself 'legate of the Senate and Roman people'.

Galba belonged to the patrician family of the Sulpicii and had enjoyed a very successful senatorial career under the Julio-Claudian emperors. He had been consul in 33, served as governor in Gaul, Germany and Africa, won the decorations of a triumph and held three priesthoods. As governor of Hispania Tarraconensis in 68, he commanded one legion but enrolled another for his

march on Rome. The praetorian troops there were bribed to declare for Galba, and the Senate decreed Nero a public enemy, a move that was quickly followed by Nero's suicide. However, Galba's position was weak, not least because he was old and lacked a successor. Indeed, he was to prove unable to cling on to power, and the year of 69 was to see three further *principes*, and is hence often known as 'the year of four emperors'.

Marble bust of Galba from the Capitoline Museum.

The issue of succession therefore bulks large in the early books of Tacitus' *Histories*. Early in 69, news reached Galba that the legions of Upper Germany were seeking a change in emperor. As a result the emperor and his advisers decided that in order to strengthen his position he should adopt a son, choosing someone who would be seen as a worthy successor. Marcus Salvius Otho felt he had a claim, since he had, as a fellow-governor in Spain, supported Galba's bid for power the previous year. However, Tacitus (*Histories* 1.13) states his belief that Galba rejected Otho as an unsuitable character and too similar to Nero, with whom he had been close. Instead, after discussion, Galba chose the well-born **Lucius Calpurnius Piso Frugi Licinianus**. Tacitus gives Galba a lengthy speech which he is supposed to have addressed to Piso upon his adoption.

Galba adopts Piso: *Histories* 1.15–17

1.15   Therefore Galba, grasping Piso by the hand, is said to have spoken to him as follows: 'If I, as a private citizen, were adopting you **according to official law before the** *pontifices*, it would be excellent for me to add a descendant of **Gnaeus Pompey and Marcus Crassus** to my own line, and a distinction for yourself to have added the ornaments of **Sulpician and Lutatian nobility** to your own. But, 5 as it is, since I have been called to power **by the common agreement of gods and men**, your outstanding character and love for your country have impelled me to offer you, who have remained uninvolved in the fighting, the position

---

Lucius Calpurnius Piso Frugi Licinianus the Pisones had remained a powerful family throughout the rule of the Julio-Claudians, but this Piso had been exiled under Nero, only to be recalled by Galba in AD 68. Tacitus describes him as 'possessing a look and a bearing that were old-fashioned, and to be judged strictly principled on a proper reckoning, but too sombre by those seeing the worst in him' (*Histories* 1.14). According to the historian this nature appealed to his rather niggardly adoptive father.

according to official law before the *pontifices* a full-scale adoption of one Roman adult by another traditionally required official sanction from the people and the priests who had special concern for family religion (the *pontifices*), since one family was being subsumed into another.

Gnaeus Pompey and Marcus Crassus the two colleagues of Caesar in the so-called 'first triumvirate'.

Sulpician and Lutatian nobility Galba was himself a Sulpicius, and on his mother's side a descendant of such notable republican figures as Quintus Lutatius Catulus, who had been a strong defender of Sulla's settlement in favour of the traditional aristocracy.

by the common agreement of gods and men whilst there had been general relief at the fall of Nero, Tacitus tells of how Galba quickly became unpopular, owing to his miserliness and brutality (*Histories* 1.4–7).

of *princeps*, which I obtained in war and **for which our ancestors competed in arms**, so following **the example of the god Augustus**: he placed in rank second only to himself Marcellus, the son of his sister, then Agrippa his son-in-law, next his grandsons, and finally Tiberius Nero his stepson. But Augustus looked for a successor within his family, I do so from the state as a whole, not because I do not have relatives or partners in war, but I did not myself accept power out of self-interest; and let not only my connections (which I have passed over for you), but also your own serve as proof of my judgement. You have a brother of equally fine birth, older than you, and worthy of this fortune, were you not to have a stronger claim. Your age is such that it has now passed the violent passions of youth, and your life is such that you have nothing to be excused in your past. You have until this point only withstood adversity: prosperity puts minds to the test with keener goads, since miseries are tolerated, but we are seduced by happiness. As for loyalty, independence and friendship, the finest qualities of the human mind, you will certainly preserve them with the same steadfastness, but others will diminish them through their deference: there will be an assault from flattery, fawning and the most destructive poison of true feelings, individual self-interest. Even if you and I today are speaking most straightforwardly between ourselves, others will speak with us more readily in the light of the positions we hold rather than as people; for to advise the *princeps* of the appropriate course of action requires a great deal of work, while toadying agreement towards any sort of *princeps* can be carried out without genuine feeling.

1.16   'If the immeasurable body of the empire could stand and balance itself without a ruler, I would deserve to be the man to mark the beginning of republican government: but as it is, it long ago reached such straits that **my old age** can provide no more for the Roman people than a good successor, and your youth can provide no more than a good *princeps*. Under Tiberius, Gaius and Claudius it was as if we Romans were the inheritance of one family: the fact that we have begun to be chosen will be a substitute for freedom; and since the dynasty of the Iulii and the Claudii has come to an end, the process of adoption will unearth whoever is best. For it is a matter of chance to be born and bred of *principes*, and it is esteemed no more than that: the decision when making an adoption is unrestricted and, if you wish to choose, public opinion shows the way. Keep Nero before your eyes, a man puffed up by the long line of Caesars preceding him, who was shaken off from the necks

---

for which our ancestors competed in arms   Piso's family had been prominent supporters of Pompey, Galba's of Caesar.

the example of the god Augustus   on the succession plans of the first *princeps*, and how they had to be repeatedly adapted, see *Annals* **1.3**, pp. 25–7.

my old age   Galba had been born in 3 BC and so was 70 years old; Piso was only 30.

of the people, **not by Vindex with his demilitarized province**, nor **by me with my one legion**, but by his own brutality and his own extravagance; nor did there exist up until that point a precedent for an emperor who had been condemned. Since we have been adopted into this position through war and as a result of the judgement of men, we shall be the objects of envy no matter how excellent we shall be. But do not be scared if **two legions are not yet settled** in this disturbance which has shaken the world. Even I myself did not come to power in secure circumstances, and when your adoption becomes known I will cease to appear an old man, which is the one complaint now laid before me. Every worst individual will always long for Nero. You and I must see that he is not also desired by good men. This is not the moment for lengthier advice, and every measure has been taken – providing that my choice of you has been a good one. The most useful criterion, and at the same time the quickest, for choosing between good and bad policies is this: to consider what you would want or not want under another *princeps*; for it is not the case here, as it is in nations that are ruled, that there is one established house to provide masters, while the rest are slaves, but you are going to command men who can endure neither complete servitude nor complete freedom.' And Galba indeed said these and other such words, as if he was creating a *princeps*, but the rest spoke with Piso as if he had already been so elevated.

1 How persuasive are Galba's arguments in favour of the process of adoption for choosing a new *princeps*? Could some of these arguments be anachronistically influenced by the period of Tacitus' senatorial career, which witnessed the adoption of Trajan by Nerva and that of Hadrian by Trajan?

2 Does Galba convince in claiming that he has made this move genuinely as a positive choice rather than out of desperation at his own weak situation?

3 What do you think were the most important qualities for Galba to look to in his choice of successor? Do you think there are any which he has overlooked?

4 How alert is Galba to the realities of his position as *princeps*?

5 Does he appreciate that the way in which he has won power has changed the nature of the principate?

6 Does the style of Galba's rhetoric suit the rather private circumstances of this speech's delivery?

not by Vindex with his demilitarized province Gaius Iulius Vindex, a Roman senator (perhaps elevated to this status by Claudius) and governor of Gallia Lugdunensis, had revolted in AD 68, probably with the intention of overthrowing the *princeps*. However, he was crushed by the legions of Upper Germany which remained loyal: Gaul itself had no legions.

by me with my one legion Galba was the only governor to respond to Vindex's call, but (as mentioned above) he had also enrolled a new legion to go with the one he had in his Spanish province.

two legions are not yet settled these were the fourth and twenty-second legions in Upper Germany, whose mutiny was finally to lead to Vitellius' march on Rome.

Tacitus notes that Piso took his elevation in a calm manner, giving the impression that he had not really desired it. He then relates the discussion which preceded the public proclamation of Piso which was to take place on 10 January.

1.17   There followed a discussion over whether to make the official announcement of the adoption **from the *rostra*, in the Senate, or in the camp.** A decision was taken to go to the camp: that would show honour to the soldiers, and although their support was not to be sought by the bad practices of bribery and favouritism, it should not be disdained when won by noble means. Meanwhile an expectant 5 crowd had gathered around the palace, impatient to hear a great secret; and those trying to suppress the rumours, which had been barely kept in check, only fanned them.

> • As a result of this decision, was the support of the praetorians really being sought 'by noble means'? Or was Galba showing contempt for the Senate and people?

After being passed over, Otho was persuaded by supporters to fulfil his own ambitions and take action to seize power for himself. His freedman Onomastus was put in charge of a plot which was centred on the praetorians: for in spite of Galba's decision to adopt Piso in the camp, he had refused to pay them the gift of money which had been promised to them. Galba ignored all indications of the coming threat.

The murder of Galba: *Histories* 1.27, 30, 37, 40–1, 47, 49–50

1.27   On 15 January, while Galba was sacrificing in front of **the temple of Apollo, the soothsayer** Umbricius gave him warning of grim entrails, an impending plot and an internal enemy, while Otho listened – for he was standing next to him – and interpreted the news in contrary fashion as being positive and favourable to his own designs. Soon afterwards his freedman Onomastus announced that the 5 architect and builders were waiting for him, the signal which had been agreed to

---

from the *rostra*, in the Senate, or in the camp   the *rostra* was the speakers' platform in the Forum, and the camp referred to here is the praetorian camp on the north-east edge of the city (see note on p. 114).

the temple of Apollo   this had been built on the Palatine by Augustus.

the soothsayer   a *haruspex* was a diviner who foretold the future by inspecting the entrails of sacrificed animals. Here the details of this investigation provided unfortunate omens for Galba.

A relief showing a haruspex (second from left) cutting open a sacrificed bull to inspect its entrails.

mark the assembly of the soldiers and the readiness of the conspiracy. Otho, upon being asked the reason for his departure, pretended that he was buying an estate that was suspect because of its age and so needed inspection before purchase. Then, **leaning on his freedman**, he went through **the *Domus Tiberiana* to the** 10 **Velabrum**, and then on to **the Golden Milestone by the temple of Saturn**. There twenty-three bodyguards hailed him as commander, panicked as he was by the tiny numbers of those hailing him. They hastily put him in a chair, drew their swords, and carried him off. Roughly the same number of soldiers joined them on the journey, some who were in the plot, the majority out of amazement, some 15 shouting and **brandishing their swords**, others silently, intending to match their attitude to the course of events.

leaning on his freedman this is a striking detail, although the Latin word may also suggest his metaphorical reliance on Onomastus. Why do you think that Tacitus has chosen to include this comment?

the *Domus Tiberiana* to the Velabrum the *Domus Tiberiana* was part of the palace complex on top of the Palatine, the Velabrum the low-lying area between the Palatine and the Capitol, from where the Forum could easily be reached.

the Golden Milestone by the temple of Saturn these lay at the western end of the Forum, where the major roads met from all over Italy.

brandishing their swords the text here is uncertain and it may instead mean 'joyfully', which perhaps suits the context better.

Otho was carried off to the praetorian camp, and when news reached Galba, he sent Piso to address the praetorian soldiers on duty at the palace. Piso began by stating his hope that there would be no bloodshed in Rome, before contrasting his character with that of the debauched Otho. He then seeks to paint the bigger picture.

1.30   'The common agreement of the human race gave Galba the name Caesar, and Galba gave it to me with your agreement. If the state, the Senate and the people are only empty names, it is to your advantage, fellow soldiers, that the worst men should not elect the commander. We have heard of instances of mutinous conduct on the part of the legions towards their leaders: your loyalty and renown 5 have remained undamaged until this day. **And even Nero abandoned you, and not you him.** Will fewer than thirty renegades and deserters confer power, when no one would tolerate them choosing a centurion or officer for themselves? Are you allowing the precedent and by your acquiescence taking a share in the crime? This lack of restraint will spread to the provinces, and whilst we will have to suffer 10 the consequences of their crimes, you will have to confront the resulting wars. No greater is the reward for killing a *princeps* than the one given to those innocent of the act: you will receive as generous a gift from us for your loyalty as you will from others for a crime.'

---

1   What do these passages suggest about the strength of Galba's grip on power? What were the factors that undermined it?

2   How persuasive are Piso's arguments to the troops? Does he fully understand the example which Galba had himself set by his actions in AD 68?

Tacitus focuses on the confusion which dominated events as they developed throughout the day. Galba's advisers split into two camps, with one urging that he should sit out the threat, while the rest urged more vigorous action, a plan which Galba eventually chose. As they set out towards the camp, news even reached them that Otho had been killed, but in fact he was strengthening his position with an address to the praetorian troops, which in Tacitus' version begins as follows.

And even Nero abandoned you, and not you him   in fact Plutarch (*Galba* 2.1–2) says that when it was clear that Nero was going to run away, the commander of the praetorian guard, Nymphidius Sabinus, had persuaded them to hail Galba as *princeps*, as though Nero had already fled.

1.37 'In what role I have come forward to address you, **my fellow soldiers**, I cannot say, since I cannot continue to call myself a private citizen when I have been hailed by you as *princeps*, nor *princeps* while another man rules. In addition, the right name for yourselves will remain uncertain as long as it remains in doubt whether you harbour the commander of the Roman people or an enemy in your ⁵ camp. Do you hear how revenge against me, and punishment for yourselves are being demanded in the same breath? So clear is it that we can neither perish nor find security except together.'

> Otho proceeds to recount Galba's crimes since seizing power, before questioning Galba's description of his own actions.

'Which provinces are to be found anywhere, which camps, **that are not bloodied and stained**, or as he puts it in his own proclamations, reformed and set straight? ¹⁰ For actions which others call crimes, this man calls cures, while **with false terminology**, he refers to savagery as strictness, to stinginess as frugality, to his punishments and insulting treatment of you as discipline.'

> • What effect does Otho suggest that the present circumstances in Rome have had upon language? Is he or Galba more to blame?

> Following his speech Otho armed all his troops indiscriminately, while Piso and Galba reached the Forum amidst mounting chaos as their supporters deserted them. Galba is portrayed as being swept along at the whim of the crowds, before Otho ordered his men to move in at full speed.

1.40 Therefore Roman soldiers, as if they were about to expel **Vologaesus or Pacorus** from the ancestral territory of the Arsacids and were not proceeding to butcher their own commander – an unarmed old man – drove their way through the people

---

my fellow soldiers the praetorians were addressed in this way also by Piso at *Histories* **1.30** (p. 182). Why do both speakers use the term? Can either of them use it with any justice?

that are not bloodied and stained this and the following accusations seem rather exaggerated when set beside Tacitus' own more moderate description of the state of the empire at *Histories* 1.8–11.

with false terminology the language Tacitus uses here echoes the words (*Agricola* 30) he gave to the British chieftain Calgacus addressing his troops before the battle of Mons Graupius, which was the crowning achievement of Agricola's governorship of Britain. He accused the Romans of dressing up the realities of imperialism with more attractive terms such as 'peace'.

Vologaesus or Pacorus Vologaesus was a Parthian king, and Pacorus his brother, who governed Media, both belonging to the Arsacid royal family. Tacitus was to narrate their involvements with Rome at length in the *Annals*.

The Forum Romanum viewed from the Capitoline.

and trampled over the Senate as they burst into the Forum, grimly armed and
riding swiftly. Nor did the sight of the Capitol, the sanctity of the temples looming 5
over them, or the thought of earlier emperors and those to come, deter them from
committing **a crime which must be avenged** by whoever succeeds to the throne.

1.41   When the column of armed men was seen close at hand, a standard-bearer of the
        cohort escorting Galba (according to tradition his name was Atilius Vergilio),
        ripped off **the likeness of Galba** and dashed it on the ground: with this indication 10
        the support of all the soldiers for Otho was clear, the Forum was abandoned in a
        flight by the people, and weapons were drawn against those who hesitated. Beside
        the Curtian lake, as a result of the panic of his bearers, Galba was thrown from

---

a crime which must be avenged   Vitellius did indeed take vengeance – Tacitus (*Histories*
1.44.2) says that he put to death more than 120 people who had asked Otho for a reward
for their services that day in helping to overthrow Galba's regime.

the likeness of Galba   this would have been on a medallion attached to the standard.

the Curtian lake   this was a sacred space in the Forum, dry by the imperial period, but
to which various traditions had been attached, dating to the early history of Rome. Livy
tells the most famous version: a chasm had opened up in the Forum and soothsayers
proclaimed that it could only be filled with 'the greatest strength of the Roman people'
(7.6). Marcus Curtius, declaring this to be Rome's military strength, rode into the chasm
fully armed, so sealing the hole and forming the pool. R. T. Scott notes the significance
of the location of Galba's murder: 'The self-immolation of Curtius closed the chasm that
threatened the destruction of Rome, but the murder of Galba can only symbolize its
reopening' (p. 58).

his chair and toppled over. His final words have been passed down in a variety of versions, according to whether each source despised or admired him. Some tell that he asked in humble entreaty what harm he had merited by his actions, begging for a few days to fulfil the payment of his gift to the troops; but most that he offered his throat to his assassins on his own initiative, bidding them to get on and strike, if this seemed to be in the state's interest. What he said was of no concern to his killers. There is no general agreement about the identity of his assassin: some say that it was the ex-praetorian Terentius, others Laecanius; the more popular tradition recounts that Camurius, a soldier of the fifteenth legion, punctured his throat by driving in his sword. Others butchered his legs and arms in a terrible fashion (for his chest was protected); a mass of wounds was inflicted on his body with a frenzied savagery once it had been reduced to a torso. 15 20 25

> • How does Tacitus seek to heighten the horror of Galba's murder?

The soldiers then turned upon Galba's associates, though the isolated example of one centurion's heroic loyalty allowed Piso to escape temporarily. Otho was said to have rejoiced in particular at his eventual death after he had been dragged out of the Temple of Vesta where he had taken refuge. The fickle loyalty of the senators and people now turned entirely against Galba and sought to win Otho's favour. However, the crime needed to be ratified by due legal process.

1.47 Once the day had been spent committing crimes, the final evil remained – the outbreak of joy. **The urban praetor** called the Senate, the other magistrates competed in their flattery, the senators rushed to attend: to Otho were voted tribunician power, the name of Augustus and **all the honours held by the** *principes*, with everyone trying their hardest to obliterate the memory of their former mockery and insults, which no one felt had stuck in his mind, since they had been bandied about indiscriminately; whether he had let the insults pass or had postponed his response remained uncertain owing to the short length of his rule. While the Forum was still filled with blood, Otho was carried through the corpses still lying there to the Capitoline and from there to the Palatine, and allowed the bodies to be handed over for burial and cremation. 5 10

The urban praetor   the two consuls had been Galba himself and his supporter Titus Vinius, both of whom had now been killed. The urban praetor was the most senior of the holders of this rank, and hence the senior surviving magistrate.

all the honours held by the *principes*   apart from the tribunician power which the *princeps* had held since the time of Augustus, these included most crucially a proconsular power superior to that of the governors of the empire, and the position of chief priest.

After obituaries for Piso and the consul, Titus Vinius, Tacitus turns to Galba.

1.49   The body of Galba was long neglected and roughly treated in numerous acts of mockery through the freedom provided by the cover of darkness. But his domestic steward, Argius, one of his former slaves, **buried him in a simple fashion in his private gardens**. His head was impaled and mutilated by the camp-followers and the soldiers' servants. It was not until the next day that it was found in front 5 of Patrobius' tomb (this freedman of Nero had been punished by Galba) and was reunited with the body which had already been cremated. Servius Galba met this end, after enjoying seventy-three years of prosperity under five *principes*, luckier during the rule of others than his own. His family was one of ancient nobility and great wealth: his own character was of a moderate standard, good 10 for the avoidance of vices rather than the possession of virtues. He neither lacked interest in, nor obsessed about renown; he did not covet the wealth of others, was parsimonious with his own and miserly with the state's; of friends and freedmen, whenever he chanced upon good ones, he was blamelessly tolerant, but if they were bad, he was blind to a fault. However, the nobility of his birth and the terror 15 of the times served as a screen, so that what was in fact his inertia was referred to as wisdom. When he was in the prime of life he enjoyed military renown in the German provinces. As a governor he ran Africa with moderation, then as an older man he held Nearer Spain with equal fairness, appearing greater than a subject when he was one, and judged by the consensus of all to be capable of supreme 20 command, had he only not held it.

---

1 What does Tacitus mean by men's judgement of Galba as 'capable of supreme command, had he only not held it'?

2 What does Tacitus' account of the senatorial debate suggest were the problems faced by men in uncertain political times?

3 Is Tacitus' obituary of Galba merely a rhetorical exercise, or do its paradoxes and antitheses offer real insight into the character of the emperor?

1.50   The city was restless and alarmed by both the atrocity of the new crime and the well-established habits of Otho, when on top of all this a fresh message about Vitellius brought panic. This had been suppressed before the murder of Galba,

---

buried him in a simple fashion in his private gardens the procedure was to cremate the body and then transfer the ashes to a suitable container for the burial proper. Note the loyalty of his freedman, and compare that of Agrippina's staff after her murder (see *Annals* **14.9**, pp. 152–3).

so that it might be thought that only the army of **Upper Germany** had rebelled. The fact that at that time it was as if the two basest of all living men in their shamelessness, laziness and luxurious excess had been selected by destiny to destroy the empire, caused the open display of grief for not only the Senate and equestrian order, who have some role and interest in the state, but even the ordinary people. No longer did they discuss **the fresh examples of the cruel peace**, but in recalling the memory of the civil wars they spoke of the city captured so many times by its own armies, the devastation of Italy, the ransacking of the provinces, **Pharsalia, Philippi, Perusia and Mutina**, the famous names of public disasters. They reflected that the world had been almost overturned even when the fight for the principate had involved good men, but that the empire had survived after the victory of Gaius Iulius, and survived that of Caesar Augustus; the state would have survived under Pompeius and Brutus: were they now to enter temples on behalf of Otho or Vitellius? Prayers for either were sacrilegious, vows for either of them execrable, two men, of whose war you would know only this, namely that it would be the worse man who won. There were those who spoke presciently of Vespasian and arms from the East, and while Vespasian was better than either, they nevertheless shuddered at a fresh war and a fresh calamity. And Vespasian's reputation was in the balance: uniquely of all the *principes* that preceded him, he changed for the better.

> 1 Why do you think that Tacitus concentrates on the feelings and reactions of the Romans of the time rather than tendering his own judgements here, as he had done with Galba's obituary?
>
> 2 How significant is the contrast between this passage and that obituary?
>
> 3 Do the historical allusions suggest that the present crisis was unparalleled or just a reversion to an earlier state of civil war, where power was won by force of arms?

Upper Germany   this lay further up the Rhine of the two German provinces, and so to the south-east of Lower Germany.

the fresh examples of the cruel peace   by this Tacitus means the cruelties inflicted on the Roman people since the civil wars by the Julio-Claudian emperors, and perhaps especially Nero as the most recent of them.

Pharsalia, Philippi, Perusia and Mutina   the battle of Pharsalus in Thessaly (northern Greece) had taken place in 48 BC, and saw the defeat of Pompey by Caesar; Philippi lay in Macedonia and saw the defeat of Caesar's killers by Antony and Octavian in 42; Perusia, an Italian town on the border of Etruria with Umbria, was burned to the ground in 40 following a successful siege by Octavian after it had sheltered Antony's brother Lucius; Mutina, lying further north and blockaded by Antony in 43, had witnessed his defeat at the hands of Decimus Iunius Brutus and the consuls, Hirtius and Pansa.

In the rest of the book, Tacitus concentrates on the advance of Vitellius' forces and reaction in Rome, only returning to Vespasian in the East at the start of the second book. Open warfare did indeed lie ahead, and Vespasian's eventual succession followed pitched battles, a threat to Rome's food supply and open fighting in the streets of the capital. The legions did indeed decide the course of political power in Rome at this juncture. AD 69 was certainly a vital year for the future of the principate – it offered a stark reminder to the powerbrokers in Rome that the legions could not be taken for granted. However, it was perhaps also vital for the hindsight which it offered to imperial historians: it encouraged men such as Tacitus to reappraise the Julio-Claudian principate and to examine in detail just how this family had manipulated the various levers of power so successfully and for so long, whether during the legionary mutinies of AD 14 or in the chaos that followed the assassination of Gaius.

Further reading and references

The works listed here (apart from those in the final section) are, in general, very accessible to the non-specialist reader.

Reference works

The essential English-language encyclopaedia of the ancient world is **S. Hornblower and A. Spawforth** (eds.), *Oxford Classical Dictionary* (3rd edition, Oxford, 1996). An abbreviated version is **J. Roberts** (ed.), *The Oxford Dictionary of the Classical World* (Oxford, 2007).

Translations

There are translations of the *Annals*, the *Histories*, *Agricola* and *Germania* available in the Penguin Classics series and the Oxford World Classics. However, the translation of the *Annals* which is by far the most faithful to the original Latin is *Tacitus, the Annals* (Indianapolis, 2004) by **A. J. Woodman**.

Roman historiography

C. S. Kraus and A. J. Woodman, *Latin Historians* (Oxford, 1997).
An excellent introduction.

A. Feldherr, *The Cambridge Companion to the Roman Historians* (Cambridge, 2009).
This offers a range of articles on specific historians as well as more thematic pieces.

Tacitus

R. Ash, *Tacitus* (Bristol, 2006).
A brief but excellent introduction.

R. Ash (ed.), *Oxford Readings in Tacitus* (Oxford, forthcoming).
This will offer a selection of important recent articles updated and conveniently collected in one volume.

J. Ginsburg, *Tradition and Theme in the Annals of Tacitus* (New York, 1981).
This groundbreaking book sets out the ways in which Tacitus exploits the annalistic structure in his narrative.

T. J. Luce and A. J. Woodman (eds.), *Tacitus and the Tacitean Tradition* (Princeton, 1993).
This contains an interesting selection of studies on a broad range of themes.

R. H. Martin, *Tacitus* (London, 1994).
Perhaps the most helpful general introduction to Tacitus and his works.

R. Syme, *Tacitus* (2 vols., Oxford, 1958).
This remains the classic study of the historian, written in a style which imitates Tacitus' own.

A. J. Woodman (ed.), *The Cambridge Companion to Tacitus* (Cambridge, 2009).
This offers a full range of articles about Tacitus' work and influence, written by about twenty different scholars.

Histories of the early principate

R. Alston, *Aspects of Roman History, AD 14–117* (London, 1998).
A good introduction to the period.

P. A. Brunt and J. M. Moore (eds.), *Res Gestae Divi Augusti, The Achievements of the Divine Augustus* (Oxford, 1967) is primarily an edition (with translation) of the *Res Gestae*, but the introduction offers an excellent summary of the Augustan principate.

M. Goodman, *The Roman World, 44 BC–AD 180* (London, 1997).
Another good introductory work on the principate.

M. T. Griffin, 'The Lyons Tablet and Tacitean Hindsight', *Classical Quarterly*, 32.2 (1982), 404–18.
This offers an invaluable discussion of the two versions of Claudius' speech to the Senate in AD 46.

M. T. Griffin, *Nero: the End of a Dynasty* (London, 1984).

B. Levick, *Claudius* (London, 1990).

B. Levick, *Tiberius the Politician* (London, 1999).

B. Levick, *Augustus: Image and Substance* (Harlow, 2010).
The above works by Levick and Griffin are excellent biographies of these emperors, but also have much to say about the principate in general.

K. Wellesley, *The Long Year, AD 69* (Bristol, 1989).
A lively account of this eventful year.

Other works referred to in the text

D. C. Braund, 'The Aedui, Troy, and the *Apocolocyntosis*', *Classical Quarterly*, 30.2 (1980), 420–5.

M. G. L. Cooley (ed.), *The Age of Augustus* (*LACTOR* 17, 2003).

H. Furneaux, *The Annals of Tacitus* (2 vol., Oxford, 1896 and 1907).

F. R. D. Goodyear, *The Annals of Tacitus I–II* (2 vols., Cambridge, 1972 and 1981).

F. Haase, 'Tacitea', *Philologus*, 3 (1848), 152–9.

B. Levick and S. Jameson, 'C. Crepereius Gallus and his *Gens*', *Journal of Roman Studies*, 54 (1964), 98–106.

R. H. Martin and A. J. Woodman, *Tacitus, Annals Book IV* (Cambridge, 1989).

N. P. Miller, *Tacitus, Annals Book 1* (Bristol, 1992).

N. P. Miller, *Tacitus, Annals XV* (London, 1973).

N. P. Miller, 'Virgil and Tacitus', *Proceedings of the Virgil Society* (1961–2), 25–34.

D. S. Potter and C. Damon, 'The *Senatus Consultum de Pisone Patre*', *American Journal of Philology*, 120 (1999), 13–41.

K. Quinn, *Catullus, The Poems* (London, 1973).

R. T. Scott, *Religion and Philosophy in the Histories of Tacitus* (Rome, 1968).

R. K. Sherk, *The Roman Empire: Augustus to Hadrian* (Cambridge, 1988).

E. M. Smallwood, *Documents Illustrating the Principates of Gaius Claudius and Nero* (Bristol, 1984).

J. J. Wilkes, 'A Note on the Mutiny of the Pannonian Legions in AD 14', *Classical Quarterly*, 13 (1963), 268–71.

A. J. Woodman and R. H. Martin, *The Annals of Tacitus, Book 3* (Cambridge, 1996).

Acknowledgements

The authors and publishers acknowledge the following sources of images and are grateful for the permissions granted.

Cover, p. 163 akg-images/Erich Lessing; pp. 12, 37, 77, 102, 120, 184 provided by Chris Burnand; p. 13 Caroline Lawrence, Roman Mysteries Ltd, www.romanmysteries.com; p. 23 Erin Babnik/Alamy; p. 24, 145 © The Trustees of the British Museum; p. 46 © 2004 TopFoto/ Woodsmansterne TopFoto.co.uk; p. 74 age fotostock/SuperStock; p. 115 The Art Archive/ Musée du Louvre Paris/Gianni Dagli Orti; p. 124 Tips Italia/Photolibrary; pp. 132, 144 New York University Excavations at Aphrodisias; p. 138 The Musée et Théâtres Gallo-Romaine de Lyon Fourvière, Lyon, France; p. 141 Per Karlsson – BKWine.com/Alamy; p. 158 The Museum of Antiquities, University of Saskatchewan; p. 159 The Art Gallery Collection/Alamy; pp. 169, 171 akg-images/Bildarchiv Steffens; p. 176 akg-images; p. 181 Haruspice consulting entrails of a bull, marble, Roman (4th century AD)/ Louvre, Paris, France/Alinari/The Bridgeman Art Library

Artworks and maps throughout by Peter Simmonett